THE
SMART
SOCIETY

THE
SMART
SOCIETY

STRENGTHENING
AMERICA'S GREATEST
RESOURCE, ITS PEOPLE

PETER D. SALINS

ENCOUNTER BOOKS
New York · London

First American edition published in 2014 by Encounter Books, an activity of Encounter for Culture and Education, Inc., a nonprofit, tax exempt corporation.
Encounter Books website address: www.encounterbooks.com

Manufactured in the United States and printed on acid-free paper. The paper used in this publication meets the minimum requirements of ANSI/NISO Z39.48–1992 (R 1997) (*Permanence of Paper*).

FIRST AMERICAN EDITION

LIBRARY OF CONGRESS CATALOGING-IN-PUBLICATION DATA

Salins, Peter D.
    The smart society : strengthening America's greatest resource, its people / Peter D. Salins.
        pages cm
    Includes bibliographical references and index.
    ISBN 978-1-59403-700-9 (hardcover : alk. paper) —
ISBN 978-1-59403-701-6 (ebook)
    1. Intellectual capital—United States. 2. Labor supply—Effect of education on—United States. 3. Education, Higher—Economic aspects—United States. I. Title.
    HD53.S243 2013
    658.4'038—dc23   2013030019

PRODUCED BY WILSTED & TAYLOR PUBLISHING SERVICES
Project manager Christine Taylor
Designer and compositor Nancy Koerner
Copy editor Nancy Evans
Proofreader Melody Lacina
Indexer Andrew Jroon

....

Dedicated to my greatest resource, my family:
Rochelle and Jonathan Salins, and
Jessica, Mike, and Marissa Malloy.

....

Contents

Preface

What impelled me to write this book? During my long academic career in planning and public policy, I have weighed in often on many critical policy issues, generally driven by an optimistic outlook on the possibilities for constructive change, offering what I have believed were reasonable solutions to long-standing local, state, or national concerns. So it is with *The Smart Society*.

What is different this time, however, is the subject matter. I have written most extensively on issues related to urbanization, specifically on policies tied to physical places: housing, land use regulation, and the economic and social vitality of New York City. My first important foray in considering policies that directly affect the welfare of people rather than places was my last book-length work, *Assimilation, American Style* (Basic Books, 1997), which looked at America's remarkable history in welcoming and assimilating immigrants. That was also my first venture in reflecting on American human capital, the focus of this book, because—as *The Smart Society* emphasizes—immigrants are above all one of its most indispensable wellsprings.

My intense interest in policies that can strengthen the capabilities of the American people (in other words, their human capital) took a quantum leap in the nearly ten years (1997 to 2006) that I served as chief academic officer—provost—of the State University of New York system (SUNY), the country's largest public collection of colleges and universities. In this role I needed to give serious thought to the university's underlying mission and how that related to the day-to-day operations of the system's institutions. Being an agency of the state of New York, heavily dependent on revenues provided by the state's taxpayers, we needed to be very clear on what the citizens and political leaders of the state expected of us and what our contribution to the state's welfare might be.

On reflection, the answer was simple: New York, like every other American state, was in a desperate competition for human capital—with other states as well as other countries—and we were the state's most comprehensive, and hopefully effective, vehicle to help New York grow its human capital and win that race. Because of the university's vast size, and the great diversity among its sixty-four campuses, SUNY touched just about every aspect of human-capital development. Our thirteen teacher training programs and thirty community colleges prepared teachers, aides, and administrators for preschool through high school; our Charter School Institute oversaw half the state's charter schools; all of our campuses together turned out the lion's share of New York's college graduates; our research universities, medical schools, and partner Cornell University conducted path-breaking research and development that enriched the human capital of American workplaces; SUNY's alliances with educational institutions and industries abroad generated human capital across the world; and, finally, great numbers of our faculty and students were immigrants, what I refer to as imported human capital.

My efforts as university provost to help our campuses succeed in carrying out their diverse missions gave me a close-up view of the places that actually generated human capital and many of the problems they faced in doing so. Let me cite just a few examples.

The university's original and still paramount human-capital contribution was in turning out tens of thousands of college graduates each year. Yet SUNY community-college and baccalaureate campuses were continually bedeviled by unsatisfactory graduation rates—a problem because the full benefits of a costly college experience depend on successful completion. Tracking that issue down, we found a nearly perfect correlation of graduation rates with the quality of students' high school preparation. Since a majority of our students come from the state's high schools, and the majority of those schools' teachers are trained in SUNY colleges, we took a hard look at our teacher training programs. What we found there was weak grounding in core subjects—mathematics being a prime case—and shockingly little classroom exposure, especially in New York City schools. This resulted partly from a dearth of student-teaching mentors, but also an unhealthy faculty bias against sending their charges to the state's urban schools (where two-thirds of New York children happen to be enrolled). In another part of our academic forest, SUNY's community and technical colleges were constantly preoccupied with ensuring that their curricula kept up with requirements of an ever-changing American labor market. Even SUNY's most prestigious institutions faced daunting challenges in fulfilling their human-capital missions: attracting the best students, retaining the best faculty, and reaching faculty agreement on a rigorous foundation of general education. In working with campuses on all of these issues and many others, I essentially underwent a thorough apprenticeship in the inner workings of America's educational system from preschool through graduate school, leading to the development of my thinking on education policy as reflected in chapters 2 through 5.

My reflections on human capital in the workplace flow from my work with SUNY's impressive research universities, including Cornell (affiliated through complex historical and financial ties) and our four medical centers. I was then—and continue to be—highly impressed by the breathtaking scientific and technological discoveries emerging from these places, which underscore how critical New York's—and the nation's—universities are in securing America's global leadership in science and technology. Further, I saw firsthand how these discoveries rapidly morphed into new products and industries, a key determinant of how much human capital is generated in the workplace: SUNY campuses gave America and the world magnetic resonance imaging (MRI) scanners; the bar code; the latest generation of computer chips; "virtual" colonoscopies; and three-dimensional printing, among countless other transformational breakthroughs. But all of the undeniable and quite awe-inspiring output of these places depended very heavily, if not in many cases exclusively, on financial support from the federal and state governments. I spent a fair amount of time and ingenuity in helping our campuses gain that support. My years toiling in SUNY's research vineyards strongly shaped my ideas in chapter 6.

Although my desire to write this book owes a great deal to my experience in Albany, it is also grounded in a deeply held conviction that has influenced all my work. Among the things I have been most certain of my entire adult life is that the United States truly is an exceptional country. Earlier in my adulthood I had plenty of company in this belief, at a time when this notion of American exceptionalism was celebrated across our nation's partisan and ideological spectrum. Today, however, the term has fallen into some disrepute, especially among America's cosmopolitan and intellectual elites. How dare we, with all our faults and shortcomings, hold ourselves apart and think of our country as better than any other?

Well, sorry, I still firmly hold on to my belief in this country's exceptionalism. Even so, it does require that I give some thought to what it is, exactly, that makes us exceptional. It begins, of course, with our founding documents, notably the Declaration of Independence, which is still the most idealistic civic charter ever written, an ongoing inspiration for freedom fighters everywhere. Certainly, being the world's oldest true democracy—at least among nations of any size—is part of the story, as is the fervent attachment of Americans to untrammeled personal freedom and individual initiative. Then there is our social egalitarianism: despite the existence at all times of great disparities of income and wealth in our midst, Americans really do believe that "all men are created equal"; that no one is intrinsically any better than anyone else; that every newborn American child should have the same shot at opportunity and success.

But the inspired civic architecture and individualistic and egalitarian values of the United States have not served just as the country's backdrop. Americans long ago realized that, for the country to remain "the promised land" (using an enduring popular metaphor), the United States needed to sustain a robust set of institutions and practices to keep its people prosperous and free; in other words, to make extraordinary—by the standards of every age—investments in the human capital of their children and fellow citizens, and to embrace human capital from abroad. That is the real basis of American exceptionalism—and the subject of this book.

I want to thank all those who made the completion of this book possible. First, I want to express my appreciation for my publisher, Encounter Books, and its staff, both for their initial confidence in my conception of the book and for their unwavering help as the book was being written and produced.

I owe an enormous debt of gratitude to the Manhattan Institute, which has provided critical support for this book, as it has for many of my previous ones. I want especially to thank its president, Larry Mone, for his ongoing faith in the project; its book director, Bernadette Serton, for her indispensable guidance throughout the long journey from the germ of an idea to finished manuscript, and my research assistant, Yevgeniy Feyman, who helped in the writing and supplied some of the book's key data.

I also want to acknowledge the many people who provided the inspiration and evidence I needed to shape my thinking on what has made the United States a smart society, from my former colleagues in SUNY System Administration to the many experts on American human capital—both scholars and practitioners—upon whose ideas, analyses, and experiences the book's arguments are based.

THE
SMART
SOCIETY

How America Became the World's Smartest Society—And How It Can Stay That Way

HUMAN CAPITAL AND THE SMART SOCIETY

The United States has, over its two-century-plus life, become far and away the world's most successful society, not only in overall economic well-being, but also in social harmony and individual happiness. As of the writing of this book, the country has emerged from the biggest economic downturn since the Great Depression, a situation that shook many Americans' deeply ingrained faith in their country's superiority and dampened their optimism concerning their own and their children's prospects.[1] With all its recent troubles, the United States nevertheless remains the richest, freest, most socially stable, and—yes—happiest nation on the face of the earth. This is not just an empty assertion; it can be documented empirically with any number of positive statistics. The United States still has the highest gross domestic product (GDP) per capita of any country over 10 million in population,[2] and in the recently published and well-respected World Happiness Report, the United States scored as the tenth happiest out of 128

1

nations surveyed—and was the only populous country in the top ten (alongside places like Denmark, Finland, and Switzerland).[3]

America's economic and social success rests in no small part on an enviable bedrock of centuries-old political, social, and economic institutions, all of which endure. Ever since the country won its independence from Great Britain in 1783, the United States has been a free-market democracy with secure personal freedoms and property rights, and that is not about to change. In addition, the country has the good fortune to possess abundant natural resources across its vast continental land mass.

Even so, the real secret to America's phenomenal success—and the subject of this book—is its extraordinarily high level of "human capital." What, exactly, is human capital? Put most succinctly, human capital refers to the sum of *acquired* personal abilities that lead any individual anywhere to be economically and socially successful. From that it follows that the greater the sum of human capital possessed by a country's adult citizens, the more successful that country will be. Thanks to far-sighted private and public investments made in the United States throughout the nineteenth and twentieth centuries, the vast majority of Americans—across lines of class, gender, religion, national origin, even race—long ago attained levels of human capital higher than those found in any other nation. As Harvard economists Claudia Goldin and Lawrence Katz note:

> Investment in physical capital became vital to a nation's economic growth with the onset of the Industrial Revolution in the nineteenth century. But the path to ongoing economic success for nations and individuals eventually became investment in *human capital* [emphasis added]. Human capital became supreme in the twentieth century and America led the way.[4]

Despite our stunning past accomplishments in generating human capital, the United States today can ill afford to rest on its laurels. Unless we rapidly revitalize our human capital capabilities we are not only in danger of seeing a growing roster of other countries overtaking us, but we also risk cheating future American generations of staggering levels of opportunity and economic prosperity. One recently published estimate of the "growth dividend" gained by upgrading American human capital (in this case through improved education) is *$77 trillion* over the next eighty years.[5]

Let me explain the title of this book. This book focuses entirely on America's human capital, why we should be worried about it, and how, with some strategic shifts in public policy, we can ensure that coming generations will accrue enough of it. Yet "human capital," a term first coined by the English economist Arthur Pigou in 1928, is jargon to the average reader, and is poorly understood by all but professional economists. Because it is the subject of the book, I cannot help but use the term, but I also want to cast its essence in layman's language. Hence my formulation of the "smart society." Just as individuals can be "smart" (not just in having a high IQ, but in any number of other functional or social ways), so can a country. Thus, I reserve the appellation "smart society" for a country where a majority of its citizens, and not just a privileged elite, possess high levels of human capital and, as will be explained later, put it to productive use. Throughout recorded history, the world's richer and more successful countries have been, to a greater or lesser degree, "smart" societies; for nearly two hundred years, the United States has been—quite intentionally—the world's "smartest."[6]

How important is human capital? Being a smart society confers huge benefits. The most obvious is material well-being (see table 1.1). Americans have long enjoyed the world's highest standard of living, however one may want to measure it. Even when compared to affluent nations in Europe and other high-income

English-speaking countries (Canada, Australia, New Zealand), Americans always have had more to eat, were the first to have electricity in their homes and streets, the first to have universal telephone service, the first to have universal car ownership, and the first to travel extensively by air. Americans have long had the world's most spacious and well-equipped homes and highest rate of homeownership. In the last few decades they were the first to enjoy the fruits of the late-twentieth-century technological revolution—computers at home and at work, large-screen and high-definition television, and electronic gadgetry of all kinds.

Rewarding as material well-being is, the more ephemeral benefits of being members of a smart society are just as important: the ability to participate responsibly as voters and officeholders in a robust democracy; the sense of personal fulfillment that comes from having a good education and occupational skills; the

Table 1.1

GDP Per Capita ($U.S.)—Historical by Country

Country	1870	1913	1973*	2011*
United States	2,457	5,307	16,607	48,100
Austria	1,875	3,488	11,308	41,700
Canada	1,620	4,213	13,644	40,300
Germany	1,913	3,833	13,152	37,900
Great Britain	3,263	5,032	11,992	35,900
France	1,858	3,452	12,940	35,000
Japan	741	1,334	11,017	34,300
Italy	1,467	2,507	10,409	30,100
Argentina	1,311	3,797	7,970	17,400

Source: Angus Maddison, *Monitoring the World Economy: 1820–1992*
(Paris: Organisation for Economic Co-operation and Development [OECD], Development Centre Series, 1995), and current data from the OECD.

*1870–1973 figures in 1990 $U.S.; 2011 in 2011 $U.S.

knowledge of other people and societies that breeds tolerance of diversity and facilitates successful social interaction; the capacity to enjoy fine literature, art, and music; the possession of habits of delayed gratification and self-discipline that lead to better life decisions and happier families—to name just a few.

Living in a human capital–rich society also confers benefits on the community as a whole. For starters, there is the issue of society-wide financial burdens. Every rich country has long ago instituted "safety-net" programs to provide for its poor, elderly, disabled, and other unfortunates. Many of the richer ones—including the United States and the countries of northern Europe—have also added other costly public "entitlements" for the not-so-poor. There is absolutely no question that the total cost of these programs is directly proportional to the percentage of the population with se-verely deficient human capital: the un- or poorly schooled, the jobless and the sick (because good health is also correlated with levels of human capital). By one estimate, federal and state gov-ernments in the United States today spend about *1 trillion dollars* annually on such programs—not counting Social Security, Medi-care, and unemployment insurance. Aside from financial consider-ations, we are all happier if our neighbors, our fellow workers, our children's classmates, and even the strangers we see in the street every day are well-off.

THE HUMAN-CAPITAL TRIPOD
What constitutes human capital, and how is it created?

Education All economists would agree that education is the single most important determinant of any person's human capital; thus a country's human capital will be largely proportional to the edu-cational attainment of its adult population. This means that, for any country, the more years of education or training its people have and the more uniformly education is distributed, the greater its human-capital endowment will be. Maximizing a country's educational potential requires establishing a national network of schools, universities, and other training facilities that are broadly accessible to the population without regard to income, and whose instructional programs meet the highest standard of the age.

However, economists specializing in the formation of human capital recognize there is more to it than education alone.[7]

Productivity The human-capital potential conferred by institutions of formal education during the early twelve to twenty years of a person's life is only realized when it is translated into *productivity* in a workplace. A country's productivity is determined by two factors. First, the actual output of workers depends on the tools and technology they have to work with. A well-educated workforce harnessed to primitive technology produces little. Therefore, a country's total annual productivity also depends on the quality of its *productive technology*. That, in turn, depends increasingly on a country's being at the forefront of scientific research and being able to quickly translate research findings into innovative technology for the production of goods and services.

Second, quite obvious when you think about it, but not sufficiently appreciated in practice, is that, to be productive, *people have to be working*—regardless of their educational endowments. A person's productivity if he or she is not working is *zero*. Projected nationally, this means that a country's total annual productivity is proportional to the number of hours per year that its adults are working.

Immigration Finally, not all human capital needs to be created at home; it can be imported from abroad by welcoming *immigrants* with strong endowments of human capital. Expanding a country's human capital through immigration is a no-lose proposition. If immigrants are educated or skilled, the country gains a human-capital windfall without having to pay for it through the costly educational system. If immigrants have less education or fewer skills, the country still gains valuable human capital because immigrants generally possess a more robust work ethic than native workers. As a bonus, immigrants generally arrive with strong family values, and strong families generate higher levels of human capital in the next generation.

Throughout this book, I refer to this mix of policies responsible for the volume and quality of America's human capital—education, productivity, and immigration—as the country's *human-capital tripod.*

THE ROLE OF GOVERNMENT

Who makes human-capital decisions and who pays for it? Obviously, since human capital is a personal attribute, individuals must decide to acquire or use it or, in the case of immigration, decide to leave their homeland. Yet, government plays an indispensable role.

Take education, for example. To begin with, the desire for education varies enormously among families in every society. Certainly, most children would not choose to be educated if the decision were left to them, and we know, from both history and life in many contemporary societies, that a large slice of parents might not care if their children were educated or not. So the only way any country can ensure that all its children get an education is to make them do so. Thus, compulsory education is now a feature of every modern country; the United States was one of the first of the world's nations to institute it.

Then there is its cost. Education is exceedingly expensive and always has been, and thus, even in affluent countries, it is beyond the financial capacity of most families. This constraint is compounded by the fact that without education, few families are able to become well-off in the first place, which creates a self-reinforcing, vicious cycle: because they lack education, parents cannot afford to pay for the education of their children, ensuring that their children will not be able to pay for that of their grandchildren, and so on. This means the government's schooling requirement must be accompanied by a willingness to pay for it. Otherwise, as was the case throughout Western history (until the United States led the way to universal, free schooling), education remains the exclusive province of the rich and wellborn, who use it to secure a privileged status for their progeny.

A country's productivity, at first blush, may not be as dependent as education on government. Most production in the United States and other rich countries is in the private sector. Nevertheless, let's look at the role of government with respect to the two determinants of productivity noted earlier: the technological quality of a country's production facilities and the country's aggregate work effort (i.e., the percentage of the population employed times annual hours worked per employee).

With respect to the former, the role of government is indirect but vitally important. Workplace technology represents intellectual property (a form of human capital) that must be protected by government through the issue of patents. Also, technology is invariably grounded in the latest scientific discoveries; for the last hundred years the pace of scientific discovery in the West has depended on a variety of government subsidies. The United States, even in the nineteenth century, found ways of underwriting scientific research, and this has contributed mightily to America's huge lead in technology.

Regarding the second, aside from the eagerness to work of a country's labor force (where the United States has a strong edge), work effort is very much hostage to government policies regarding income support based on disability and unemployment, national old-age pension provisions, mandatory retirement and minimum wage requirements, collective bargaining rules, allowable hours of work, public employee pensions, and a host of other government restrictions on working.

That said, I know that many readers of this book have a visceral distrust of government, or at the very least share a high degree of skepticism as to its efficacy. I share this skepticism. Nevertheless, it is an unarguable certainty, in any country at any time, that if the generation of human capital were left entirely to the decisions and resources of individuals, families, and private enterprises, there would be much less of it. This is not an issue of ideology, but of standard economic theory, subscribed to by economists across the ideological spectrum.

All of these governmental intrusions, especially in education and basic research, involve what economists call "public goods." Public goods are expenditures that generate enormous benefits to the community beyond those realized by any individuals willing to pay for them in private market transactions. In the instance of education, for example, while it is clearly beneficial to the individuals who possess it, it also confers great benefits on society as a whole: it results in more skilled and efficient workers, better citizens, informed voters, better parents, and so on. Education's status as a public good is compounded by the fact that, for most of the educational cycle, its immediate beneficiary—the child—has no capacity to pay for it. Well, why can't parents pay for it? Parents are only indirect beneficiaries of their children's education, and, while many parents may want the best for their children, they may not have the money, or they may not be willing to forgo a large portion of their own needs to pay for it. Even if all parents sacrificed equally to finance their children's education, the quality of education any child received would then still be dependent on their parents' income. Therefore Americans a long time ago, and all developed countries today, have come to accept education as a collective responsibility, to make sure that the lifetime well-being of their children does not depend on the good fortune of having rich—and altruistic—parents.

An even purer instance of a public good is basic scientific research. As will be discussed at length in chapter 6, basic research is one of the most fruitful and cost-effective generators of *applied* human capital, which is why the United States has for decades invested so much in it, and why China, Japan, Korea, and the most advanced countries of Europe are doing so now. The only alternative funding sources for basic research would be private firms or private universities. However, if industrial firms picked up the tab, its benefits would easily spill over to "free-riding" competitors who would be able to take advantage of its findings (say, in new product development), without having had to contribute anything. If universities paid for basic research out of their own funds (for prestige and as a lure for top faculty and students) they would have to push the cost onto their tuition-paying students, who would receive no direct benefit at all. In summary, nearly all the specific components of human-capital investment involve public goods; as such, they are either paid for by the public (through one or another government action), or they just are not produced at the scale needed or, in some cases, produced at all.

Finally, there is one aspect of American human-capital development, immigration, where we must look to government because government—in this case at the national level—is the sole arbiter of whether to admit immigrants into the country, and under what criteria. Most countries in the world do not permit immigration on any meaningful scale. Others, like the richer countries of Western Europe, have welcomed immigrants only recently, and generally grudgingly, and those immigrants who make it in are likely to become poorly assimilated, second-class citizens. In sharp contrast, America, founded by immigrants, has welcomed them from the beginning (except for some notable but time-limited gaps), with the result that immigration has provided the United States with one of its most unique and long-standing advantages in human capital. However, as chapter 8 discusses in detail, the full human-capital benefit from immigration does depend on the details of which immigrants are admitted, and that necessarily is determined by the Congress and the president of the United States.

Although government has an indispensable role in creating human capital, not everything that governments do is wise. Governments—very much including the federal, state, and local governments of the United States—can also destroy human capital, or hold back its development. In taking the reader through all the ways that American human capital is created or used, this book will show where our governments might do more, but also where they might do less and, most often, where they should do things differently.

THE REST OF THIS BOOK

Given the indispensable role of government in generating human capital and making America the world's smartest society, it matters a great deal how, specifically, government executes that role. Happily, the United States has long been a leader in developing vast amounts of human capital and for a few more years it can still be characterized as the world's smartest society. But this is only because it continues to benefit from human-capital investments made in the nineteenth and twentieth centuries. The rest of this book will delve in some detail into each of the three legs of America's "human-capital tripod"—its schools, its workplaces, and its immigration policy—and recommend important changes in policy that could substantially and rapidly increase the country's human capital. As noted earlier, most of these changes would neither expand the role of government in the United States—a highly fraught issue these days—nor increase its overall cost.

Education America's educational supremacy is being threatened by several factors. Large numbers of young Americans, mainly from disadvantaged backgrounds, are getting an exceedingly poor education, and have been for a long time. America's middle-class youth are getting a middling education that used to be good enough for them to get by but, in the competitive twenty-first-century economy, will soon leave them in the dust. America's colleges and universities, once the envy of the world, cost too much, teach too little, and are increasingly distracted from their primary mission.

The American adult population is still the best educated in the world (see table 1.2) but only because our older generations (over thirty-five years of age) are better educated than their counterparts in Canada, Europe, or Asia. The sad fact is that the current generation (under thirty-five) is outshone by its peers in a dozen or so countries—including Canada. (Throughout this book I will be using Canada as a comparison for many of the human-capital issues under discussion. Canada is an excellent benchmark for comparative purposes because among all the nations in the world it is the most like the United States. In their history, population composition, primary language, popular culture, economy, housing, civic beliefs, and many other ways, Canadians are like Americans.) Americans used to lead the world in years of school completed, high school graduation rates, college attendance and graduation rates, and international tests of school performance. We no longer do. Even more disturbing, the current generation of young Americans is not doing as well in some key measures as that of its parents. All of these indicators are especially disheartening given the extraordinary efforts directed at educational reform these days.

Behind these unsatisfactory indicators lie several stories. The most compelling is the continuing large discrepancy in academic performance between white and Asian children (higher) and African American and Hispanic children (lower). This per-

Table 1.2

School Years Completed and Percent of College Graduates among Adults in Selected Countries, 2010

Country	School years (adults over 25)	% College graduates (ages 30–34)	% College graduates (adults over 25)
United States	12.4	21.7	20.0
Germany	12.2	11.7	12.8
Australia	12.0	37.7	22.4
Canada	11.5	26.6	21.1
Japan	11.5	40.0	23.9
Netherlands	11.2	22.2	16.5
France	10.4	19.1	10.6
Great Britain	9.3	30.6	14.4

Source: R. J. Barro and J. W. Lee, "A New Data Set of Educational Attainment in the World, 1950–2010," Working Paper 15902 (Cambridge, Mass.: National Bureau of Economic Research, April 2010).

formance gap has been receiving public attention—and efforts at remediation—for over half a century now, beginning with the 1954 *Brown v. Board of Education* Supreme Court case that ended formal school segregation. On its heels, as part of the late 1960s Great Society legislation, Congress instituted federal aid targeted to school districts with large numbers of poor minority children. In the 1980s, publicly funded, privately operated "charter schools" were launched to give poor minority children access to a presumably more effective alternative to their local public schools. Most recently, President George W. Bush persuaded Congress to pass the No Child Left Behind Act, which made federal aid conditional on local districts implementing rigorous annual testing regimes, with the specific—and mandated—goal of closing the ethnic performance gap. The sad truth is that half a century of efforts dedicated to closing this gap have borne only modest fruit. In chapter 3 I will address this issue and put forward policy recommendations that, if implemented, may finally give poor minority children a decent chance of catching up with their more successful white and Asian peers.

But the ethnic performance gap is not the only reason that American children are losing the global education race. The largely unacknowledged fact is that the majority of white (and some Asian) students in most American school districts are not learning as much as they should, or as much as they are capable of. In other words, a large share of the "not left behind" face a substantial performance gap vis-à-vis their upper-middle-class peers in the United States, and their mainstream counterparts in northern Europe and East Asia. The children subject to this gap fall into two categories. The least worrisome component is made up of the vast cohort of schoolchildren who are insufficiently challenged today because of low academic expectations. Happily, this gap should be relatively easy to close. All it will take is the will, on the part of the fifty American states and their fourteen thousand school districts, to toughen up their school curricula and demand more effort from their schoolchildren.

More troubling is the growing army of white children who perform poorly in school because, like low-income African-American and Hispanic children, they are being raised in single-parent households where they receive insufficient stimulation or motivation. No amount of social engineering, which would not be politically viable in any case, can change these circumstances. But the right kind of school environment and academic program can effectively compensate for them. How to help both subsets of these ostensibly "not left behind" schoolchildren will be taken up in chapters 3 and 4.

The last stage of formal education's contribution to the smart society is post-secondary education, "college" in ordinary parlance. The importance of a college education in today's global, information-age economy is now taken for granted. Accordingly, most state governments and our national one are working hard to raise college attendance rates while also increasing student "diversity" (i.e., increasing rates of black and Hispanic attendance). If these efforts succeeded, American human capital would in fact be significantly enriched—assuming the new collegiate enrollees actually graduated and mastered college-level material.

Unfortunately, while the percentage of high school graduates aspiring to a college education, 62 percent, is bigger now than it ever has been, and may be even bigger than in any other country, the United States now lags in college graduation rates. A growing number of young Americans do not even make it out of high school and many of those who do are not ready for college. As a result, only two-thirds of American baccalaureate enrollees today graduate after six years, and less than a third of those attending community and technical college earn any degree at all, including those who transfer to baccalaureate schools.

These low academic success rates can be traced to several root causes. Perhaps the greatest is the inadequacy of the typical student's high school preparation, something that colleges alone cannot cure—even when they devote heroic resources to "remediation." Thus, meaningful higher education reform must begin in high school, with a thorough subject-by-subject, college-led integration of high school and college curricula and a refusal by colleges to admit underprepared students. Much of the blame can also be placed on the shoulders of the colleges. Too many institutions are far more interested in the numbers of students who enter (on whose tuition and federal aid dollars they depend for survival) than on the numbers who graduate, and most colleges are hardly interested at all in how well any of their former students do after they leave. How American higher education can become both more accessible and effective as the human-capital foundation of the next generation is the subject of chapter 5.

Productivity It is not enough for the adults in a society to be well educated if their education is not put to good use and if no further growth in their capabilities takes place after they graduate from school or college as young men and women. For a society's human capital to flourish, it must be applied and strengthened in its workplaces. As noted earlier, this means that as many adults as possible should be working, and their effort should be amplified by high-quality production technology. Consider the dismal productivity of Russia and some countries of the Middle East, where the people are quite well educated, but where the economies are so dysfunctional, and workplace technology so out-of-date, that their societal human-capital investments in the young are largely squandered by adulthood.

As it happens, the strongest leg of America's human-capital tripod today is its workplace productivity, but that, too, may not be true for much longer. American workplace technology is still the world's most advanced, but will start falling behind in the years ahead unless the United States maintains its lead in scientific research. American workers, long the world's "workaholics," are working less these days, some because of the dismal state of the economy, others due to misguided public policies.

Early on, American civic and political leaders understood that a modern, high-growth economy depended not only on a flourishing free-market economy uninhibited by stifling regulations, high taxes, or restraints on competition but also on the most modern productivity-enhancing technology. To this end, among the U.S. Constitution's handful of explicitly cited powers of Congress was the "Power . . . To promote the Progress of Science and useful Arts."

Taking a long historical perspective, we can see that the United States has ushered in transformational workplace technologies for more than two hundred years: mechanized textile production and other basic manufacturing in the late eighteenth century; a range of stunning new transportation technologies (canals, roads, steam-boats, and railroads) in the early nineteenth century; scientific agriculture and steel-making in the mid-nineteenth century; electrification, telecommunication, advanced construction (long-span bridges, high-rise buildings, underground transportation), and petroleum extraction and refining in the late nineteenth century; assembly-line manufacturing of automobiles and a wide array of consumer products from the early twentieth century on; highly efficient mass-market media and retailing at all times; and, most recently, information technology and biomedicine in the late twentieth century. From minor innovations such as safety pins, zippers, and soft drinks, to iconic breakthroughs such as telegraphs, telephones, electric lighting, automobiles, airplanes, and the Internet, American inventors and scientists have been responsible for each of these technologies and, just as important, American businesses and consumers have been quick to adopt them. *However, in most cases, direct or indirect government subsidies played an important catalytic role.*

For America's human-capital leadership in the workplace to continue, the pace of technological innovation—grounded in scientific discoveries—must accelerate and its businesses must find it profitable to apply new technology rapidly in commercial applications. In his book *The Great Stagnation*, Tyler Cowen notes the centrality of American-led technological innovation in fueling the economic ascendancy of the United States over the last century and a half—and also suggests (hence the book's title) that U.S. technological progress since the 1970s has slowed so much that it has led to most of the country's current economic woes.[8] While Cowen may be too pessimistic about U.S. prospects, and also mistaken in believing that we have already maximized potential gains from education and other aspects of human capital (like immigration), he is surely correct in asserting that unless the U.S. technological enterprise is in high gear there can be only limited progress in further workplace productivity—and concomitant rising American incomes.

Unquestionably, high-technology workplaces result from the decisions of far-sighted entrepreneurs. But most entrepreneurs are not inventors, or necessarily even tech savvy (there are very few contemporary Thomas Edisons or Henry Fords). They rely, instead, on the emergence of new technologies arising from research in the nation's laboratories operated by universities, corporations, and branches of the federal government. Universities are the most dynamic generators of new research and have been since at least the nineteenth century. While universities divert some revenue from their main line of business, teaching undergraduates, to finance faculty scholarship, academic research funding depends heavily on government grants, primarily federal ones. Corporations focused on new product development, like those in the pharmaceutical and computer industries, have a strong incentive to invest in laboratory research but they also count on government support, through both grants and favorable corporate tax treatment. The federal government engages in research more directly through its national laboratories (such as Brookhaven National Laboratory, affiliated with my university), which are overseen by the Department of Energy, the Defense Department, and other federal agencies.

Has federal support for university and corporate research been worth it? Unlike the often uncertain outcomes of government-led educational reforms, when it comes to science and technology, the connection between government inputs and measurable results is much more direct and predictable—albeit less immediately apparent. A nation's investments in scientific research invariably generate proportional increases in scientific discoveries. A nation's increment of scientific discoveries spawns proportional gains in technological applications. And, barring excessive or ill-designed taxation or regulation, new technological applications will most quickly be commercially adopted in the workplaces of the nations where they are conceived. This simple syllogism has served the United States well, and, together with the nation's long-standing (but now eroding) educational leadership, it is the bedrock of the country's centuries-long economic success. How America's lead in workplace technology can be sustained, even in the face of fierce international competition, is the subject of chapter 6.

Among workers in the world's advanced economies, Americans have long exhibited the strongest work ethic. Given Americans' eagerness to work—at all ages and under nearly all circumstances (for example, while attending school, raising children, suffering from disability)—one of the easiest ways to raise the aggregate human capital of the United States, and American workers' corresponding income, is to encourage them to work as much as they are able. After all, payment for work is by far the largest source of family income—far outpacing social security, pensions, or any other kind of income transfer, and the longer people work, the greater the lifetime return on initial educational or other human-capital investments to both the individual and society.

Although Americans still (just barely) work longer and harder than workers in most other rich countries (accounting for the United States' continuing productivity superiority—despite the relative decline in educational achievement), a growing percentage of working-age men are not in the labor force. Adult male labor participation, which in the 1970s averaged 78 percent, fell to 71 percent in 2010 and even before the recent economic collapse was only 73 percent. While some of this is because more men are in college, and the impact of this shift on the overall American labor force is partially offset by a big increase in the percentage of working women, if men returning to the workforce were to join the growing cohort of women workers, the United States would realize a painless human-capital windfall.

The decline in labor force participation is the result of both an institutional "push" and personal calculation "pull" dynamic.

Workers are pushed out of the labor force by the impact of periodic downturns in the business cycle, such as the unusually severe one that began in 2008. In response to such economic conditions, too many decision makers in the government and labor unions, guilty of overly simplistic economic reasoning, foolishly subscribe to the "fixed lump of labor" view of the economy: a belief that keeping potential workers out of the labor market is a viable way to reduce the official unemployment rate. This leads them to promote "early retirement" and indiscriminate authorization of disability eligibility. On the pull side, fully capable workers who are laid off or discontented with their jobs are quick to jump at pension or disability stipends when these become too readily available. At the epicenter of these dynamics are federal entitlement programs and state and local public employee contracts. How these can be realistically restructured to let the American workplace take full advantage of our workers' natural propensity to work—and to work hard—is the subject of chapter 7.

Immigration Immigration has also been one of America's most singular human-capital advantages; we have always admitted far more immigrants, and assimilated them more thoroughly, than any other country on earth. Now, after years of complacently tolerating immigration policies that are simultaneously incoherent, unfair, and unenforced, ordinary Americans are thoroughly confused about the issue, and their political leaders are having a hard time agreeing on sensible reforms.

Most obviously, immigrants were needed in the nineteenth century to settle the United States' expanding western frontier and operate its rapidly growing number of farms, factories, and shops. But regardless of the circumstances of the time, immigrants have built American human capital uninterruptedly from the first settlers to the present day, and at every level of the economy. Each year around the Fourth of July, *The New York Times* carries a full-page advertisement celebrating the contributions of eminent immigrants, past and present. The page is dense with iconic names from Joseph Pulitzer and Andrew Carnegie in the nineteenth century, Albert Einstein, Samuel Goldwyn, and Irving Berlin in the mid-twentieth, to Henry Kissinger and George Soros today. Throughout American history, immigrants were the indispensable Americans, building railroad, manufacturing, financial, and entertainment empires; making the world's most notable breakthroughs in scientific research and technological inventions; and cementing the United States' renown in music, the fine arts, and literature. Other immigrants entered politics and throughout American history have occupied every political office, at every level of government—federal, state, and local—except for the presidency.

How well the nation benefits from immigration does depend, however, on the contours of national immigration policy. Until the 1920s, American immigration policy was essentially an open door to any and all who wished to come (with the occasional exception, such as the exclusion of the Chinese in the 1880s). At a time when most of Europe was quite poor, and when migrating meant leaving one's native land forever, immigrants to the United States were most likely to be Europe's—and, to a lesser extent, Asia's—most talented and venturesome people. Further, coming to an America that had not yet instituted a social welfare safety net or labor protections, immigrants had to be extremely hardy and hard-working—highly valuable attributes in a rapidly industrializing society. In other words, America was attracting the world's best and brightest without even trying.

Because America's borders are no longer open to all comers, if the United States wants to replicate its earlier success in attracting highly capable immigrants, it must now do so through the design of its immigration quotas. While most debates on immigration policy today concern the not unimportant question of what to do about the country's 10 to 12 million illegal immigrants, a more fruitful policy discussion would focus on the politically less sensitive issue of which immigrants we should seek to admit in the future. In recent years the United States has admitted, on average, more than 1 million immigrants a year. Among legal immigrants, over 65 percent were sponsored by families, 15 percent were admitted as victims of persecution, and 14 percent were skilled workers sponsored by employers. The small remainder span a number of admission categories including 4 percent selected by lottery. While most family-sponsored and persecuted immigrants are hard-working and many have useful talents, the overwhelming majority are nevertheless poorly educated and unskilled.

That need not be the case, however, for future immigrants. The United States could, by restructuring its immigration admissions criteria, quickly realize an incremental human-capital bonanza. Even holding to current aggregate quota levels, by bending the immigrant admissions trajectory in favor of the hundreds of thousands of better-educated, skilled (and perhaps even English-speaking) immigrants, the United States would gain an instantaneous infusion of talent. This infusion would significantly enlarge the pool of intelligent, creative, and motivated workers to supply American firms on the technological and biomedical frontiers with new scientists, engineers, physicians, and nurses; schools and colleges with new teachers and scholars; the financial industry with new analysts and managers; and the dominant service economy with new supervisors, technicians, and troubleshooters. Some of these immigrants, following in the footsteps of Andrew Grove of Intel and Sergey Brin of Google, are bound to launch the exciting industries and technological breakthroughs of tomorrow.

Beyond dramatically upgrading America's labor force today, an immigration policy focused on admitting more capable immigrants would reinforce a virtuous human-capital cycle for future generations. All the empirical evidence suggests that an influx of better-educated immigrants, raising their children in predominantly stable families and encouraging high achievement in school, would generate human-capital outcomes much greater than those currently characterizing American immigrant children. These children, in turn, as adults would provide rich human-capital nurturing grounds for subsequent generations. If the United States is ever to meet the educational achievement goals of No Child Left Behind, it must recognize that fully half of the "left behind" are the children of recent immigrants.

In the process of retooling immigration policy, we must not forget the importance of *assimilation*. As noted earlier, America's overwhelmingly positive immigration history has depended on the fact the United States was able to, quite uniquely, assimilate wave after wave of its immigrants for centuries. Undeniably, the historical record shows periods when Americans exhibited hostility to certain immigrant groups and, at all times, many immigrants have clung to their native tongues and customs for at least a while. But true assimilation depends much more on immigrants' acceptance of *America's values* than their adoption of all facets of its contemporary culture, and on natives eventually welcoming them with generosity and tolerance. Both of these conditions clearly prevailed—until the 1960s. Since then, America's assimilation ethos has fallen on hard times because of strong resistance—not from the native-born or even the immigrants themselves—but from America's intellectual elite and its leading institutions, regrettably including urban public schools. Our long-standing national faith in the assimilation process must quickly be restored because, regardless of the mix of immigrants the United States admits, immigrants will be able to contribute fully as members of America's smart society only if they are thoroughly assimilated.

The smart-society implications for American immigration policy going forward are crystal clear. Because immigrants at all times and in all places in the United States have invigorated the country economically and socially, the most rapid and certain way to build and regenerate American human capital is to admit more of them and, most critically, to admit them *legally* under sensible, strategic admissions criteria—and to do everything we can to encourage their rapid assimilation. How this can be done is the subject of chapter 8.

SUMMING UP

Thoughtful Americans are becoming increasingly alarmed by signs that the human capital of the United States is deteriorating, either in absolute terms or relative to our international rivals in the hypercompetitive global economy. And they are right to worry. We should worry that a growing share of young Americans are failing to receive the education they need to succeed—both economically and socially—in the demanding environment of the twenty-first century. We should worry that not enough Americans are working. We should worry that, unless we keep our place at the scientific frontier and invest enough in emerging technologies, we will lose out to the Asian Tigers, the European Union, and eventually China and other emerging economies. Finally, we should worry that someday soon, the flow of immigrants may dry up, and those who still want to come will be drawn increasingly from the bottom of the immigrant pool.

The most concrete manifestation of our human-capital worries can be seen in the bitter partisan debates in Congress and state capitals about growing income inequality, the scope of the American welfare state, and the size of federal and state deficits. What both sides (and the public at large) fail to understand is that all of these problems—and many others—are really caused by the ongoing erosion of Americans' human capital. Most of the things the American left is exercised by these days—high unemployment, stagnant wages, rising poverty, homelessness, and diminished access to health care—result from human-capital deficiencies of the lower third of the population. At the same time, so do the concerns of the American right—the rising cost of welfare-state entitlements, subpar economic growth, alarming rates of out-of-wedlock child rearing (even among formerly middle-class whites), and idleness and criminality among the young.

Failing to appreciate the degree to which human-capital erosion is at the root of their complaints, both the left and the right look to implement unproductive policies. The income redistribution favored by the left and partial dismantling of the safety net favored by the right are both politically infeasible and economically counterproductive—and they do nothing to make Americans any smarter. Even the favorite nostrums of the political center, best characterized as attempts at social engineering, may be more politically palatable but are equally ineffective.

Americans do not have to choose between diverting a growing share of national resources to the welfare state (displacing other essential government spending and running up the deficit) or inhumanely letting many less fortunate Americans needlessly suffer. In this book, I argue for a third way. We can restore the status of the United States as the world's smartest society by retooling all three legs of its once invincible human-capital tripod: reform American education, rebuild the American workplace, and welcome to America the world's most capable immigrants.

The rest of this book is dedicated to thoroughly examining each leg of America's human-capital tripod, identifying its strengths and weaknesses, and recommending strategic changes for national, state, and local governments to adopt in programs already entirely under their jurisdiction. All of my policy recommendations meet two criteria: they do not expand the scope of American government and they are not too costly relative to the benefits they promise to generate.

American Education

THE KEYSTONE OF A SMART SOCIETY

Building a smart, high-human-capital society begins with making sure that all children get a good education. A century and a half ago, within decades of its independence, America became the world's most human-capital-rich—i.e., smartest—country by establishing the world's best education system and having the world's most-educated people. That is no longer true. While most young Americans today—across all ethnic and socioeconomic categories—are better educated than their parents or grandparents, they are not necessarily educated well enough for the contemporary, globalized knowledge economy. In contrast to only a few decades ago, they are no longer better educated than their peers in other advanced—and some not-so-advanced—countries. Some of this international comparative deficiency is due to "the rise of the rest," but, whatever the reason, it is a condition that should rightly concern all Americans. Also, the quality of education across the United States varies far too widely—among Americans of different backgrounds and among the fifty states. How America's educational shortcomings can be remedied is the subject of this and the following three chapters.

Americans can once again become the best-educated people in the world through a few strategic interventions at key points in the schooling trajectory. One set of reforms should be aimed at closing two key academic performance gaps plaguing the country's K–12 public schools: the vast gulf separating the achievement of disadvantaged American youngsters of all ethnic groups from that of the vast majority of non-disadvantaged mainstream children (which I discuss as the "Megagap" in chapter 3), and the smaller but much more pervasive one separating the achievement of mainstream students from that of the most privileged American youngsters and their mainstream foreign peers (the "Mainstream" gap discussed in chapter 4). Reforms of higher education should be aimed at enabling all qualified American high school graduates to go to (and complete) college or other relevant post-secondary training, and making sure that this experience is academically or professionally rigorous.

AMERICA'S HISTORIC LEAD

What is considered to be the right number of years to spend in school and what should be taught there obviously changes over time. Two hundred years ago, when Americans first laid the groundwork for a system of universal education—universal in that it was not limited to the children of the rich—being an educated person required about six years of school, what we today would call an elementary education. One hundred years ago, to be well educated meant completing high school. After World War II, the educational gold standard became a college education. Now, increasingly, to be at the educational frontier requires a graduate or professional degree.

Whatever the contemporary educational threshold, Americans always got there first: building the institutional infrastructure, providing for public funding in whole or in part, and establishing the ancillary quality-control processes (like testing and accreditation). As noted in the previous chapter, even before the Colonies won independence from England, American schools were always accessible to all children in their catchment area, at a time when England and continental European countries restricted schooling to children of the aristocracy or the more affluent members of the merchant and professional classes. Throughout the nineteenth and twentieth centuries, from the Land Ordinance of 1785 through the G.I. Bill of 1944, American education for students of all ages expanded in leaps and bounds, always staying far ahead of even the most enlightened European countries and somewhat ahead of America's neighbor to the north, Canada (table 2.1).

From the time of the revolution through the early decades of the nineteenth century, most American schoolchildren were

....

Table 2.1

**Public Elementary School Attendance
in the United States and Selected Countries,
1870–1900 (percent of all ages 5–19)**

Country	1870	1880	1890	1900
United States	54.8	56.7	59.2	61.1
Canada	53.4	54.7	57.6	61.3
Germany	–	–	–	56.1
France	40.9	44.9	49.8	50.7
Austria	28.8	36.6	45.2	50.2
Great Britain	17.4	36.7	43.9	51.5

Sources: For U.S.: Thomas D. Snyder, ed., *120 Years of American Education: A Statistical Portrait* (National Center for Education Statistics, January 1993). *For Canada:* B. R. Mitchell, *International Historical Statistics: The Americas, 1750–2000* (New York: Palgrave Macmillan, 2003). *For Europe:* B. R. Mitchell, *International Historical Statistics: Europe, 1750–2000* (New York: Palgrave Macmillan, 2003).

taught in what educational historians label "district schools" because they were organized and paid for by local school districts, and generally territorially compact enough so that all pupils could walk to the nearest school. Characterized now as "one-room schoolhouses," these district schools were unquestionably quite primitive by later educational standards, having fairly rudimentary 3-R (reading, writing, arithmetic) curricula, mixing children of all ages and abilities in the same classrooms, and employing teachers whose own education was quite limited. Nevertheless, even these basic educational facilities were revolutionary for the time. They were open and usually free to all local children and they brought together children not only of all ages but of all social classes as well, because all but the very richest families sent their children to them.[1]

In one of the most striking educational developments of the young United States, district schools throughout the new states were determined to stifle at an early age the kind of speech-related class distinctions that then and now have plagued the people of England. Strongly influenced by Noah Webster, they *consciously and universally* propagated a uniform way of writing (including spelling) and speaking that we today recognize as Standard American English.[2]

Beginning in the 1830s, spurred on by the enormously influential educational reformer from Massachusetts, Horace Mann, and responsive to the growing educational requirements of a rapidly industrializing country, a powerful national education reform movement strove to substantially upgrade the curricular content, teaching effectiveness, and time span of America's public schools.[3] In Mann's own words,

> After the State shall have secured to all its children, that basis of knowledge and morality, which is indispensable to its own security; after it shall have supplied them with the instruments

of that individual prosperity, whose aggregate will constitute its own social prosperity; then they may be emancipated from its tutelage, each one to go whithersoever his well-instructed mind shall determine.[4]

This effort, referred to by education scholars as "the common school movement," took on great momentum and spread like wildfire across the new nation. Illinois imposed universal schooling along these lines in 1825, followed by New York in 1830, Massachusetts in 1837, and by the 1860s, so had all northern, Midwest, and frontier states. Only in the South was the movement thwarted before the Civil War, where affluent whites sent their children to private schools, and poor whites and blacks (then enslaved) received a meager district school education at best. In the Reconstruction period after the Civil War, unsegregated common schools open to both white and black schoolchildren were established in all southern states, but with the collapse of Reconstruction after 1875 and the adoption of Jim Crow laws throughout the South, these became segregated and remained so until the passage of civil rights legislation in the 1960s.

Many of the characteristic aspects of American schools today, most particularly elementary schools, were set in stone by the common schools of the nineteenth century. Among the most distinctive at the time—and the most enduring—was the belief that teachers should receive specialized training, which resulted in the establishment of "normal schools" to prepare them with supposedly scientific methods of teaching (i.e., "pedagogy"). America's first normal school was launched in Boston in 1838, and by the end of the century the lion's share of the national teaching force was trained in such places.[5] The professionalization of teacher training got a huge boost in prestige and public acceptance with the founding in 1887 of the national citadel of teacher training, Columbia University Teachers College. By the early twentieth century, most normal schools had mutated into state teachers colleges, and, after World War II, into comprehensive public liberal arts colleges dominated by their teacher education programs. To this day, a majority of American elementary schoolteachers as well as a large share of high school teachers are graduates of such teacher education programs, the descendants of the normal schools of the common school era.

The common school movement introduced many other familiar features of public schools. While originally dedicated only to making access to elementary school universally mandatory and free, by the end of the nineteenth century the movement had extended its reach to encompass universal secondary education. The common school template fostered the strict assignment of students to classrooms by age (something quite novel in the nineteenth century) and by academic ability. In the wake of the movement's influence, many other American public school characteristics also came to be nationally consistent. Despite being under the jurisdiction of state education departments, with almost no federal government input until recently, the curricular content of schools, subject for subject, became relatively uniform across the country. This was most likely due to the influence of national (but nongovernmental) accreditation organizations that first arose at the end of the nineteenth century; the standardized doctrines of the teachers colleges; and the sales policies of textbook publishers that profit from nationwide adoption of their offerings. Even the physical specifications of American schools quickly became homogenized, with consistent class and classroom sizes, and a familiar repertoire of ancillary facilities: gymnasiums, auditoriums, cafeterias, and so on.

By the early twentieth century, the common school movement had succeeded in making its vision of access to a professionally delivered, practical education for all Americans a reality in every state. But it took a while for the education establishment to agree on the precise format and academic content of a typical school system's elementary (and later, secondary) schools. In the case of elementary education, there was always general agreement (even internationally) on the educational foundations to be taught. However, in the early decades of the twentieth century, John Dewey and other "progressive" educators challenged the rigidly structured rote learning and focus on academic content practiced in most American elementary schools at the time—and still pervasive in the rest of the world—charging that it was pedagogically ineffective and, worse, stifled child development and creativity.[6] By the middle of the twentieth century, the progressives had won this argument, first in the training of teachers in state colleges, and then in the classrooms of most districts. In a strong backlash, there arose a powerful countermovement in the 1950s against progressivism led by such national figures as Harvard President James Bryant Conant, University of Chicago President Robert Maynard Hutchins, and Admiral Hyman Rickover, all of them calling for higher academic standards and more rigorous instruction.[7] This debate continues to the present day, with the teacher training establishment and the National Education Association still promoting progressivism, and a host of prominent critics opposing it, including luminaries such as the late Boston University President John Silber, former Assistant Secretary of Education Chester Finn, and several notable public school chancellors in Chicago, New York, and Washington.

The spread of American secondary schools at the turn of the last century raised other questions. First, at what age should elementary education end? The study of early adolescent psychological development that surfaced at the time, and the high dropout rates of children who went to four-year high schools right after eight years of elementary school, persuaded educators that there had to be a transitional, intermediate institution. Thus, beginning in 1909 in Columbus, Ohio, and 1910 in Berkeley, California, secondary education came to be articulated into two segments: a transitional school for early adolescents (called junior high or middle school) and high school for older teens. But the precise age at which to set cutoffs to begin the transition (ten, eleven, or twelve) or to end it (fourteen or fifteen) has yet to be settled. Given the uncertainty of the subjects to be taught—and how they are to be taught—in the transition years, and the painfulness of teaching anything to early adolescents, few districts have been happy with any of the many variations they have tried out over the years.

More seriously, educators needed to agree on what should be taught—and to whom—in high school. From their widespread introduction in the early twentieth century until the 1960s, the national consensus was that high schools should sort students by academic ability, as measured by standardized aptitude or IQ tests (administered in elementary or middle school), and tailor each student's coursework to reflect his or her intellectual and occupational capacities. This sorting led inexorably to channeling students of different abilities—and, to a lesser extent, boys and girls—into different academic and, ultimately, career paths. The cognitively gifted were to be prepared for college; the less gifted taught enough to function competently in lower- and mid-level white-collar jobs (such as girls being groomed for secretarial work); and the least academically oriented (mainly boys) trained for vocational or technical trades, either in comprehensive high school vocational tracks or in specialized vocational schools.[8]

There were certain undeniable benefits to having academically stratified high schools. They could require rigorous courses for college preparatory students, assuring a very high degree of academic readiness for the college-bound, and they supplied the middle and lower tiers of the labor market with an army of competent secretaries, clerks, and skilled tradesmen. They were also reasonably effective in matching the abilities of young people to career paths in which they were likely to succeed. And though American high schools were internally stratified academically, in other respects they were consistent with the country's democratic, egalitarian values. Unlike stratified secondary school systems in Europe, all local children attended the same high school, and the American high school experience always included a wide range of social and athletic pursuits open to all students—ones in which the non-cognitively or non-socially advantaged could excel. On the negative side, scholastic stratification was bound to reinforce prevailing patterns of class and racial differentiation, especially for African Americans and poor children generally.

PARADIGM SHIFTS

The rapid diffusion across the United States of a standardized national template for universal education, beginning 150 years ago, can be seen for most of American history as a great triumph, and is largely responsible for the United States being, until the day before yesterday, so far ahead of the rest of the world in giving all of its citizens a sound education. But this historical paradigm is no longer adequate. If the United States wants to remain the world's best-educated country, it must revamp the entire set of institutions and policies, from preschool through college, that constitutes the American educational system.

Over the last five decades, with accelerating force, America's long-settled educational paradigm has been transformed by four major developments. The first was a new self-consciousness regarding the nation's international standing in indicators of educational achievement. Until the Cold War, without giving the matter much thought, Americans were supremely complacent about the superiority of their educational system relative to that of any other country. For much of the last century, most of the world was barely literate and even the richer countries of Europe clearly lagged behind the United States in how well their people were educated (as indicated in the data cited earlier). However, the launch of the world's first space satellite, *Sputnik*, by the Soviet Union in 1957 was a wake-up call that suddenly cast into doubt America's vaunted global technological superiority and, by extension, the quality of its schooling in science and mathematics. The immediate result of this new sense of vulnerability was to increase significantly public school funding and efforts in these subjects. The long-term effect was to instill in Americans a gnawing anxiety and inferiority complex about the quality of their schools in any international matchup.

The second, and perhaps most important, paradigm shift affected the way professional educators (and the public) looked at—and took responsibility for—the academic success or failure of public school students. Before the 1960s, everyone unquestioningly believed not only that every American child's academic (and, therefore, career) prospects were shaped by some combination of their genetic endowment and family status, but also there was not much that could—or should—be done about it. This kind of cognitive and socioeconomic fatalism is no longer acceptable (except, maybe, among teachers). Out of the social upheaval of the 1960s and the civil rights movement, a new national consensus took hold that insists that no youngsters, including those from underprivileged minority groups, should be doomed to a bad education or an inferior career merely because of their genes or familial disadvantage.

Third, the increased reliance on testing to gauge American educational progress has buttressed these paradigm shifts. A number of tests developed by two international education agencies working with the U.S. Department of Education measure how well American schoolchildren are doing compared to their international peers. The International Association for the Evaluation of Educational Achievement (IEA) conducts two periodic assessments. The older one, Trends in International Mathematics and Science Study (TIMSS), has measured, at four-year intervals beginning in 1995, the mathematical and science proficiency of fourth- and eighth-grade schoolchildren in sixty or so countries. The other, Progress in International Reading Literacy Study (PIRLS), has been given at five-year intervals since 2001 to fourth graders in forty-two countries to assess reading comprehension. Starting in 1997, and at three-year intervals, the Organisation for Economic Cooperation and Development (OECD) has been assessing the mathematical and science proficiency of fifteen-year-olds in more than seventy countries in its Programme for International Student Assessment (PISA) tests. The United States participates fully in all of these international assessments and, to date, American schoolchildren have not done especially well in any of them (I will review the findings later in this chapter), a widely cited fact that accounts for much of the current American educational angst.

Testing has become even more important in gauging academic achievement *within* the United States, primarily to address—and remedy—disparities among schoolchildren of different ethnic and socioeconomic groups. While common for decades, public school testing took a quantum leap forward with the passage of the Elementary and Secondary Education Act of 2001 (No Child Left Behind, or NCLB). NCLB requires all states, as a condition of receiving federal school aid, to test all third- to eighth-grade students annually to determine their achievement levels in reading and math. For certain student cohorts (especially black and Hispanic schoolchildren) that test below benchmark proficiency levels, states and school districts must show "adequate yearly progress" in test results or risk losing some portion of their federal aid. Testing is also a key element of local school accountability to parents and other "stakeholders," as most states now issue district-level and individual school student achievement "report cards."

One of the unfortunate political compromises made by the George W. Bush administration to secure passage of NCLB was to permit each state to develop and use its own tests. This almost guaranteed a kind of testing "race to the bottom," because if a state implemented really rigorous tests it faced a greater risk of falling short of its own (and national) achievement benchmarks and triggering federal sanctions. Therefore, for anyone wanting to know how well students are doing in any American state, the only reliable set of academic achievement tests is that administered by the U.S. Department of Education: the National Assessment of Educational Progress (NAEP), dubbed "the nation's report card."

Fourth, and finally, the most recent and urgent reason for comprehensively revising American educational practice is the growing recognition that, for the United States to remain a global economic power, Americans must excel in the global "knowledge economy." The knowledge economy, both in the United States and abroad, puts a labor market premium on brains over brawn and, even among brains, on keen analytical abilities (requiring stronger mathematical and scientific proficiency) and communication skills (requiring greater literacy).

All of these concerns have coalesced in a new educational paradigm that obligates America's schools and colleges to:

1. Instill higher academic expectations backed by more rigorous curricula to meet the demands of the knowledge economy and to restore American global educational preeminence.

2. No longer allow the scholastic achievement of their students to depend on good genes and good fortune, with the corollary that all students—including the most disadvantaged poor and minority children—must be brought to some satisfactory level of academic proficiency.

3. Keep track of their educational progress through frequent and reliable testing, and be prepared to continuously revise their educational policies accordingly, implementing proven "evidence-based" strategies.

Some features of the new paradigm have not gone unchallenged. The abandonment of cognitive and socioeconomic educational determinism and its companion, holding schools and teachers accountable for student performance based on testing, while pretty much "the law of the land," face resistance from two quarters. Schoolteachers, standing as they do at the front lines of accountability for satisfactory levels of student achievement, not only are understandably anxious about what this means for their job security and pay, but also not so secretly question the basic premise. They say, not without reason, that it is naive and unfair to put the entire burden of student achievement—especially for the poorest or most handicapped children—on their shoulders. As one commentator observes, regarding the New Orleans school system:

> The criminal justice and health care systems may be broken, living-wage jobs in short supply, and families forced to live in unstable or unsafe conditions. But the buck supposedly stops in the classroom. Thus teachers can find themselves charged with remedying an impossibly broad set of challenges that go far beyond reading at grade level.[9]

They have a point. In chapters 3 and 4 I address ways in which we can significantly boost student achievement and, while not letting teachers off the hook, also not impose on them the entire burden of eliminating performance disparities.

The other opposition comes from a segment of contrarian opinion that believes that education reform efforts aimed at closing achievement gaps are largely futile because schoolchildren's cognitive and cultural disadvantages are too deep-seated to overcome. Instead, they argue that not all Americans need to be educated to the level of college readiness, and that this goal is not achievable in any case. The policy prescription we are to infer from this bleak assessment is that we should go back to the old paradigm of cognitive and social stratification: stop wasting money or energy on school reform and focus education efforts on those most likely to succeed academically with the goal of preparing them—and only them—for college, and, as in the old days, steer the educational losers into industries and occupations that may require specialized training (e.g., hair stylists, telephone installers) but not a thorough general education.

Are the contrarians correct? First, their position is not new; it is merely a rationale for reestablishing the status quo that prevailed in the first two-thirds of the last century. Taken to its extreme, it echoes the educational elitists of every era to justify the kind of educational rationing and stratification that used to be endemic throughout the world—something repugnant to the egalitarian American ethos. But the best *empirical* refutation is found in the academic fortunes of upper-middle-class American children. Central to the contrarian's view is the argument that half of all children must be—in terms of statistical logic—below average and therefore should be automatically disqualified from aspiring to or getting a college education. Yet this same logic should also apply to children from the upper middle class. Countless studies refute the notion that just because upper-middle-class adults engage in "assortative" (i.e., class-based) mating, their children have any *genetic* advantage in intelligence.[10] Yet, despite not being necessarily "smarter" than the general population—or even than the majority of disadvantaged children—nearly all upper-middle-class children graduate from high school and most go on to and graduate from college—*mainly because their well-educated parents see to it.* Bottom line: if upper-middle-class kids of middling (or even inferior) ability can get—and benefit from—a good education, then all other kids should be able to as well. So, despite the doubters, we need not abandon the idealistic new American public education paradigm; we just have to make it work.

MILESTONES ON THE ROAD TO THE NEW PARADIGM

Widespread acceptance of America's new educational paradigm did not occur overnight; it is the product of a half century of study and reconsideration. Perhaps the first crack in the old paradigm was the 1954 Supreme Court decision in *Brown v. Board of Education*, which ended de jure school segregation in the South. Clearly, the court's ruling was primarily grounded in the flagrant unconstitutionality of state-mandated segregation. But a key element in the court's motivation was the desire to raise the academic achievement of black schoolchildren. The court's thinking was influenced by the research of sociologist Kenneth Clark and others that for the first time challenged the prevailing socioeconomic determinism that took the poor school performance of blacks—segregated or not—for granted.[11] Thus *Brown* might be considered the country's first step on the path to holding schools, not children, responsible for educational outcomes.

As noted earlier, the Soviet Union's launch of the *Sputnik* space satellite in 1957 suddenly made Americans aware that the United States was in danger of losing the global race for technological superiority, the one domain in which Americans had long displayed unchallenged leadership. The fact that the country might be overtaken not by a friendly Western competitor but by its dangerous Cold War adversary heightened Americans' anxiety and sense of inferiority. The response of the Eisenhower administration was to launch a host of committees and studies and, ultimately, to sharply increase federal aid for public school instruction in science and mathematics.

In 1965, as part of the Lyndon Johnson administration's "Great Society" reforms, Congress passed the Elementary and Secondary Education Act (ESEA), which, for the first time, specifically directed federal school aid to raise the academic achievement levels of underperforming schoolchildren, most of them poor, urban, and minorities. In terms of policy, this was the first concrete attempt to decouple student achievement from socioeconomic or cognitive determinants. This legislation also established Head Start, the first (and still the largest) federal foray into promoting preschool education for disadvantaged youngsters. (The importance and design of an effective preschool experience is the subject of chapter 3.)

A singular aspect of the new paradigm story is the expanding role of the federal government in education policy. In fact, to a large extent it is the "federalization" of education that has defined the new paradigm. The old paradigm, although strongly impacted by national intellectual and advocacy currents like the common school movement, nevertheless was implemented entirely by the individual states and localities. In contrast, every element in the new paradigm depends on national perceptions and national action. The U.S. Supreme Court ended school segregation. National Cold War anxieties and national civil rights advocacy prompted federal aid to address their concerns. One key advance in this march toward the federalization of education policy—along new paradigm lines—was the creation of a cabinet-level federal education agency. A modest movement in this direction had already been taken during the Eisenhower administration in the establishment of the U.S. Department of Health, Education, and Welfare (HEW) in 1953. The definitive step, however, was the transfer of national education policy and oversight from HEW to an independent Department of Education under President Jimmy Carter in 1979.

A cascade of influential reports and popular books has both shaped and responded to federal education policy. Two books in particular that highlighted the failings of American public schools caught the public imagination: *Death at an Early Age* by Jonathan Kozol and *Why Johnny Can't Read* by Rudolf Flesch.[12] These works drove yet more nails into the coffin of the old paradigm of socioeconomic and cognitive educational determinism. But the most influential of all the postwar education reports by far was *A Nation at Risk: The Imperative for Educational Reform*, authored by a blue-ribbon commission of prominent educators under the auspices of the Reagan administration in 1983.[13] The report charged that "the educational foundations of our society" were being "eroded by a rising tide of mediocrity that threatens our very future as a Nation and a people" and "If an unfriendly foreign power had attempted to impose on America the mediocre educational performance that exists today, we might well have viewed it as an act of war." Beyond its hyperbolic rhetoric, the report was one of the earliest to note the poor performance of American students on international tests in mathematics, science, and language arts. Among its many other indictments, it asserted that 23 million Americans (about 14 percent of all adults) were "functionally illiterate" and a majority of the rest lacked "'higher order' intellectual skills"; that Scholastic Aptitude Test scores for college-bound seniors had fallen over the previous twenty years; and that colleges had to offer remedial courses to a high proportion of their underprepared entering students.

Federal spending on education has grown dramatically as Congress has continually tweaked the various provisions of the ESEA under its successive reauthorizations. Federal aid to state and local public schools has grown from $2 billion in 1965 to more than $56 billion in 2008.[14] But the reauthorization of ESEA in 2001—optimistically titled No Child Left Behind—exponentially increased the intensity of federal intervention in state and local school policy. This legislation, more than any of its predecessors, has already impelled states and their local school districts to introduce reforms that only a few years ago were unthinkable: the widespread establishment of charter schools; more rigorous evaluation of teachers, including assessing their effectiveness through pupil test scores; recasting of curricula; lengthening of school days and years; and a host of locally idiosyncratic experimental interventions. Chapter 3 will review in detail the value and costs of implementing the most pervasive of these reform initiatives.

The Obama administration has tried to speed up the pace of educational reform by dangling before states and localities the prospect of winning competitively awarded federal grants. Originally part of the American Recovery and Reinvestment Act (ARRA) of 2009, and now funded through annual appropriations, the Race to the Top initiative has distributed, in three competitive cycles, more than $4 billion—with another half billion in the pipeline—to states that agree to implement more aggressive school reform measures. Success in winning a Race to the Top grant (or its size) has depended primarily on the willingness to implement a rigorous, student test–driven teacher evaluation system and substantially increasing the number of charter schools, while gaining the acquiescence of local teacher unions.

In parallel with the steady stream of publications that view American education with alarm and pieces of federal legislation, there have been substantial developments of the reforms themselves. The first truly new idea was the "charter school," a tuition-free, publicly funded school available to parents dissatisfied with the zoned local district school, and operated free of the constraints imposed by unionized teachers and district administration. The idea of permitting independently operated schools to receive public funding is said to have originated with University of Massachusetts, Amherst, professor Ray Budde in 1988, and was embraced soon after by Albert Shanker, then president of the American Federation of Teachers. In 1991 Minnesota became the first state to authorize charter schools, followed by California in 1992. Today charter schools exist in forty-one states and the District of Columbia. The success to date of charter schools nationally will be considered in chapters 3 and 4.

Another independently developed but highly significant educational reform initiative is Teach for America (TFA), which was founded in 1990 by Wendy Kopp and based on her 1989 Princeton University senior thesis. Its idea is to break the prevailing monopoly on teacher training of state teacher colleges—and their mediocre private collegiate brethren—by recruiting "the best and the brightest" graduates of U.S. Ivy League and other prestigious universities to become teachers, especially in the country's most troubled neighborhoods. The TFA program involves, first, going to America's best colleges and universities to attract teaching candidates—none of whom has ever taken any "education" courses—and then giving them a crash course in pedagogy so they can qualify to teach in public school classrooms in most U.S. states. TFA has by now become hugely successful in carrying out its mission; each year it currently attracts more than 46,000 candidates and trains and places about 4,500.[15]

It is indeed curious that, given the stress our national dialogue about public school reform has placed on the importance of recruiting and retaining highly effective teachers, there has been so little interest in where teachers are being trained. Kopp's brainstorm was to recognize that the overwhelming majority of U.S. teachers today are being educated in second-rate institutions, and consequently America's public schools are losing out in the competition for first-rate talent. We don't know yet how well teachers' effectiveness is correlated with their intellect, or the quality of their undergraduate education, but there is good reason to believe that brighter, better-educated individuals might also be better teachers. Beyond this yet-to-be-proven hypothesis, there is the important issue of teachers' prestige. Among the countries that outrank the United States in educational outcomes there is one common factor: their teachers are better educated and, consequently, better respected.

The last significant educational milestone is the effort to institute across the country a more rigorous—and more nationally uniform—public school curriculum. Launched by two nonfederal organizations—the National Governors Association and the Council of Chief State School Officers—and based on studies going back to 1996, the Common Core State Standards Initiative encourages every state to adopt its highly subject- and grade-specific recommended curriculum. As of 2012, all but five states are on board.[16] While very promising conceptually, it remains to be seen whether the common standards are academically sound and whether they will actually be implemented as envisioned and prove to be educational game changers.

All of the milestones noted so far have been national. One important addition to the list, however, is state initiated. The Massachusetts Education Reform Act of 1993 imposed a rigorous, statewide K–12 core curriculum and a somewhat longer school day and school year; in 2005, the state began piloting an even longer school day in certain districts. Perhaps because of these measures, Massachusetts now leads the nation in K–12 education gains. A recent Harvard study, examining results from international math and reading tests, found that Massachusetts eighth graders not only scored highest among American states on the tests but also outscored test takers in all but a few countries (see table 2.9).[17] Other encouraging statistics: 61 percent of Massachusetts high school freshmen proceed to college, and 53 percent of its young adults have college degrees; both are the highest proportions of any American state.

MINDING THE (ACHIEVEMENT) GAPS–AND CLOSING THEM

For America to regain its status as the world's smartest society, it must have the world's best educational system. Yet, as noted earlier, looking at metrics of educational achievement internationally, we see that the United States is rapidly falling behind, being overtaken by an increasing number of other countries with each passing decade. Most of this can be ascribed to the rapid educational progress being made by other places. The advanced rich countries of Europe have largely abandoned their educational elitism and are making good on their own version of "not leaving any children behind." Other countries with the will to become smart societies needed only the means. The former Soviet satellites of Eastern Europe no longer have their educational potential held back by the yoke of Soviet communism, and the "Asian tigers" no longer suffer from the scarce resources of early-stage economic development. Although we are losing the educational race mainly because others have learned to run faster, that is no excuse; we must learn to run even faster ourselves.

The inferior standing of the United States is evident in all three of the international tests, in all three subjects (reading, math, and science), and at all ages (fourth grade, eighth grade, and age fifteen) as shown in tables 2.2 and 2.3.

A detailed analysis of the data behind these dismal statistics reveals that the deficiencies in American school achievement are

Table 2.2

PIRLS Test Scores for Reading (fourth grade)

Country	2006	2001
Russia	565	528
Canada (Ontario)	555	548
Italy	551	541
Hungary	551	543
Sweden	549	561
Germany	548	539
Netherlands	547	554
United States	**540**	**542**
England	539	553
France	522	525
International Average	500	500

Source: OECD, Programme for International Student Assessment, 2009.

Table 2.3

**TIMSS Test Scores for Mathematics
(fourth and eighth grades)**

Country	Fourth grade		Eighth grade	
	2007	1995	2007	1995
South Korea	–	–	597	581
Japan	568	567	570	581
Hungary	510	521	517	527
Great Britain	541	484	513	498
Russia	–	–	512	524
United States	**529**	**518**	**508**	**492**
Australia	516	495	496	509
Sweden	–	–	491	540

Source: National Center for Education Statistics,
Trends in International Mathematics and Science Study.

Table 2.4

PIRLS Percentiles for Reading (fourth grade), 2006

Country	Median score	25th percentile	75th percentile	95th percentile
Russia	569	523	612	671
Hong Kong	567	527	605	655
Canada (British Columbia)	561	513	606	668
Canada (Ontario)	557	510	603	666
Hungary	555	507	599	658
Italy	554	507	599	658
Sweden	554	512	592	647
Germany	553	508	593	647
Netherlands	549	513	584	631
England	546	486	598	673
United States	**545**	**494**	**592**	**653**
France	525	478	568	626

Source: OECD, Programme for International Student Assessment, 2009.

present not just in the bottom cohort of schoolchildren (the "left behind"), but also in those at higher levels of ability. As shown in table 2.4, even America's brighter youngsters, those in the 75th and 95th percentile of test takers, do poorly relative to their peers in other advanced countries. This suggests that the fastest way for American political and educational leaders to restore the country's historic international educational supremacy is to direct much more attention to increasing the academic performance of mainstream schoolchildren, a subject elaborated on later and addressed in chapter 4.

The country's greatest contemporary educational failure is the shockingly uneven level of academic achievement among Americans in different circumstances and in different places. The most familiar comparison is that white children are doing much better than blacks and Hispanics, and Asians are doing a little better than whites. Less frequently noted, white children whose parents have a college education are doing much better than those who don't. Overall, suburban children are doing better than those who live in cities, and *much of this disparity remains even when we hold race and parent education levels constant* (table 2.5)! Among city children with the same profile, those going to school in smaller cities (or poor suburbs) do better than those in the biggest. But the most startling finding, and actually the most hopeful in terms of effective educational policy reform, is the enormous difference in academic performance from state to state—even after one adjusts for each of the socioeconomic and locational distinctions mentioned above. In fact, as

Table 2.5

NAEP Eighth-Grade Reading Scores for Whites by Location and Parent Education, 2011

	College graduate	High school graduate
Suburb	281	261
City	278	257

Source: U.S. Department of Education, National Assessment of Educational Progress.

Table 2.6

NAEP Eighth-Grade Reading Scores by Race and State (top and bottom five), 2011

State	White	Black	Hispanic	Asian
New Jersey	284	256	257	291
Connecticut	283	255	255	282
Massachusetts	282	255	248	288
Maryland	282	255	262	294
Colorado	278	257	254	285
National average	**272**	**248**	**251**	**275**
Arkansas	267	238	253	–
Oklahoma	265	247	251	–
Tennessee	265	240	255	–
Louisiana	264	241	249	–
West Virginia	256	249	–	–

Source: U.S. Department of Education, National Assessment of Educational Progress.

table 2.6 shows, achievement-lagging demographic cohorts in some states do better than leading ones in others. This is hopeful because, if such academic achievement disparities cannot be attributed to socioeconomic disadvantage, and the statistical distribution of cognitive ability should be the same everywhere, then the only explanation for such differences lies in the schools themselves.

The project of fixing America's educational system should begin with a strategic analysis of where, in the interaction of children and schools, we find our most serious academic problems; and where, in the educational pipeline, those problems can be most effectively addressed. While the achievement of major educational gains for all categories of youngsters remains challenging, the gaps to be closed can be parsed into just two broad categories, and these can be addressed at just a few promising intervention points, all replicable at a national scale, and all affordable—measuring affordability in terms of their long-term, rather than short-term, cost-benefit ratios.

The largest academic achievement gap, one that has long consumed the energies of U.S. national, state, and local education agencies, remains the one separating poor minority children from mainstream whites (see table 2.7). Closing that gap has so

Table 2.7

NAEP Test Scores by Race and Location, 2011

A. READING

Fourth grade	White	Black	Hispanic	Asian
Suburb	234	210	209	238
City	231	202	203	230
Difference (%)	1.1	4.0	2.8	3.7
Eighth grade	**White**	**Black**	**Hispanic**	**Asian**
Suburb	275	251	254	279
City	273	246	248	271
Difference (%)	0.8	2.1	2.4	2.9

B. MATHEMATICS

Fourth grade	White	Black	Hispanic	Asian
Suburb	252	228	230	257
City	251	221	228	254
Difference (%)	0.7	3.0	0.9	1.1
Eighth grade	**White**	**Black**	**Hispanic**	**Asian**
Suburb	296	263	271	306
City	294	261	268	299
Difference (%)	0.7	0.8	1.1	2.1

Source: U.S. Department of Education, National Assessment of Educational Progress.

far proven to be beyond the reach of the most prevalent education reform policies. To date, despite the expenditure of billions of dollars and the implementation of countless experimental reforms—affecting teachers, class sizes, school organization, high-stakes testing, and so on—progress has been very limited and geographically sporadic. Not far behind poor minority children in school performance is a growing cohort of lower-income white children—most often those raised in single-parent families, a phenomenon largely ignored by reformers obsessed with ethnically correlated performance differences.

Increasingly noticeable is the academic achievement gap between girls (higher) and boys (lower) among schoolchildren of all class and ethnic backgrounds, as indicated in table 2.8. Some recent reports on male/female school performance disparities ascribe them to likely differences in brain wiring, and therefore conclude they might be lessened by using gender-differentiated teaching strategies, and perhaps hiring more male teachers. This is most certainly wrong; effective schooling can be—and should be—gender-blind. When Lawrence Summers, as president of Harvard, suggested something similar, that women's underrepresentation in mathematics and the sciences was due to gender-based cognitive

Table 2.8

NAEP Eighth-Grade Reading Scores by Gender and Race

Year	Gender	White	Black	Hispanic	Asian
2011	Male	267	242	248	270
	Female	277	253	255	280
1998	Male	261	234	235	252
	Female	276	249	248	273

Source: U.S. Department of Education, National Assessment of Educational Progress.

differences, he was booed off the stage and ultimately lost his job. Cognitive determinism is no more defensible when it is used to justify why so many boys are lagging academically. For children growing up in poor families—white or black—a better explanation is that being raised in fatherless households disproportionately undermines the school performance of boys. Girls often have a positive role model—and achievement motivator—in their mothers, while boys in the absence of fathers are apt to look to delinquent older males (who most likely show contempt for any evidence of academic striving) for guidance.[18]

The one American school cohort that is *not* being left behind academically is made up of *upper-middle-class white* children. Even here, girls do better than boys, but the boys easily do well enough to succeed in college and later in their working careers. Obviously, it is no surprise that socioeconomically advantaged kids do well in school, and disadvantaged ones do badly; we have always known this intuitively and statistically have confirmed it repeatedly since the publication of the Coleman Report in 1966,[19] but we have had a hard time translating this knowledge into a plan of educational action. Until the 1960s, we simply shrugged and accepted differential school outcomes as the unavoidable byproduct of social stratification. After the Supreme Court ended de jure racial segregation in 1954, we naively assumed that racial mixing—and, by extension, socioeconomic class mixing—would trump the disparities in home environments. When that didn't work, we decided that compensatory resources would do the trick—for example, giving school districts with large numbers of disadvantaged children more money to pay teachers more, run smaller classes, hire paraprofessionals, and engage educational "experts." When that didn't work either, we launched the current generation of reforms that will be reviewed in detail in chapter 3.

Although the strongest predictor of academic performance

for *all* schoolchildren is family social and economic status, and this explains not only the inferior academic performance of lower-income minority schoolchildren but also that of lower-income whites, with the greatest impact falling on boys in both groups, there is not much we can do about that. Decades of failed experiments have conclusively shown that it is nearly impossible for government to level the socioeconomic playing field through interventions in the home. The inevitable policy conclusion to be drawn from this fact is that if we are to raise the academic performance of disadvantaged children, we must do so in school.

But which kind of school? It is becoming increasingly obvious that all of these apparently discrete school performance gaps—affecting African American and Hispanic children, lower-income white children, and lower-income boys of all ethnic backgrounds—have their origins in the same underlying condition: cultural deprivation at an early age. If that is so—and the work of E. D. Hirsch and other scholars of cognitive development persuasively documents the validity of this hypothesis—it is a problem that *can only be successfully remedied at an early age*. All efforts to date that have attempted to close the academic gap in high school and college have yielded only marginal gains. Even elementary school may be too late. There is a growing body of evidence that the best place to address this issue is in preschool. But not any old preschool, as the country's disappointing experience with Head Start, the nation's largest preschool program for disadvantaged youth, has demonstrated. However, with the right kind of preschool curriculum, and the right kind of preschool teachers, and with sufficient time—in school-day hours and school-year days—a very large share of these heretofore intractable gaps can be closed. Why and how this is to be done is discussed in detail in chapter 3.

But it is not just children from poor minority families who are being "left behind." Looking at the previous tables, we can see that currently the *majority* of American schoolchildren are falling short relative to their potential and the education they need to excel in the twenty-first-century knowledge economy. This is the gap separating "normally" performing American middle-class schoolchildren from their more successful European and Asian peers and their affluent—often privately schooled—upper-middle-class American ones. This Mainstream achievement gap affects the largest number of American schoolchildren and also happens to be the easiest to close, yet it has gotten practically no notice at all. This gap can and should be closed later in the educational cycle—that is, in high school and college—and we have good evidence on how to do it. Since this gap is not grounded in hard-to-overcome handicaps of poverty, racism, family structure, or cultural disadvantage, we need only look for guidance to places where mainstream students are doing well—like Massachusetts in the United States, or Japan abroad. Indeed, the most irrefutable evidence that the Mainstream gap can be closed is in the marked variation among American states in the performance of their white, middle-class, suburban schoolchildren. For example, those in Massachusetts taking the NAEP eighth-grade reading test in 2011 outscored their California peers by an entire proficiency level. Indeed, as table 2.9 confirms, the educational performance disparities among American states, even after accounting for demographic variables, are as great as those that differentiate school performance among nations.[20]

This is actually a piece of very good news because these interstate differences can be tied to differences in state educational practices, and *educational practices can be easily changed*. Further, by showing *what can be done*, these data represent an irrefutable counter to the educational determinism of reform skeptics. What educationally successful school districts, states, or countries tell us is that the most important determinants of high academic achievement for non-disadvantaged students is offering them demanding academic content and instilling high academic expectations. This

Table 2.9

Comparing U.S. States (top and bottom five) and Sixty-six Foreign Countries in Reading and Mathematics Proficiency, 2011

State	% Proficient in mathematics	% Proficient in reading	Number of countries that outperformed the state*	Similar countries*
Massachusetts	50.7	43.0	1	Canada, Finland
Vermont	41.4	42.1	3	New Zealand, Singapore
New Jersey	40.4	39.0	5	Australia, Japan
New Hampshire	37.9	37.2	8	Belgium, Netherlands
Minnesota	43.1	36.6	8	Belgium, Netherlands
West Virginia	18.5	22.9	28	Croatia, Greece
Alabama	18.2	21.2	31	Slovakia, Spain
Louisiana	19.0	19.4	35	Latvia, Lithuania
Mississippi	13.6	17.4	37	Bulgaria, Turkey
New Mexico	17.4	17.3	39	Bulgaria, Turkey

Source: Paul E. Peterson et al., *Globally Challenged: Are U.S. Students Ready to Compete?*, Harvard's Program on Education Policy and Governance, August 2011.

*On reading proficiency test.

is well understood by those parents who spend enormous sums sending their children to elite private schools (whose success is based on these factors and *not* on their social cachet) and by the majority of Catholic schools, which serve less affluent children.

THE EDUCATIONAL CAPSTONE: POSTSECONDARY EDUCATION

Probably the best overall qualitative measure today of a society's educational system is how many of its young adults complete a program of higher education—in other words, college. American international superiority was once dramatically evident in this educational arena, even more so than in elementary and secondary schooling. As noted in chapter 1, Americans established colleges and universities—public and private—at a rapid pace from the seventeenth century through the twentieth and aimed at educating not just the children of the affluent (as was the case in the world until very recently), but all who had the desire and (ideally) the aptitude. As a result, throughout the nineteenth and twentieth centuries, a higher percentage of Americans had a college education than the citizens of any other country.

Despite this impressive heritage, by many indicators the United States is now lagging increasingly behind its global peers. In 1970, when 19 percent of American young adults (i.e., age thirty to thirty-five) had gotten a college education, the United States was well ahead of all other countries in the world, including Canada (11 percent), Japan (7 percent), France (4 percent), and Germany (3 percent). By 2010, the latest year for which comparative data are available, the proportion of young Americans with college degrees had risen modestly (22 percent), but the United States had been overtaken by Japan, Australia, Canada, Britain, the Netherlands, and even Spain. Comparing American college *graduation* rates (of those entering college) to the average for all the advanced OECD countries, in 1995 the U.S. rate of 33 percent was well above the

Table 2.10

High School Graduation Rates by State (top and bottom ten)

State	2008–9	1990–91
Wisconsin	90.7	85.2
Vermont	89.6	79.5
North Dakota	87.4*	87.6
Minnesota	87.4	90.8
Iowa	85.7	84.4
New Jersey	84.6	81.4
New Hampshire	84.3	78.6
Massachusetts	83.3	79.1
Missouri	83.1	76.0
Nebraska	82.9	86.7
National average	**75.5**	**73.7**
Arizona	72.5	76.7
California	71.0	69.6
Alabama	69.9	69.8
Florida	68.9	65.6
Georgia	67.8	70.3
Louisiana	67.3	57.5
South Carolina	66.0	66.6
New Mexico	64.8	70.1
Mississippi	62.0	63.3
Nevada	56.3	77.0

Source: U.S. Bureau of the Census.

*Italics indicate that rates have fallen since 1990–91.

OECD average of 20 percent. Today, at 37 percent, it is slightly below the OECD level.

Thus, school reforms in elementary and secondary schooling need to be focused single-mindedly on having *all* schoolchildren graduate from high school and then preparing them for life *after* high school. Overall, current high school graduation rates fall far short of this goal, but, as in student performance generally, there is wide variation among the states (table 2.10).

Currently, two-thirds of those who do graduate from high school go on to some kind of higher education. The problem is that no more than one-third of these students are actually ready for college, something evident in today's low college-completion rates (tables 2.11 and 2.12). While U.S. colleges and universities are not blameless in this, they are very much at the mercy of how well American high schools prepare their graduates—meaning that the link between high school and college academic expectations must become considerably tighter, an issue calling for more stringent college admissions policies and greater cooperation between colleges and their feeder high schools.

This problem has been bedeviling American higher education for decades, and mere exhortations to resolve it have proven futile. To reform higher education comprehensively, we need to generate more potent incentives for both students and the collegiate institutions. The most efficient and scalable way to do this is through the funding of college education, most of it directly or indirectly

Table 2.11

College Enrollment by Gender and Status, 1970–2021

Gender/Status	1970	1990	2010	2021 (projected)
Number (thousands)	7,369	11,959	18,079	20,597
Male	57.7%	45.0%	43.3%	41.6%
Female	42.3	55.0	56.7	58.4
Full time	71.7	58.3	63.3	62.2
Part time	28.3	41.7	36.7	37.8
Public	76.3	81.2	75.8	75.9
Private	23.7	18.8	24.2	24.1

Source: National Center for Education Statistics, Digest of Education Statistics.

Table 2.12

College Graduation Rates of 2004 Entering Cohort (percent by race and gender)

	Total	White	Black	Hispanic	Asian	Male	Female
Graduation in six years							
All four-year	58.3	61.5	39.5	50.1	68.7	55.5	60.6
Open admission	29.2	35.4	18.1	27.5	34.4	27.7	30.4
Highly selective	87.2	88.9	63.2	85.7	92.7	85.3	89.4
Public four-year	56.0	58.9	38.3	47.8	66.2	53.0	58.5
Open admission	28.8	32.9	17.0	28.4	34.4	25.7	31.6
Highly selective	82.2	83.0	49.2	80.0	90.2	79.2	86.2
Not-for-profit	65.4	67.9	44.9	60.5	76.2	63.0	67.3
Highly selective	90.5	92.7	69.2	90.7	95.5	89.9	91.2
Graduation in three years							
Community college	29.9	29.5	25.3	33.4	33.6	26.4	32.7

Source: National Center for Education Statistics, Integrated Postsecondary Education Data System (IPEDS).

underwritten by the federal government. Changing the basis of that aid should motivate students and colleges to raise their game. Chapter 5 will review the extent to which college attendance and completion (by years of study) adds to individual and national human capital, how much of the population might actually benefit from going to college, how the quality of a typical American college education can be strengthened across the board, and how federal financial aid to students and colleges can be comprehensively restructured to ensure that most American college students are college-ready, that all who are can get a college education, and that they and the colleges are motivated to see that they graduate.

Closing the Megagap

The most conspicuous of America's human-capital failures, and the one that to date has been resistant to remedy on any kind of sustained basis, is the disappointing school performance of socioeconomically disadvantaged children, including a majority of those who are African American and Hispanic. As noted in chapter 2, lower-income white children are also performing well below their potential, and boys from low-income families of all ethnic backgrounds are doing worse than girls. These disparities are especially worrisome because when these children (especially the boys) grow up, their inferior education relegates them to low-paying (or no) jobs, poor marriage prospects, and possibly trouble with the law; when they have children they are very likely to be absent fathers or distracted mothers perpetuating a cycle of intergenerational educational and social dysfunction.[1] For the purposes of discussion in this chapter and throughout the book, I will refer to this complex of low academic achievement affecting poorer Americans of all ethnicities as the country's educational "Megagap."

If it could be accomplished, no other measure would so completely transform American society as significantly narrowing the Megagap. A host of societal ills from poverty, poor health, crime, and child neglect would be sharply reduced; the economic significance of income inequality would virtually disappear; and the United States would truly become in reality what it has always imagined itself to be: an almost universally *middle-class* country. In the pursuit of just such a breakthrough (and as a collateral aspect of the civil rights movement), generations of political leaders and educators have, for more than fifty years, launched a long and varied sequence of policies aimed at transforming the American public school system—from *Brown v. Board of Education* (1954) to No Child Left Behind (2001) and Race to the Top (2009). The problem is that, by and large, the policies haven't worked, at least with respect to their stated goal of enabling disadvantaged schoolchildren to catch up with the rest. While the scores of African American and Hispanic test-takers have actually risen modestly over the most recent decades, the spread separating them from those of mainstream whites is stubbornly persistent. In today's information-age economy, the human-capital failure this represents is more problematical than ever. What, if anything, can be done?

We have long known that the educational Megagap is deeply rooted in familial socioeconomic circumstances, but since these are beyond the reach of government to change, we have counted on decades of educational reform efforts aimed at attacking it in school. We have strong proof that the Megagap *can* be significantly narrowed, if not eliminated altogether, *with the right kinds of school interventions.* One reason our progress on this front has been so disappointing is that education reformers have been too indiscriminate—and inconsistent—in their choice of reforms. The half-century-long Megagap closing effort has by now yielded an education reform garden so overgrown that, in classic Gresham's

Law fashion, the bad (meaning ineffective) ideas often overwhelm the good. In the pages that follow, I will review the most frequently adopted of these reforms (roughly in the chronological order of their popularity), and summarize what we have learned regarding their effectiveness. I will conclude by highlighting the two proven educational strategies that, where and when they have been properly implemented, have measurably increased the academic performance of Megagap children and permitted them to succeed, in later grades and beyond, at or near the level of their mainstream peers: namely, *effective preschool education* and *expanded learning time.*

DECADES OF EXPERIMENTATION

Racial Integration In the long sequence of ameliorations specifically focused on raising the scholastic achievement of African American schoolchildren, the first was racial integration. Driven initially by the constitutional imperative of the Supreme Court's 1954 *Brown v. Board of Education* ruling, court-ordered integration of de jure segregated schools in the South was followed soon after by court-ordered integration of de facto segregated schools in the north. The overwhelmingly dominant rationale behind these court decisions (promoted by liberal educators and racial advocates) was a firm conviction that integration would have a significant positive impact on the academic performance of African American children. The remedy most frequently imposed by the courts was intra-district busing, sending black schoolchildren to formerly majority-white schools and (less often) sending whites to formerly majority-black schools. Other attempts at fostering school integration have included the establishment of "magnet" schools with enriched facilities and programming to attract white students without coercion and, in already racially diverse municipalities, redrawing attendance-zone boundaries and permitting open enrollment across the district on a first-come-first-served basis.

After a half century of trials, all available evidence shows that the impact of integration on the African American Megagap has been limited at best. Desegregation initially resulted in increased funding of schools attended by blacks, most notably in the South, where it modestly lowered black dropout rates.[2] Over time, however, the gains from desegregation efforts diminished significantly, especially outside the South. Most critically, it has been almost impossible to get whites to go along with integration on any meaningful scale. The most common consequence of integration initiatives, especially court-ordered busing, has been white flight to nonracially diverse suburbs.[3] But even where, through chance or the good-faith efforts of liberal communities, racial integration has been possible, gap-closing progress has been minimal.

Three kinds of "natural experiments" might tell us whether racial integration raises the academic performance of minority (black or Hispanic) schoolchildren. Where school districts integrated their schools at a particular point in time (either through court order or voluntarily) we can look for positive changes in minority test scores and whether the white-minority performance gap narrowed. In suburban regions where the majority of districts are racially homogenous but some districts are integrated, we can see if minority children in integrated places do better than those in majority-minority districts. Along the same line, within districts whose schools vary in the extent of their racial integration, we can see if black and Hispanic student academic performance is positively correlated with greater integration.

Under these circumstances, the greatest benefit of racial integration has initially come from transferring black schoolchildren out of inferior neighborhood schools into ones with better teachers and better management. Holding that effect constant, however, the academic benefits to minority children of integration per se have been limited to nonexistent. Most troubling, whatever integration does occur is short-lived, as such schools are inevitably re-segregated when white parents send their children to private schools or move out of the community.[4]

Equalizing Expenditures The evident failure of integration as a panacea led inexorably to another Megagap-closing fix, this one designed to help all educationally disadvantaged children, regardless of ethnicity: reducing disparities in school expenditures. Beginning in the 1960s, courts around the United States began demanding that school funding—typically hostage to differences in the value of local taxable property—be equalized within states or intrastate regions. Their motivation is not unreasonable, given that schools in many poor communities have been financially shortchanged; when school expenditures fall below a certain threshold, academic outcomes are bound to suffer. Nevertheless, decades of expenditure equalization initiatives have borne little fruit in the way of higher student achievement.

The most extreme national example of such an initiative is New Jersey's "Abbott" court-imposed school expenditure equalization, named after the New Jersey Supreme Court case *Abbott v. Burke* (a Camden, New Jersey, student and the state's Commissioner of Education, respectively). Through numerous rulings running from 1981 to 2003, the state's courts have mandated that per-pupil funding be equalized throughout New Jersey and, given the inability or unwillingness to cap spending in the state's affluent suburbs, this has required substantially greater taxpayer support for schools in its poorer cities. Costing more than $40 billion since 1998, state Abbott-formula funding allows places like Newark, Camden, Jersey City, and Asbury Park to spend more than $20,000 annually on each of their schoolchildren—*with no discernible gains in their performance.* Indeed, as measured by National Assessment of Educational Progress (NAEP) reading scores, New Jersey's

Megagap has not budged after funding equalization and now exceeds that in the rest of the country.[5] If school-funding equalization has not lessened the Megagap in New Jersey—America's most stringent experiment—there is no reason to expect it to do so anywhere else.

Reduced Class Size Even if generalized school-funding parity has been shown to be of little benefit, it is still possible that certain particular categories of school spending might lift the performance of disadvantaged schoolchildren. Throughout the reform era, teachers and liberal education advocates have insisted that one of the keys to raising the academic outcomes of disadvantaged students is to reduce class size, arguing that smaller classes allow teachers to devote more attention to each schoolchild. The largest national experiment in class-size reduction was conducted by California after legislation to that end was adopted in 1996. Costing more than $1 billion per year, the state conditioned supplemental state aid to school districts on their implementing significant (but not necessarily uniform) class-size reductions. Yet both before 1996 and currently, California is one of the lowest-performing states in all the NAEP tests. Among the several studies that looked specifically at the impact of the state's class-size reduction initiative, most have concluded that it made no difference at all and one (using a different evaluation methodology) claimed to find some positive impact.[6] The distinguished education researcher Eric Hanushek, evaluating class-size reduction initiatives across the country over a period of years, concludes categorically that there is no evidence that they reduce the Megagap while they do squander resources that might better be devoted to more effective reforms.[7]

Teacher Pay Teacher pay has been another perennial education reform issue for decades—in two respects. Teacher unions and many educational professionals assert that raising teacher salaries across the board would attract more and better teachers to the country's schools—especially to those serving the lowest-performing children in the Megagap schools. However, most respected education researchers doubt that broad-based teacher pay increases can make any qualitative difference. They point out that U.S. teacher compensation levels (including consideration of total hours worked and generous fringe benefits) are already higher than in just about any other advanced country (including those that outperform us) and, even more damningly, among U.S. school districts currently, there is no evident correlation between teacher pay and student performance—with some of the best-paying places, like Washington, D.C., having the most dismal academic outcomes.

But another aspect of teacher compensation *has* generated considerable backing from reformers: paying teachers more if they achieve notable student performance gains, usually referred to in shorthand as "merit pay." To date there is too little empirical data to definitively validate or repudiate merit pay as an effective strategy for closing the Megagap, but the preliminary findings from places that have instituted it are not encouraging. The most thorough evaluations of teacher merit pay have been conducted by Vanderbilt University's National Center on Performance Incentives, looking at the impact of such initiatives on disadvantaged student achievement in Nashville, Tennessee, and various districts in Texas and New York City. In all cases that the Center studied, the impact of performance-based teacher pay bonuses was nonexistent to negligible.[8]

Distinguished educators participating in a recent forum on the issue indicated why this was to be expected: The academic success of disadvantaged students is dependent on too many factors beyond a teacher's control (as will be discussed later in this chapter). The size of typical performance bonuses adds little to most teachers' intrinsic motivation to succeed. The prevailing accountability environment already provides strong incentives for teachers and administrators to raise student performance. And, not unimportant, teachers' anger at having merit-pay schemes imposed on them (and the challenge to their professionalism that this implies) can offset any potential benefit that might otherwise occur.[9] That said, teacher competence is in fact critical to school success, and not just for those serving the disadvantaged. In chapter 4, I address a more reliable—and replicable—way to recruit American schoolteachers who are up to the job.

School Choice (Charter Schools and Vouchers) With the exception of merit pay, all of the earlier proposed reforms have been (and mostly still are) heartily championed by the teacher unions and other liberals. Beginning in earnest in the 1990s, an entirely different approach to the problem entered the education reform arena—one that the usual education advocates have generally opposed—giving parents a choice of schools for their children. The purest, but only rarely implemented, form of school choice has districts issuing vouchers to parents that enable them to send their children to any school that accepts them. Much more common—and expanding rapidly—has been the establishment of "charter" schools. Charter schools are institutions managed by nonpublic organizations (usually not-for-profit) but authorized by state educational departments and funded out of local education revenues, usually at or near the level of comparable public schools. By the end of 2011, forty-one states have authorized 5,600 charter schools, enrolling more than 2 million students across the country, with 400,000 potential charter-school enrollees on waiting lists.[10]

Offhand, it would seem that vouchers and charter schools should be the perfect vehicles for closing the Megagap. Where they have been established, these schools are largely free of the constraints alleged to hold back disadvantaged children academically in typical local public schools: they can hire, evaluate, reward, or fire (mostly non-unionized) principals and teachers at will; they have great latitude in curricular and instructional design; and— more than most ordinary public schools—they seek to intensively involve parents as supportive partners. What they are expressly *forbidden* to do in most places is to cherry-pick their student bodies (a frequent but unproven accusation of charter-school opponents), and they are held to the same statewide content and testing standards as their publicly operated peers.

Nevertheless, despite these advantages, school choice has not been nearly as successful in closing the Megagap as its advocates have hoped, with some notable exceptions. Looking first at vouchers, the largest voucher experiment in the United States has been conducted by the Milwaukee, Wisconsin, school district. Beginning in 1990 and now enrolling 15,000 students, with a state-mandated cap of 22,000, the program is popular with parents; but all evaluations that have compared voucher students with comparable Milwaukee peers find little or no evidence of academic gains. Like all such programs in other places, the dollar value of the vouchers is far short of the full annual per-student cost of a typical elementary or secondary education, limiting potential placements to subsidized religious (generally Catholic or Lutheran) schools.[11]

The record for charter schools is somewhat better but falls short of expectations. This is particularly disappointing because they are designed quite specifically to close the Megagap, and operated according to principles long championed by the conservative education reform movement—free of local district and teacher union rules inhibiting staffing, teacher evaluation, classroom management, or educational content. (On a personal note, for the ten years I spent as the university provost of the State University of New York [SUNY], which authorizes roughly half of the state's charter schools, I was able to get a front-row view of their operations and oversight. SUNY's monitoring of charter-school applications and performance, which encompassed roughly half the charters in New York City, has been noticeably more rigorous than the national norm.)

There have been numerous evaluations, nationally and locally, of charter-school effectiveness, with the two benchmarks for comparison being national academic standards and the performance of comparable local public schools. What these studies show is that charter schools vary enormously in quality, and while many have been notably successful—like those in New York City and those operated by the Knowledge Is Power Program (KIPP)—the majority of their students do no better academically than those in local district schools.[12] There are several reasons why. The leading expert on the success of charter schools, Caroline Hoxby, in a methodologically rigorous study, found that in New York, students who "attended a charter school for all of grades kindergarten through eight would close about 86 percent of the 'Scarsdale-Harlem achievement gap' [equivalent to the Megagap] in math and 66 percent in English."[13] That is good news, and a tribute to the city's charter schools (many overseen by SUNY), but the hitch, of course, is that a great many of these students do *not* stay in charter schools for that many grades and thus, according to Hoxby, "A student who attended fewer grades would improve by a commensurately smaller amount."[14] Another reason that charter schools may not meet expectations is lack of rigorous adherence to one of the reform's fundamental premises: that schools that do not demonstrate superior academic results should be closed. But in too many states that doesn't happen; often—as I observed in SUNY—because charter parents want to keep them open despite their academic performance (usually because of their superior facilities).

The fact that such plausibly beneficial measures as merit pay and school choice, or smaller class sizes and greater resources, haven't made much of a dent in narrowing America's educational Megagap doesn't necessarily mean that they are without merit, or that K–12 education reform is a lost cause. Undoubtedly, even when they have not increased academic performance, many of these reforms have made schools better in other ways. Smaller classes and greater resources obviously can result in a richer and more personalized school experience. Charter schools and those attended with vouchers are undeniably safer, better managed, and usually in nicer facilities. *It is just that these reforms have been sold as surefire ways to raise the academic achievement of disadvantaged schoolchildren, and they have not been able to do that.* Where these kinds of broad-based public school system changes *can* prove their value is in *sustaining* any academic gains made by Megagap children before they enter first grade and bringing *mainstream* students up to twenty-first-century global standards. To close—or at least narrow—the Megagap, we need something entirely different.

TWO MEGAGAP STRATEGIES THAT HAVE BEEN PROVEN TO WORK

Countless studies have indicated what causes disadvantaged children to do so badly in school later on. The families in which they are raised—poor and predominantly headed by single mothers— fail to give them the kinds of cognitive and emotional stimulation necessary for early childhood development that their more fortunate upper-middle-class (usually white or Asian) peers on the far side of the Megagap are able to get at home. These early age disparities are then magnified throughout the years of formal schooling because of radically different experiences outside of school. Most mainstream children return after school and in the summer to a home setting conducive to study and parents determined to have them do well academically. Disadvantaged children, however, even those who have the ability to keep up with their classwork, return to households where both the physical setting and family circumstances make study difficult and unappreciated, with peer influences that are downright hostile to academic achievement.

This initiates a self-reinforcing vicious cycle of scholastic un-derperformance and mounting academic failure that only gets worse as these children get older. Being less prepared when they enter first grade, Megagap schoolchildren have an increasingly dif-ficult time keeping up with the demands of their classwork as they ascend the K–12 ladder. Many do so badly that they are left back a grade or two—or would be, if academic standards were enforced. Bitter at their lack of success—after all, everyone resents and dis-parages tasks that they are not good at—they develop a hostile at-titude toward schooling altogether, and celebrate those classmates who have the temerity to challenge teachers and disrupt classes. Once they reach high school as adolescents, they either drop out of school altogether, or graduate with too little academic profi-ciency to succeed in college or a cognitively demanding job. To top it off, for reasons ranging from bad role models and raging hormones to damaged male pride, this cycle of failure takes its greatest toll on boys.

The diagnosis is clear enough, but what is the remedy? Disad-vantaged children need *more time—well-spent—in school*, by start-ing school at an earlier age, spending more time in school each day, and going to school in the summer. What follows is the develop-mental rationale for why this is necessary, empirical evidence of its efficacy, and how it might be implemented in practice.

E. D. Hirsch, one of the most brilliant education research-ers in the United States, and for decades an insufficiently heeded voice in the wilderness of educational reform, has offered the most persuasive analysis yet of the roots of the Megagap, defining the problem as one of "cultural literacy." In putting forward the cul-tural literacy hypothesis, Hirsch argues that:

1. Differences in cultural literacy, more than any other single factor, separate socioeconomically disadvantaged children from the rest.

2. For them to catch up, this cultural deficit must be addressed by instilling in these children the "core knowledge" that middle- and upper-middle-class children are exposed to at home, beginning at as young an age as possible, and then continuing through at least the early years of formal schooling.

Therefore, to narrow the Megagap and give disadvantaged children a running start so they can succeed in grades one through twelve, much of their cultural literacy deficit must be erased *before they enter first grade* by enrolling them in *preschool*, with continued reinforcement of cultural literacy in the elementary school grades.[15]

There is powerful empirical evidence documenting that giving all students at risk (and maybe all children, period) an *effective* preschool program can compensate for deeply rooted familial socioeconomic circumstances. According to a 2009 RAND Corporation Policy Brief:

> Evaluations of ... *high-quality* [emphasis added] preschool programs show that such programs can advance school readiness and lead to higher test scores through at least [the] third grade. The benefits of preschool are more pronounced for disadvantaged children, but there are positive effects for children across the socioeconomic spectrum.[16]

An even more ringing endorsement of the need to address the later academic difficulties of poor children in preschool can be found in a definitive study by Nobel laureate James Heckman and Dimitriy Masterov:

> An accumulating body of knowledge shows that early childhood interventions for disadvantaged young children are more

effective than interventions that come later in life. Because of the dynamic nature of the skill formation process, remediating the effects of early disadvantages at later ages is often prohibitively costly.[17]

Most professional educators now favor the expansion of preschool programs (after all, it increases their business) but at the same time too many of them fail to understand the underlying premise for doing so. Although a growing volume of empirically solid research confirms the cultural literacy deficit hypothesis, this finding has been largely ignored or rejected by the American educational establishment. And because a large share of early childhood educators and administrators are skeptical or at best indifferent when it comes to cultural literacy, they fail to base their preschool or elementary school curricula on its precepts.[18] *This has led to a nationwide profusion of ineffective preschools, undermining the rationale and broad-based public support for significantly expanding the preschool enterprise.*

Head Start, America's largest preschool program, enrolling more than 1 million poor, primarily minority, children and costing $9.5 billion currently, is the most conspicuous case in point. Even though a few Head Start locations across the country have (with supplemental funding) implemented curricula and staffing based on Hirsch's work—and have seen positive outcomes as a result—the vast majority primarily function as day care centers. Of the over 1 million children currently enrolled in Head Start, fewer than half are in "center-based" full-day/full-week programs. The remainder are in part-day/part-week and home-based programs. The educational content across the Head Start system is enormously varied, locally determined, subject to few mandated content or staffing requirements, and only rarely succeeds in giving its enrollees the eponymous "head start" enshrined in its mission. Numerous evaluations (including the most recent conducted by the Brookings Institution in 2010, based on the latest data from the U.S. Department of Health and Human Services, which administers the program) document that Head Start students make minimal academic gains while they are in the program, and that whatever little benefit there is vanishes by first grade.[19] As one of the leading experts in the field of preschool education has noted: "Head Start is locked into a program model that fails to focus on intensive education . . . [and] has failed every true experimental test."[20]

Nevertheless, in this chapter, I will make the case that giving *all* American children access to publicly funded preschool is one of the few proven ways for the United States to narrow its educational Megagap—as long as it is done according to *curricular and other specifications shown to have been effective*. At the same time, Head Start should be ended—not "mended"—for several reasons. First, preschool should be seen as the first rung on the educational ladder for all children, not a day care program exclusively for the poor, as Head Start is. Second, as an educational program, preschool should be operated under the oversight of local, state, and national educational agencies, not the social welfare system, as Head Start is. Most important, after decades of operation, Head Start has clearly failed in its central ostensible mandate: enabling its charges to catch up with mainstream children on the other side of the Megagap. But the failure of Head Start should in no way be mistaken for a failure of preschool.

In table 3.1 we see fairly straightforward evidence that preschool can raise scholastic achievement for all ethnic groups and Head Start does not. The National Assessment of Educational Progress (NAEP) (the only consistent metric we have for consistently evaluating American student performance over time and place), in its long-term trend statistics on reading achievement of thirteen- and seventeen-year-old schoolchildren, tabulates results

Table 3.1

**Reading Scores by Prior Attendance
in Preschool or Head Start**

A. AGE 13

	Year	Yes Preschool	No Preschool	Yes Head Start	No Head Start
All	2004	278	259	257	264
All	1994	273	264	–	269
White	1984	270	259	258	264
Black	1984	247	235	238	241
Hispanic	1984	243	240	240	240

B. AGE 17

	Year	Yes Preschool	No Preschool	Yes Head Start	No Head Start
All	2004	305	291	–	295
All	1994	303	290	–	297
White	1984	305	295	289	299
Black	1984	271	260	260	264
Hispanic	1984	275	267	267	268

Source: U.S. Department of Education, National Assessment of Educational Progress.

by whether they previously attended Head Start or some other preschool; in its survey for 1984, it cross-tabulated this data with ethnicity (white/black/Hispanic). The results speak for themselves.

WHEN, WHY, AND HOW DOES PRESCHOOL WORK?

There is now incontrovertible evidence that, when done properly (explicitly or implicitly attacking the cultural literacy deficit), *preschool can narrow the Megagap.* One of the more comprehensive reviews of preschool effectiveness asserts:

Multiple meta-analyses conducted over the past 25 years have found preschool education to produce an average immediate effect of ... the equivalent of 7 or 8 points on an IQ test, or a move from the 30th to the 50th percentile for achievement test scores. For the social and emotional domains, estimated effects have been somewhat smaller but still practically meaningful. ... To put these gains in perspective, it's important to realize that [these gains are] enough to reduce by half the school readiness gap between children in poverty and the national average [i.e., the Megagap].[21]

This optimistic conclusion is based on a synthesis of research on specific preschool programs of widely varying quality, including the largely ineffective Head Start. The real payoff from preschool will come if we substantially scale up the most successful preschool models.

The most frequently cited—and for many preschool researchers, most definitive—proof of the value of preschool lies in three specific, intensively studied preschool programs. Let me briefly summarize each one.

The HighScope Educational Research Foundation's Perry Preschool Study conducted a comprehensive longitudinal analysis of five consecutive classes of children enrolled in the Perry Elementary preschool in Ypsilanti, Michigan, from 1962 to 1967, a group with marked "at-risk" socioeconomic characteristics (i.e., typical Megagap children). The study sought to determine the impact of the preschool experience in improving their later academic and quality-of-life outcomes; in other words, how much did it raise their human capital? The overall sample included 123 three- and four-year-old children, all of them African American, from poor households, with below-average IQ scores. The strength of the study lies in its methodological rigor, following the children who attended the Perry preschool and comparing their outcomes with those of a precisely matched control group that was not enrolled in any preschool program. As longitudinal studies go, this one was unusually extended, with both groups followed until they reached age forty-one, and with most of the study subjects staying in the panel to the end.

The results are strikingly positive with respect to outcomes. The preschoolers consistently outscored their control group peers on in-school academic performance tests well into high school—although the gap narrowed with time. Significantly, the preschoolers did substantially better in later outcomes—a key finding with respect to the smart society issue of *lifetime* human-capital attainment. Perry children graduated from high school at a rate 30 percent higher than the controls and by age twenty-seven had had 80 percent fewer arrests, were four times as likely to earn middle-class incomes, three times as likely to own homes, and 25 percent less likely to ever go on welfare. One of the other most important findings was the extent to which the preschool experience closed the male/female achievement gap. Perry males were *seven* times more likely than those in the control group to hold middle-income jobs and one-fifth as likely to ever be arrested.[22]

Another widely cited study of preschool effectiveness is the Abecedarian Project, an experimental preschool experience operated by an affiliate of the University of North Carolina, Chapel Hill. Launched in 1972, the program enrolled low-income African American children living in Chapel Hill. The longitudinal study, conducted by UNC researchers from 1972 to 1985, followed 111 healthy children from age 4.4 months through age 21, with 104 of the subjects remaining in the panel to the end. Of the sample, 57 children were randomly assigned to the Abecedarian program and the other 54 were assigned to the control group. The preschool experience of the treatment group was both longer and more intensive than in the Perry study, involving more parental involvement and more early elementary grade interventions. Again, the results were consistently positive, with the preschool enrollees scoring considerably higher than the controls in nationally normed in-school reading and math tests and almost half as likely to be held back in any 1–12 grade. Looking at metrics reflecting later life human-capital impacts, the Abecedarians were three times as likely to attend a four-year college, half as likely to become teenage parents, and twice as likely to hold a skilled job.[23]

An interesting ancillary finding has particular relevance to the issue of the best age at which to address the Megagap. The Abecedarian program, unlike most experimental preschool initiatives, included both preschool and early grade interventions, with methodologically careful reassignment of subjects so that the impacts of the two settings could be analyzed separately. What the follow-up studies found is that almost all of the positive results were associated with the preschool portion of the program, and the early grade interventions made little difference. Supporting the hypothesis that preschool can erase much of the overall handicap associated with socioeconomic class differences, another finding was that for Abecedarian preschool participants: "the program mitigated any negative effects of a low-quality home environment."[24]

The last of the most frequently cited studies is the Chicago Longitudinal Study. The Chicago study follows 1,539 children born in 1980 and drawn from Chicago's highest-poverty neighborhoods. Of this sample, the treatment cohort consisted of 1,150 children enrolled in twenty of Chicago's Child-Parent Centers (CPCs), operated by the Chicago city school system, generally housed in regular school buildings. The CPCs offer intensive educational and socialization experiences to children and counseling services to parents, from preschool through first grade—including full-day enriched kindergarten. Another 389 children with comparable socioeconomic backgrounds, randomly selected from non–CPC kindergartens in high-poverty neighborhoods constituted the control group. All children were followed for nineteen years (i.e., to when they were twenty-three to twenty-four years old) and, as in the other studies, assessed with respect to both grades

1–12 academic achievement and later life socioeconomic outcomes. About 90 percent of the original cohort subjects remained in the study to the end.

As social science research, the CPC study is something of a mess. Among many other methodological defects, there are unequal numbers of children in the treatment and control groups; the treatment children have been subject to a highly varied set of experiences in preschool, kindergarten, and the early grades; and the preschool curriculum lacks consistency. Nevertheless, the study is valuable because it does survey a large cohort of inner-city children (the heart of the Megagap) and assesses the benefits of a program *embedded in the public school system*—the model that I believe is more appropriate for widespread replication than the kind of idiosyncratic prototypes represented by Perry and Abecedarian.

The findings: First, just as in the Abecedarian study, almost all the positive outcomes were associated with the preschool, rather than early grade interventions. In academic achievement outcomes, the CPC preschoolers significantly outscored the controls in reading and math tests through the sixth grade; were considerably less likely to repeat grades; and were less apt to ever need special education. In later life outcomes, the CPC preschoolers were much more likely to complete high school; considerably less likely to be arrested or incarcerated; somewhat less likely to receive welfare; and more likely to have health insurance. Because the follow-up surveys ended at age twenty-three, they did not fully capture possibly significant differences in college enrollment and completion, and later employment and income profiles.[25]

I have referred to these three studies because they are so often cited in the literature on the positive effects of preschool, and because their findings are so consistent. Nevertheless, if we are to count on a large-scale expansion of preschool to close America's Megagap and to strengthen the academic achievement of mainstream children, we need to set much tighter specifications than those present in these model programs. Happily, there is an enormous body of methodologically rigorous research, much of it sponsored by the U.S. Department of Education, which has pains-takingly evaluated dozens of preschool program designs. Not so happily, the results are less than conclusive when it comes to iden-tifying ones that actually deliver game-changing outcomes. One piece of good news, however, is that *almost all of the serious preschool formats do deliver positive results*, even if some of them are modest. The most serious shortcoming of these studies is that, of necessity, they follow children attending the evaluated programs for only a few years out of preschool.

Perhaps the most empirically solid validation of universal preschool *based on cultural literacy concepts* lies outside the United States, in France. France has one of the most comprehensive pre-school programs in the world, enrolling nearly all four-year-olds, a majority of three-year-olds, and even a sizable number of two-year-olds. What makes a study of the French system particularly relevant, however, are the ways in which it addresses—and to some extent overcomes—France's own Megagap problem. Studies conducted by France's education ministry in the 1970s and 1980s highlighted enormous disparities in K–12 academic achievement, largely correlated—as in the United States—with social class and ethnicity (e.g., children of France's large North African immigrant community). This led to the introduction of the country's univer-sal, public, free preschool system, open to (but not compulsory for) all children age two to five. Beyond making preschool universally available, its French designers and managers—strongly influenced by the work of Hirsch—specified a rigorous and consistent cul-tural literacy curriculum, well-trained teachers, reasonable staff ratios, and good facilities.[26]

Numerous evaluations since then have documented that France's preschool initiative has been remarkably successful in raising later academic achievement and high school graduation levels, especially among disadvantaged children. A 1992 French government survey of children entering preschool in 1980 found that preschool attendance significantly reduced the school retention (i.e., non-dropout) rate disparity between the children of privileged and disadvantaged families, with the size of the reduction precisely proportional to the length of the preschool experience.[27] Hirsch has repeatedly stressed the applicability of France's experience to the American case based on his analysis of this data.[28]

BUILDING THE RIGHT KIND OF PRESCHOOL SYSTEM
Given the growing evidence that the best—or maybe the only— way to help children from poor, single-parent families (regardless of ethnicity) catch up academically with their mainstream peers is to give them *an effective preschool experience of preferably two years*, the national policy challenge is finding a way to accomplish this at some meaningful scale. As noted earlier, attempting to do this by expanding Head Start would be fatally counterproductive. What needs to happen instead—if it can be sold politically and afforded financially—is to *fully incorporate preschool within the regular district educational system.* Under this rubric, all states would extend their educational ladder by two years below kindergarten, creating an integrated pre-K to grade 12 curricular program. Here are the benefits of such an approach: First, while absolutely essential to close the academic achievement Megagap, preschool can benefit *all* schoolchildren—thus helping to close the growing educational gap separating middle-class American K–12 students from their upper-middle-class and advanced foreign peers (the subject of chapter 4). Second, to succeed in giving children academic skills that survive into later grades, preschool programs need to be integrated into the K–12 school curricula and overseen by state and district educators. Finally, to get national and local taxpayers to agree to support preschool as an integral component of district school systems, it needs to be tuition-free and not means-tested.

With such an institutional structure in place, the entire Head Start enterprise should be phased out.

Calling for universal preschool might appear at first blush to be merely endorsing a growing reality. Even President Obama, in his 2013 State of the Union address, asked Congress to consider it.[29] Looking at current preschool attendance figures, 72 percent of all American children are now exposed to some kind of pre-school experience by age four and 43 percent by age three. Forty-three percent of four-year-old children and 14 percent of younger ones, totaling 2.5 million children, are enrolled in one or another publicly funded program (local, state, or federal), with Head Start being by far the largest in attendance and cost. Aside from Head Start, a very limited number of publicly funded preschool programs are offered in thirty-eight states and the District of Columbia. Of the remaining 6.3 million preschool-age children, 2.5 million or 29 percent go to some kind of private facility.

However, preschool in the United States as currently constituted is unacceptably fragmented and inconsistent. More than 50 percent of preschoolers are enrolled in part-day programs, many with no educational content whatsoever. In the publicly funded realm, almost all programs—not just Head Start—are means-tested, with eligibility varying widely by program and locality. To be eligible for Head Start, a child's family must have an income below the federal poverty level or be on public assistance. Most state programs also restrict eligibility to households whose incomes fall below the official poverty threshold or some fraction of the state's median income. Seven states offer limited (partial day/partial week) preschool experiences to all four-year-olds; only Oklahoma has something like universal—but still time-limited—access to preschool for all three- and four-year-olds.[30] The variation in quality and school time among private preschools is even greater than that found in publicly funded programs.

The bottom line: for the cohort of American children three to five years of age, access to a preschool experience and the educational benefit they gain from it is currently so varied and uneven that the American preschool system, such as it is, cannot possibly be expected to make a game-changing impact on later academic achievement—and, overall, it doesn't. This is because, when it comes to preschools in the United States today, we are at roughly the same stage of educational maturity as the elementary schools of the early nineteenth century when they were mainly district-operated one-room schoolhouses.

America's nineteenth-century public education revolution only truly got off the ground when, after intense advocacy by Horace Mann and the common school movement, the country's educationally erratic district schools were replaced with higher-quality and nationally consistent public schools in most American states. So too today, we will only close our intractable educational Megagap—and help mainstream students as well—when our current incoherent preschool system is replaced by a national network of preschools that are for the most part publicly funded, non–means-tested, accessible, and tuition-free to all children within a school district, and, most critically, *based on specifications proven to be effective in leveling the cultural literacy and academic readiness playing field for children of diverse socioeconomic backgrounds.*

Clearly, implementing such a revolutionary change in American schooling will be not only expensive but also controversial in other respects. Some (including a large number of parents) will argue that young children should not be herded into formal institutional settings at such an early age; that they would be happier and better adjusted at home, or engaged in structured play. (This view doomed an early education initiative forty years ago, when Congress passed—and President Nixon vetoed—legislation that would have paid for states adding up to two years of preschool to their K–12 educational sequence.)[31] Others will say that we cannot afford it, or that at the very least we should take advantage of the fact that most middle- and upper-middle-class families already pay for private preschool, and only subsidize poorer preschool children on a sliding means-tested scale. Then, regardless of the size of the new increment of public support, there is the question of who should pay for it: the federal government, the states, or local school districts. But the greatest political obstacle of all will be convincing skeptics that universal access to preschool really can sharply increase the prospects of academic success for disadvantaged youngsters. Despite the evidence cited earlier, gaining bipartisan support for the kind of vastly expanded—and locally integrated—preschool initiative called for here requires hard evidence of its prospective benefits. That, in turn, requires fairly rigorous specification of its key substantive features.

Curriculum As noted earlier, there is widespread agreement with Hirsch's argument that America's academic Megagap arises from vast disparities in cultural literacy among two- to four-year-olds of different economic and ethnic family backgrounds, and that subsequent K–12 academic success depends critically on leveling the cultural-literacy playing field before kindergarten. This, then, is the most important function of preschool, one that depends on using the right curriculum. At this moment in the evolution of preschool programs in the United States, there is a daunting array of curricula in use, more being developed to choose from, and scant evidence on which to base the choice. What little evidence exists is not all that helpful. For example, the What Works Clearinghouse of the Institute of Education Sciences (a unit of the U.S. Department of Education considered to be one of the more reliable referees of educational practices), in a methodologically rigorous review of widely adopted preschool curricula, found only three that appeared to have a significant longer-term impact on subsequent academic achievement: *Bright Beginnings, Doors to Discovery*, and *Literacy Express*. At the same time, the Clearinghouse acknowledges that many of the available curricula (including, regrettably, the *Core Knowledge* curriculum of Hirsch's protégés) have not yet been thoroughly studied.[32]

Teachers Regardless of curriculum, if we want preschool to launch young children—and most especially culturally disadvantaged young children—on a successful academic trajectory for the rest of their school years, we need good teachers. To be a good preschool teacher requires—just as it does for kindergarten and later grades—a sound college education and specialized training. Accordingly, the National Institute for Early Education Research (NIEER), one of the country's most respected centers in this field, insists that the minimum qualifications for preschool teaching should be a baccalaureate degree and specialized training in early childhood instruction and programming.[33]

However, this is very far from the current reality. For starters, fifteen U.S. states have no preschool teaching requirements at all. Head Start and twenty-nine states require only an associate degree in child development (a CDA), the qualification possessed by the majority of working preschool teachers today. Eighteen states mandate a baccalaureate, but only nine follow the full NIEER specifications, demanding specialized training along with the baccalaureate. The net result is that while 87 percent of teachers in state-operated programs (generally in states with more stringent teaching requirements) do have baccalaureates, they serve only a small proportion of all public preschool children. Among Head Start teachers, serving 84 percent of all public preschoolers, only 30 percent have a baccalaureate. By way of comparison, 100 percent of U.S. K–12 teachers have at least a baccalaureate, and over 90 percent have specialized training in pedagogy and classroom management. If—despite such credentials—we are unhappy with

K–12 teaching outcomes in the later grades, how can we possibly be satisfied leaving preschool instruction to teachers with even weaker credentials?

Then there is the issue of what the preschool teaching force is paid. Along with their substandard qualifications, most preschool teachers also earn substandard pay. According to U.S. Labor Department data, the median annual salary for U.S. preschool teachers in 2010 was $25,700, about half what elementary school teachers got that year: $51,700. Even those *with baccalaureates* earned only $36,000.

Do teacher qualifications and pay make a difference? There is convincing evidence that they do. On the subject of educational credentials, Steven Barnett, one of the leading experts in the field—citing the voluminous research on this subject—asserts categorically: "studies of state-supported preschool programs have found that quality is higher in programs where more teachers have at least a four-year college degree."[34] Regarding pay, research shows that low pay—even by local public school standards—impairs morale, motivation, and turnover.[35] And, of course, it can't be separated from the issue of raising teacher qualifications, because it is highly unlikely that better-educated teachers will work for bargain-basement wages.

Age, Time, and Class Size Three other factors can affect the long-term human-capital benefits of a preschool experience. The most important is the age at which children are first exposed to it. Typically, preschool can begin at age three and continue through age four. Hirsch and other preschool proponents, who see it as essential to leveling the cultural-literacy playing field, want all culturally disadvantaged children to begin when they are three. Buttressing their concern over class-based early childhood educational disparities, that happens to be the age at which the majority of upper-income children with college-educated parents currently enter private—mostly unsubsidized—preschool programs. Yet only a small share of other three-year-olds are currently served by any public program (including Head Start). Even at age four, only a third of low-income American children are enrolled in a public preschool program (again, predominantly in Head Start).[36] Hirsch has studied the impact of French preschool on that country's educational Megagap—mainly related to its large North African population—and noted how much better those enrolled at age three did later on in French K–12 grades.

Regardless of age, for preschool to make a difference, children must spend enough time at it every weekday. Currently the majority of preschool programs—public and private, Head Start and others—are part day. While full-day programs allow for more enriched programming and are more helpful for working parents, they also cost more and may be too exhausting for the youngest children. Here is a case where quality may matter more than quantity; the NIEER and other evidence-driven proponents of expanded preschool access consider 2.5 hours a day, five days a week, adequate—if those hours are well-spent.

Since the benefits of preschool depend very much on the interaction of children with teachers and classmates, class size and staffing also matter. The consensus in the field, supported by studies of effective programs across the country, is that classes should have no more than twenty children (comparable to kindergarten in most places), with at least two professional staff—a highly qualified teacher (per the specifications noted above) and an appropriately trained aide.

GETTING TO UNIVERSAL PRESCHOOL

We have reams of empirical evidence giving us reason to hope that vastly expanding preschool accessibility can narrow—perhaps even close—the Megagap holding back disadvantaged children, especially those from African American and Hispanic families.

For all other children, regardless of race or class, it can dramatically raise U.S. educational performance, along with all the other human-capital gains that a better education generates. We also have convincing arguments for accomplishing this expansion by extending the district public school instructional ladder down to age three—with universal eligibility and at no cost to parents (as opposed to the means-tested, largely independent preschools operating today). But such a breathtaking change in American educational policy cannot be entered into lightly. Obviously there is a fairly hefty price tag, at least in the short run. The more serious issue, as noted earlier, is making sure that when preschool is scaled up, it can deliver the same promising outcomes seen in the as yet quite limited field experiences. Aside from the challenge in convincing national and state politicians to take the plunge and authorize the initiative, we cannot risk public disappointment or, worse, outright disillusionment, with its results down the road. Disappointing results will inevitably ensue unless universal preschool is done properly wherever it is instituted. This means that all children under this initiative should attend preschools that are:

1. Managed by local school districts as the earliest rungs of a pre-K–12 educational ladder.

2. Using an academically sound curriculum.

3. Deploying teachers with baccalaureates and specialized preschool training.

4. Offering at least 2.5 hours of instruction a day for five days a week (during the normal school year).

The only way for universal preschool along these lines to become a reality is for it to be operated under the auspices of each state, but funded—at least initially—by the federal government. If it is funded federally, it can and should have its design specified, and performance monitored, federally. We actually have a good example at hand of another educational reform initiative that can serve as a model. The Race to the Top grant program of the U.S. Department of Education, begun in July 2009, has, with financially modest competitive awards, managed to get states to institute serious K–12 reforms that would have been unthinkable only a few years ago. Federal preschool grants to the states could be handled the same way. Federal financial assistance to the states would be conditioned on state applications that followed the kinds of specifications noted above. Further, federal aid should also require states to carefully monitor the performance of preschoolers in subsequent grades—all the way to high school graduation—with statistically valid longitudinal studies. States that are not able to demonstrate significant academic achievement gains at least up to the third grade might lose some or all of their federal aid.

PAYING FOR UNIVERSAL PRESCHOOL

If Congress agreed to a national universal-access and free preschool program, where would the (mainly federal) money come from? In calculating its cost, we need to factor in what we are already spending on Head Start and other public preschool programs, what we spend later in the K–12 grades to try to offset the Megagap, and the lifetime human-capital costs (to individuals and society) when millions of Americans have an incomplete education. In 2011, the total publicly supported preschool enrollment nationally was 1.3 million children, costing the federal government over $9 billion on Head Start, with the states spending an additional $5.5 billion to supplement the federal program or on a variety of local preschool initiatives. Another $14.5 billion is spent annually in federal aid to elementary and secondary schools directed almost entirely to raise the academic performance of disadvantaged children. The largest relevant national expenditure, however, is neither for preschool nor for disadvantaged children generally, but for special education:

totaling over $50 billion. Although most of this money is spent on educational services for children with explicit physical or developmental handicaps, at least a third is used to provide enriched education to underachieving disadvantaged children with no true disability.[37]

All of the funds aimed (explicitly or implicitly) at Megagap children together total $44 billion. The entire national population of three- and four-year-olds currently is 8.2 million. However, even if preschool across the country were tuition-free and available to all age-eligible children without means-testing, many families would want to keep their children at home (especially three-year-olds), and others, for financial or perceived quality reasons, would enroll their children in private programs. Therefore, the most generous estimate of likely preschool enrollment would be 90 percent of four-year-olds (3.7 million) and 50 percent of three-year-olds (2.1 million), giving us an aggregate cohort to be served of 5.8 million. Thus, if we wanted to fund a universally accessible program for all American children of preschool age *only* with money currently devoted to disadvantaged preschoolers (mainly Head Start) and money used in later grades to compensate for early childhood educational deficits, we could spend $7,500 per enrollee, 80 percent more than we devote annually to each preschool child today. If implemented on a national scale, initially—perhaps for a decade— the entire marginal cost of nationally universal preschool might be borne by U.S. Department of Education grants to local school districts, channeled through state education departments. And, as indicated earlier, Head Start should be phased out, with all of its funds redirected to the new initiative.

EXTENDED LEARNING TIME

Out of habit or inertia, the established national norm of 180 school days, 6.5 hours per day, is a facet of American public school policy that has been pretty much frozen in place for more than a century. Recently, some states have looked into lengthening the instructional calendar as a way of lifting student achievement, but to date this has usually taken the form of modestly increasing the proportion of time devoted to academic subjects (as opposed to meals, transitions, homeroom, recreation, or electives) from two-thirds to three-quarters of the school day. Yet, as a strategy for raising academic performance, what educators refer to as "extended learning time" (ELT) needs to be taken much more seriously, with the proviso that the school time needs to be extended in very specific ways, and the way in which the extra time is spent matters a great deal.

While ELT may be beneficial for all schoolchildren, it has proven to be especially effective in raising the academic performance of Megagap schoolchildren and for keeping them on track once they have begun to catch up with those in the mainstream. For that reason ELT also happens to be one of the core elements in the Massachusetts reform playbook, a key feature of the more successful charter schools, and it is now being aggressively promoted by the U.S. Department of Education.

The theory behind ELT for Megagap schoolchildren rests on two somewhat distinct ideas. The first might be described as "practice makes perfect." As Malcolm Gladwell documents in his bestselling book *Outliers*, in every field spending more time at an endeavor leads to greater success.[38] Applying this notion to children at an educational disadvantage because of their families' social and economic circumstances, ELT should produce academic gains first by giving them more time to process and do practice exercises in challenging subject matter, especially in mathematics, science, or serious literature; second, by exposing them to class material in greater detail, using a wider range of teaching aids and media; third, by allowing their teachers to spend more time on important subjects like history, geography, and the social sciences (the single-minded focus of federal and state education departments on raising proficiency in math and language arts—as exemplified by No Child Left Behind—results inevitably in hard-pressed Megagap schools shortchanging everything else); and, fourth, by enabling their teachers to spend more time with them when they have difficulty.

The second idea rests on the Hirsch thesis that school can compensate for the cultural deficits in the home and neighborhood environments of poor children. While a core knowledge preschool experience may be an absolutely necessary first step in reducing the cultural deficit of Megagap children, it is also necessary to sustain their academic gains as they move up the schooling ladder. In this endeavor, longer school days may make a big difference, but even more important is countering the academic backsliding occasioned by the typical ten- to twelve-week summer break.

Both kinds of ELT have extensive empirical validation. Here again, the experience of Massachusetts is worth noting. The state's original reform legislation normalized—and modestly lengthened—instructional time across all local districts, so one could reasonably ascribe a small portion of the state's impressive academic gains since then to this aspect of the reform package. However, more methodologically convincing validation can be found in what happened a decade later. In 2006, Massachusetts launched its Expanded Learning Time to Support Student Success initiative, which gives 10,500 of the state's Megagap schoolchildren, attending nineteen schools in ten districts, three hundred additional hours of instruction per year. The initiative grew out of a carefully structured pilot experiment, conducted in ten schools in five districts, as well as research on the impact of ELT in selected schools across the country. To cite just one example of ELT efficacy, some of the extra time in the Boston and Lawrence pilot schools was spent on doubling the hours devoted to math, with striking results: in 2003–2004, compared to similar students in these cities' regular schools, students in the pilot schools were twice as likely to demonstrate basic levels of understanding (with near 100 percent passing scores) and three times as likely to reach the higher standard of "proficient."

Among other evidence, one rigorous meta-analysis of the issue (summarizing a large number of empirical findings) was conducted by David Berliner in 1990 that concluded that instructional time made a great difference in the academic performance of at-risk schoolchildren and that the greater the time spent in class, the better the educational outcomes. But how that time was spent mattered as well, and the most successful models were those that made sure that students were actually engaged in active learning.[39] A recent report by the National Center on Time and Learning, *Time Well Spent*, undertook a detailed review of thirty "Expanded-Time" schools spread across the country (nineteen of them charters, eleven conventional district-operated), all of which reported significant learning gains.[40] The typical school in this sample expanded instructional time by about three hundred hours per year—about the same as in the Massachusetts ELT initiative—representing an increase over the prevailing norm of 21 to 31 percent. As important, most of the additional time was dedicated to core classroom academics (as opposed to meals, transitions, homeroom, recreation, or electives), and the lion's share of that was spent on math and English language arts subjects.

The most comprehensive review of the benefits of expanded learning time is a 2012 report commissioned by the Wallace Foundation, which looked at a comprehensive array of ELT programs across the country, encompassing a wide variety of approaches: longer school days, longer school years, varying amounts of time added, varying amounts dedicated to specific academic subjects, as well as added time spent on tutoring and extracurricular activities.[41]

SUMMING UP

Education agencies and school districts in the United States, with the courts intervening on the sidelines, have devoted the better part of half a century to close (or at least narrow) the gap between the academic performance of America's disadvantaged schoolchildren, often poor and minority, and the majority of those, usually white, from the middle-class mainstream—what I have characterized in this book as the Megagap. As indicated earlier, after spending billions of dollars, experimenting with a broad array of thought-to-be-promising reforms, the results are beyond disappointing.

But buried in this extensive repertoire, two reforms *have* been proven to work, at least when they have been tried on a limited scale: quality preschool education and extended learning time. I propose that both of these not just thought-to-be-promising but empirically validated reforms be given a comprehensive nationwide trial. Implemented on a national scale, these initiatives might also deliver disappointing results, but if they worked, they would revolutionize American education and produce a quantum increase in American human capital.

For political and financial reasons, both ideas might first be implemented on a pilot basis. In a pilot preschool initiative, the U.S. Department of Education might invite applications from districts around the country that wish to introduce a free, open-access preschool program for three- and four-year-olds. Federal funds would underwrite the full cost of implementation for a period of years (maybe five to seven), with districts chosen based on the proven effectiveness of the proposed curriculum, the qualifications of teachers, and adequacy of facilities. Applicant districts must maintain thorough records documenting the progress their preschool children make in later grades. Districts that can show real gains would have the grants renewed for a limited number of years; those that can't would have the grants terminated. If the pilot is widely successful, the program should be expanded on a national scale.

Similarly, in a pilot extended learning time initiative, districts that wanted to implement this would be invited to apply for U.S. Department of Education grants, with awards given to districts that present empirically validated formats for using the extended learning time and an agreement to carefully monitor the progress of children in the ELT program. The department might invite a variety of alternate ELT formats to determine which are the most educationally effective, and make this the basis for a nationwide expansion of ELT.

Closing the Mainstream Achievement Gap

The U.S. public school reform enterprise is now over a half century old—taking the *Brown v. Board of Education* Supreme Court ruling as the starting point. From 1954 to the present day, this effort has focused almost exclusively on closing the achievement gap separating disadvantaged minority schoolchildren from the rest— what I refer to as the Megagap in chapter 3. As well-intentioned and admittedly important as this effort has been, it has fallen far short of delivering on its high hopes despite the expenditure of tens of billions of dollars.

Largely forgotten, meanwhile, has been another education reform objective that is much more achievable—sometimes with the same means that didn't work on the Megagap—and arguably just as worthwhile: that is, closing the growing gap between what most *non-disadvantaged* American youth are capable of learning (and what their European and Asian peers *are* learning) and what is actually expected of them in the typical U.S. public school. I call this the "Mainstream" learning gap; this deficiency is chiefly responsible for America's mediocre standing on international achievement tests and it frustrates American employers looking to fill jobs requiring advanced literacy and analytical ability. Mainstream students make up 70 to 80 percent of the U.S. K–12 student body (depending on precisely where one sets the mainstream/disadvantaged threshold). Closing the Mainstream gap would not only quickly catapult the United States into first place in global educational performance rankings but would also electrify the capability of the American labor force and in countless ways expand the well-being of the American middle class.

A thorough review of the empirical evidence points to a surefire and easily implemented path to achieve strong school-performance gains for most American schoolchildren who are not otherwise handicapped by poverty, family breakdown, or poor physical or mental health. It turns out that all it will take to close the Mainstream gap is for the typical American public school district—and most particularly its high schools—*to demand more of its students in the way of academic work.* In practice this will mean:

1. Accelerating the pace at which subject matter is covered in each grade—especially in grades nine through twelve, with more rigorous coverage of science (including physics), math (including advanced algebra), English, geography, and history.

2. Holding students to high performance standards through continuous low-stakes, feedback-oriented testing and challenging homework requirements.

3. Making sure that teachers are qualified to teach these subjects (a topic addressed later in this chapter).

4. Issuing *college preparatory* high school diplomas conditioned on courses taken and passing scores on a college-ready exit exam.

The beauty of this prescription is that, given the preeminent role and jurisdiction of the fifty state education departments, it can be implemented rapidly and consistently across entire states at, as they say, "the stroke of a pen." This is in sharp contrast to the laborious, highly contentious, frequently costly, and only marginally effective school reforms being advocated and tried on a more-or-less random, district-by-district basis across the country. I am referring primarily to the single-minded focus on new teacher performance evaluation protocols being vigorously advocated by education reform conservatives, but also to the favored nostrums of education reform liberals: smaller class sizes, "diversity" initiatives, and increases in school funding.

That the Mainstream gap can be closed without heroic exertions is empirically demonstrated by the enormous variation in academic achievement among and within the fifty American states, when looking exclusively at the National Assessment of Educational Progress (NAEP) scores of *white, suburban* schoolchildren. (As indicated in chapter 2, NAEP tests are the best, nationally uniform basis for making interstate and intrastate comparisons.)

Table 4.1 shows eighth-grade test scores in reading and math for suburban whites in the top five and bottom five U.S. states. At the extremes, the gap between white suburbanites in the highest- and lowest-achieving states is almost as great as that separating minority and white test takers nationally.[1] There is no way that any particular genetic or cultural handicap can account for this amount of interstate variation, leading to the inescapable conclusion that the best explanation lies in interstate differences in the characteristics of schools attended by these children. If one looks closely at what goes on in the various states to account for these performance differences, one finds that the more successful states engage in some or all of the practices enumerated above. And among the higher-performing states, one clearly stands out: Massachusetts.

Table 4.1

NAEP Eighth-Grade Reading Scores of White Suburban Children (top and bottom five states), 2011

State	Average score	Level
New Jersey	284	Proficient
Connecticut	283	Proficient
Massachusetts	283	Proficient
Maryland	282	Proficient
Virginia	281	Proficient
California	265	Low basic
Oklahoma	265	Low basic
Louisiana	264	Low basic
Nevada	262	Low basic
West Virginia	262	Low basic

Source: U.S. Department of Education,
National Center for Education Statistics.

THE MASSACHUSETTS MIRACLE

The leading position of Massachusetts in these interstate comparisons is most striking—it is no mere accident or momentary fluke. While Massachusetts is unquestionably an affluent state, with a high proportion of well-educated adults (read parents), so are any number of other states that do not score as well on the NAEP. When it comes to suburban whites in particular, there is absolutely no reason to assume that the children in this cohort in Massachusetts possess any advantage over their counterparts in, say, California, Ohio, or Michigan, other than going to better schools. Further, the superiority of school achievement in Massachusetts is relatively new, dating to the period after the early 1990s.

The reason that Massachusetts has overtaken other equally affluent states in school performance since then can be attributed to a sharp turn in *state education policy* that was undertaken two decades ago. The trigger was the work of a blue-ribbon state commission appointed by Massachusetts Governor William Weld in 1993 and chaired by the president of Boston University, John Silber. This commission, defying the stereotypical anodyne and rarely implemented output of such elite problem-solving bodies, issued a hard-hitting, highly detailed policy document that not only recommended striking changes in K–12 education practices but also saw to it that they were faithfully executed.

The Massachusetts Education Reform Act of 1993 consisted of a number of reform initiatives, but four of them stand out in their impact on state educational outcomes, and it is these that can be easily replicated by other states—and should yield the same beneficial results:

1. The requirement for all state school districts to adhere to rigorous curriculum specifications (grounded in world-class academic standards) that impose detailed lesson plans for all key subjects in every grade.

2. A new statewide diagnostic testing protocol, the Massachusetts Comprehensive Assessment System (MCAS), to ensure that students achieve proficiency in the new curricular standards.

3. More rigorous testing of new teacher candidates to ensure that they demonstrate mastery of subject matter as well as literacy skills before they enter a state classroom.

4. A statewide uniform high school graduation standard requiring that all tenth-grade students must take—and pass—a comprehensive, multi-subject MCAS test battery to receive an academic diploma.[2]

As a result of these reforms, Massachusetts now leads the nation in most state-level head-to-head comparisons on the NAEP tests and, perhaps even more significant, in the pace of achieve-ment gains in key subjects. As table 4.2 indicates, the state's own annual assessment reports show that between 1998 and 2012, tenth graders' proficiency rates jumped from 38 percent to 88 percent in reading and writing and from 24 percent to 78 percent in math.[3] These results are particularly impressive because the state's own tests—the MCAS—are closely aligned in rigor and scoring with the national NAEP exams, meaning these gains are not just the product of testing "grade inflation."[4] Further, a recent Harvard study, examining results from international math and reading tests, found that Massachusetts eighth graders not only scored highest among American states on these tests but also outscored test takers in all but a few countries. Some other encouraging sta-tistics from Massachusetts: 61 percent of high school freshmen there proceed to college, and 53 percent of the state's young adults have college degrees, both the highest proportions of any Ameri-can state.[5] In contemplating these gains, remember that the de-mographic profile of the state's schoolchildren has not changed during this period, meaning that *all* of the improvement can be attributed to changes in education policy!

The success of Massachusetts contrasts sharply with condi-tions in most other American states, where too many high school students—even those with no discernible socioeconomic or cogni-

Table 4.2

Percent of Students Scoring Proficiency or Higher, MCAS (tenth grade)

Subject	1998	2001	2004	2008	2012
Mathematics	24	45	57	72	78
English Language Arts	38	51	62	75	88
Science/Technology	–	–	–	57	69

Source: Massachusetts Department of Elementary and Secondary Education.

tive handicaps—fail to graduate and those who do aren't prepared for college. A February 2011 report issued by New York's Board of Regents, for example, found that in 2009, only 77 percent of the state's students who had been ninth graders four years earlier managed to get a high school diploma; further, only 41 percent of students who went on to college were "college ready."[6]

COMMON ACADEMIC STANDARDS

The most burning question posed by the "Massachusetts miracle" is whether its reforms—and the resulting outcomes—can be replicated, state by state, across the United States. As it happens, a multistate initiative is currently in play that is designed to do exactly that with respect to the most substantive of the Massachusetts reform measures: instilling a more rigorous curriculum in all grades based on carefully specified academic content standards. This is the Common Core State Standards Initiative (CCSSI), a decades-long effort sponsored by the Council of Chief State School Officers and the National Governors Association, which commits its forty-five enlisted states to setting stringent English and math content standards from first through twelfth grades. (The states that have not yet signed on are Alaska, Minnesota, Nebraska, Texas, and Virginia.)[7] Given the success of Massachusetts, it is tempting to celebrate the near-universal adoption of the CCSSI as a great victory and a breakthrough in closing the Mainstream learning gap nationally.

The Thomas B. Fordham Institute, one of the nation's most highly respected education policy organizations, issued a report on the CCSSI in 2010 summarizing its conclusions and concerns. With respect to the academic rigorousness of the CCSSI standards for math and English language arts (ELA, also known as reading and writing), its verdict was "good but not great." The Institute considers them better than those currently in force in the majority of states and, overall, gives the math standards a grade of A– and the English standards a B–. As two of the Institute's scholars, Chester Finn, former U.S. Assistant Secretary of Education, and Michael Petrilli, have noted: "standards are the foundation upon which almost everything else [in raising student achievement] rests. . . . They should guide state assessments and accountability systems; inform teacher preparation, licensure, and professional development; and give shape to curricula, textbooks, software programs and more."[8]

At this early stage, however, celebration of the CCSSI as a game-changing national reform might be premature—depending on its state-by-state implementation.[9] As conventional wisdom has it, "God is in the details," and there are many details here to contend with. There are a host of ways in which many states may not be able to ensure that the standards actually close the Mainstream learning gap. For one thing, as of now the standards only affect mathematics and ELA; truly stringent academic content standards—like those in Massachusetts—should cover the natural and social sciences, history, and geography. Then there are some other really big questions: Are the standards sufficiently rigorous? How thoroughly will they be enforced at the state level? Since the standards are quite specific by subject and grade level, all schools in the subscribing states will need to extensively revise their classroom lesson plans, textbook requisitions, and teacher training. This might be fairly costly, and may be resisted (or sabotaged) by many district principals and teachers who resent the added work and fear the possible accountability consequences if students don't do well under the new standards. Crucially, the state tests in these subjects will need to be revised, and probably made more rigorous, risking high failure rates that will generate angst among parents, teachers, and school administrators. And the most daunting hurdle of all: a large share of a state's teachers, if not a majority, may themselves never have mastered the material required in the CCSSI.

A preview of what might be in store for states implementing

the CCSSI can be seen in New York State's experience when, at the end of the 2012–13 school year, it revised its third- to eighth-grade mathematics and ELA achievement tests to conform to the new curricular expectations. Statewide passing (i.e., "proficiency") scores in both subjects and all grades were from 44 to 52 percent lower than in the previous year's (non-CCSSI linked) tests, triggering great alarm among both educators and parents. Even in affluent and typically high-performing Long Island—the very epitome of a mainstream school locale—proficiency percentages in math dropped from 75 in the previous year to 38, and in ELA from 67 to 40. To quell anxieties—and to avoid having the CCSSI standards derailed at their birth—state and national education officials, notably including Arne Duncan, the U.S. Secretary of Education, have been busily assuring everyone that when the new CCSSI curricula are actually taught in the classroom, all students will do considerably better. But the most important of their messages has been—echoing the argument of this chapter—that the current poor exam performance only shows how far behind twenty-first-century global educational standards (their precise formulation) American students have fallen. In Secretary Duncan's words: "Too many school systems lied to children, families and communities. Finally, we are holding ourselves accountable as educators."[10]

With respect to its adoption by Massachusetts—and perhaps a few other states—there is another important issue: the CCSSI might represent a step back in terms of curricular rigor. It is on exactly these grounds that Massachusetts education officials and nationally respected education experts oppose the "one size fits all" nature of the CCSSI standards. The issue of potential disparities between the CCSSI and more demanding state standards is exacerbated by the U.S. Department of Education's determination to condition a portion of federal school aid on state adoption of the CCSSI—exactly as written. Both to keep Massachusetts from having to in any way erode its extremely successful curricular model, and to encourage other states to match Massachusetts in rigor, the national education bureaucrats would be well-advised in their promotion of the CCSSI to treat it as a set of *minimal* standards, allowing the states to modify it if they can show that their home-grown version is superior.

Let me conclude this section, however, on a positive note. The post-reform experience of Massachusetts is a brilliant vindication of the proposition that *curriculum matters*, and that curriculum reform is *one of the most easily replicable ways of closing the Mainstream learning gap*. Whatever their shortcomings, the CCSSI standards are a vast improvement over what most states currently teach. Over the medium to long haul, we can expect (or hope) that with experience and refinement, the CCSSI standards will become more rigorous, cover more subjects, and be ever more consistently implemented nationally.

ACCOUNTABILITY TESTING

Accountability-based education reform, for both Megagap and Mainstream schoolchildren, depends on putting in place a feedback loop to both provide incentives for and measure achievement gains: as education reforms (of the sort reviewed in this and the previous chapter) are implemented, students are tested to gauge their academic progress at the individual, class, school, and district level; if standards are not being met, teachers and administrators are expected to modify educational strategies accordingly (with rewards and sanctions providing the motivation); the next round of testing determines the effectiveness of these changes, and so on in a benign cycle of continuous improvement.

This is the logic behind the central feature of the 2001 federal Elementary and Secondary Education Act (also known as No Child Left Behind, or NCLB), which requires all states to periodically test public school students to gauge their proficiency in math and ELA and, if they are falling short, to undertake remedial measures. Technically, these are "low-stakes" tests in that students aren't directly affected by how well they score. But they do pose higher stakes for the states—and, by extension, their local districts and schools. In its original form, the law specified that unless 100 percent of its students reached proficiency levels in these subjects by 2014, a state would lose a sizable chunk of its federal school aid—a policy that has now been effectively scrapped through state-specific waivers and indefinite postponement. This provision looked good on paper, but suffered in practice from being both too inconsistent (it left the choice of tests—and their difficulty—to the states, giving them a powerful incentive to make tests less rigorous) and too unrealistic (no state—even with dumbed-down tests—could have been expected to meet this criterion). Another provision of NCLB, however, does allow us to get a good idea of how each state's students are actually doing. While free to base student proficiency assessments on their own tests, the states are also required to administer the national NAEP Math and ELA tests to a representative sample of their students, yielding a reliable benchmark against which to judge state test results.

Against this backdrop, the nation's most comprehensive and well-thought-out framework of educational accountability is the Massachusetts Comprehensive Assessment System (MCAS) cited earlier. MCAS was adopted as a key component of the state's comprehensive 1993 education reform act, nine years before passage of the federal NCLB law. It also goes much further than NCLB in the subjects it covers, in marked contrast to NCLB's widely criticized single-minded focus on math and English language arts: in addition to these subjects, MCAS tests students in biology, chemistry, physics, engineering technology, history, and social science. The other distinction of MCAS is that its tests are tightly aligned with the state's curriculum standards, so that this is one instance where "teaching to the test" is something to be desired rather than being a mere stratagem to avoid accountability sanctions.

The most striking feature of MCAS is its rigor. A 2004 evaluation of MCAS looked at how its math and ELA test results stacked up next to NAEP results for the same subjects, grade levels, and time of administration. They found that:

1. The MCAS scores closely mirrored those of the Massachusetts administered NAEP tests, meaning the results can be interpreted as a valid barometer of student proficiency, unlike the case in virtually every other state.

2. From 1992 (the year before the start of MCAS) to 2003, Massachusetts students made striking gains in both MCAS and NAEP scores, especially in math.

3. The NAEP scores and the gains over this period were greater than those for the nation as a whole (table 4.3).[11]

Table 4.3

Percent of Eighth Graders Scoring at or above Proficiency Level

A. MATHEMATICS

Test site	Basic and above	Proficient and above	Advanced
Massachusetts 1996/98	68	28	5
U.S. 1996/98	61	23	4
Massachusetts 2005	80	43	11
U.S. 2005	68	28	6

B. ENGLISH LANGUAGE ARTS

Test site	Basic and above	Proficient and above	Advanced
Massachusetts 1996/98	79	38	3
U.S. 1996/98	71	30	2
Massachusetts 2005	83	44	5
U.S. 2005	71	29	3

Source: Massachusetts Department of Elementary and Secondary Education, 2005 NAEP Tests: Summary of Results for Massachusetts.

In many respects MCAS is the critical linchpin in the Massachusetts reform initiative: because its tests are designed to follow the state's prescribed curricula, teachers are motivated to adhere closely to their standards; for the same reason, its results are useful diagnostic tools to help struggling students; and, since the state makes passing the MCAS tests a condition for graduating from high school with an academic diploma (as noted in the next section), Massachusetts high school graduates are among the country's best prepared for college. Clearly, MCAS is the accountability-testing model that should be followed by all states working to close their Mainstream learning gap.

TEACHER TRAINING

Even if the current education reform orthodoxy exaggerates the centrality of teacher quality, there can be no question that this can heavily impact education outcomes. Translating this truism into meaningful policy, however, depends on knowing how to train and identify good teachers. After-the-fact evaluations of teacher performance in the classroom, no matter how thorough—the only arrow in the current teacher-quality quiver—are not enough.

Giving American public schools the best possible teachers depends on three things: first, attracting highly capable individuals into the profession; then making sure that they have mastered the subjects they will be teaching; and, finally, appropriately rewarding the better teachers in the field and quickly dismissing the poorer ones. None of these criteria is being met currently, nor can even the most stringent post-hoc evaluation protocols make up for these deficiencies.

At the center of the teacher-training problem are the places that have, for the last hundred years or more, secured the monopoly on teacher training and recruitment: formal teacher education programs, the direct descendants of the country's normal schools. When they were established in the mid to late nineteenth century as a key component of America's path-breaking push to universalize public education, the normal schools were admirable in many respects: they professionalized teaching, which heretofore had been hit-or-miss as to teacher qualifications, and they provided a secure and prestigious career path for educated women, a rarity at that time elsewhere in the world.

Most selective American universities, both public and private, have stayed away from teacher training, and those that once offered it have long since closed their teacher education programs or restricted them to graduate study. Thus, second-tier, unselective state and private colleges—the progeny of the normal schools—are now just about the only places left that specialize in the training of teachers. These are, with few exceptions, exceedingly mediocre institutions—in the scholastic aptitude of their students, in the rigor of their curriculum, and in the scholarship of their faculty. To cite no less an authority than the U.S. Secretary of Education:

By almost any standard, many if not most of the nation's 1,450 schools, colleges and departments of education are doing a mediocre job of preparing teachers for the realities of the 21st century classroom.[12]

Even the head of one of the two national teachers unions concurs:

Today, despite many efforts at reform, teacher preparation is still inadequate for the realities of urban classrooms.[13]

Aside from their mediocrity, teacher education programs are falling short for some very concrete reasons. The most pervasive critique concerns what prospective teachers actually learn there. Two-thirds of a typical teacher education curriculum consists of what is broadly called *pedagogy*, a wide array of courses that ostensibly teach teacher trainees *how* to teach. Included are courses in child development, the history of education, various subject-specific techniques, and "classroom management." If these courses actually ensured success in the classroom, their curricular dominance might be justified. But countless studies have shown that exposure to pedagogy courses does not translate into better teaching.[14]

Because so much time is devoted to studying pedagogy, teacher education students spend very little time taking the courses they need to master the subjects they themselves will be teaching, especially in more demanding fields: mathematics, the sciences, even history, geography, and literature. Even the courses in those subjects they are required to take are usually watered-down versions tailored specifically to education majors—facetiously dubbed by faculty in the relevant fields as "math (or biology or geography) for poets."

Given the focus on pedagogy, one would expect that teacher education programs would at the very least give their trainees extensive exposure to classroom experience through student teaching in local school districts. But owing to the difficulty in finding enough qualified student teaching instructors and classroom mentors, student teaching requirements—usually set by state mandates—are typically light, often just one semester or less. Thus, this limited experience is usually of little value in instilling real-world teaching proficiency.

This critique applies pretty much to all such programs across the country because, despite the great variation among American states along so many other dimensions, when it comes to teacher education, almost all places follow roughly the same format. This is to a large extent due to the role that teacher education accreditation plays—all states make graduation from an accredited program a condition for obtaining teacher certification—and the inherent long-standing prejudices of the nation's leading accrediting organization: the National Council for Accreditation of Teacher Education (NCATE). To be fair, NCATE has been stung by the critique and has responded by encouraging teacher education programs to become more selective in their admissions policies and ramp up their subject-matter content. NCATE has in recent years been facing competition from a rival accreditor, the Teacher Education Accreditation Council (TEAC), established specifically to get teacher education programs to address the problems noted above. As of this writing, NCATE and TEAC have merged, creating a single, ostensibly more rigorous, national teacher training accreditor: the Council for the Accreditation of Educator Preparation (CAEP).[15] If CAEP lives up to its billing, some of the most serious shortcomings of traditional American teacher training institutions may be remedied. One can only hope for the best.

The states play two critical roles in shaping the quality of their teachers: the requirements they impose to be eligible for teacher certification and the rigor of their certification exams. Generally speaking, the former—very much aligned with the curricula of traditional teacher education programs—have been too rigid in their specification of required pedagogy courses, repelling many of the most talented prospective teachers; and the latter have been too lax, allowing many of the least talented graduates to enter the classroom. Raising the bar on the Massachusetts teacher certification exam was one of the important—and highly controversial—features of the Massachusetts 1993 education reform initiative.

The great alternative to the traditional teacher education program, Teach for America, has had stunning success in luring some of America's brightest and most idealistic college graduates into careers as teachers. The easiest part of this venture has been recruiting teaching candidates; Teach for America has from the outset been flooded with applications from graduates of America's best colleges. The hardest part has been getting them credentialed to teach, bypassing the sclerotic rules of state education departments. The formal name for this end run is "alternative certification," something that is—happily—gaining increased acceptance in states across the country. New York City, for example, under Chancellor Joel Klein (who loathed traditional teacher education programs and loved Teach for America) received New York State permission for an expedited path to certification for bright, motivated, recent baccalaureates who had never taken a single pedagogy course.[16] Under the terms of an optimal alternative certification program, potential teachers are selected on the basis of their own proven scholastic ability (as measured by subject matter mastery), then trained in the most relevant pedagogical techniques, and, most critically, tested in the classroom. The best hope for getting a truly high-quality teaching corps into America's classrooms in the future rests with a quantum expansion of this model.

HIGH SCHOOL GRADUATION REQUIREMENTS

The most pervasive failing of American high schools is their inability to adequately prepare their graduates for college-level work. Readers may be surprised to learn that this is not just a problem in poor inner-city districts (the ones coping with the achievement Megagap addressed in chapter 3), but one affecting a majority of high schools whose students are middle class—even a large share of those in wealthy suburban districts. A 2012 study by ACT (formerly the American College Testing Program), evaluating college readiness in five subjects, found that nationally only 52 percent of *all* American high school graduates met the benchmark for reading, 46 that for math, and 31 the benchmark for science (table 4.4).[17] Even in the hyper-affluent New York City suburb of Pelham, New York, according to the New York State Board of Regents report cited earlier, only 55 percent of high school graduates are prepared for college. This wouldn't be a problem if, as in the past, high school graduates who weren't prepared for college work didn't go. But today the vast majority of high school graduates *do* aspire to go to college—and most at least begin. In Pelham's high school, for example, 95 percent of its graduates ended up enrolling in college, a majority in selective four-year institutions. When these inadequately prepared students arrive, however, a huge number need to take remedial courses in English and math and, when that doesn't overcome their academic deficiencies, they drop out— or flunk out.

State education departments have long been aware of this problem and have attempted to address it with high school exit exams (of the kind on which the New York Regents based their college-readiness assessments). The gold standard is the Massachusetts MCAS-based exit exam, which requires students to demonstrate college-level ability in math, ELA, the key sciences, history, and social science as a condition for graduating with an academic diploma. As of this writing, twenty-nine other states make students who are about to graduate from high school take an

Table 4.4

Percent of College-Ready ACT Test Takers by Subject (Massachusetts and ten largest states)

State	Mathematics	Reading	Science
United States	46	52	31
Massachusetts	73	72	48
New York	67	67	47
Pennsylvania	59	62	38
California	58	58	35
North Carolina	56	58	34
Ohio	49	58	34
Illinois	44	47	30
Texas	48	48	29
Georgia	40	50	27
Michigan	36	45	26
Florida	37	46	22

Source: ACT, *The Condition of College and Career Readiness*, 2012.

academic proficiency "exit" exam; and twenty-five make the high school diploma conditional on passing it.[18] The test takers in these states account for 76 percent of all high school students, 78 percent of all students from poor families, and 84 percent of all blacks and Hispanics. Despite these large numbers, only 65 percent of all high school students nationwide have the receipt of a diploma conditioned on *passing* the local exit exam.

Given the pervasiveness of high school exit exams specifically designed to weed out the college-unready today, why are so many entering college students still so woefully unprepared? The primary reason is that these tests are, for the most part, not closely aligned with college academic expectations; thus, most colleges ignore them and are indifferent to student exit exam scores when making admissions decisions. In only one state, Georgia, do the state's colleges base admissions on exit exam results.[19]

If the goal of high school exit testing is to make sure that all college-bound students are truly ready to do college work, the best approach would be to replace all current exit exams with one of the two prevailing national college entrance exams: the College Board's Scholastic Aptitude Test (SAT) or the ACT test. As it happens, this is under consideration in eleven states. I would strongly urge *all* states to adopt these tests—and to issue *academic diplomas* only to students that score at benchmark levels. This would be a powerful academic motivator for both high school educators and students. Students with lower scores might earn other kinds of diplomas, but at least both they and any colleges that admitted them would be aware of the academic pitfalls that lay ahead.

Obviously, exit exam testing will not by itself make mainstream high school students college-ready. What *will* accomplish that goal is *taking the right high school courses and enough of them.* The ACT report clearly documents the difference that course-taking makes: in mathematics, for example, students taking three years of recommended core high school math courses (in algebra, trigonometry, solid geometry, etc.) were *six times* as likely to meet college-readiness benchmarks; those taking three years of core science courses, 2.5 times as likely; and those exposed to the four-year English core, 50 percent more likely.[20] Let me stress again that we are not talking here about academically handicapped Megagap schoolchildren, but typical middle-class American high school students who should easily be able—were they so advised—to take and pass such courses. The importance of rigorous high school curriculum design—accompanied by smart student course choices—is now a staple of the voluminous college-readiness literature, along with the hope that the near-universal adoption by states of the Common Core curriculum will result in its realization.

SCHOOL CHOICE

Reforms such as those reviewed above are often resisted—or subverted—at the district level by teachers, principals, and their collective-bargaining agents, either despite state education department intentions, or because the state departments have been lobbied to forgo them. Under these circumstances, perhaps the fastest way to see such reforms enacted is to turn over their implementation to schools outside the reach of the reigning education establishment—namely, charter schools or, less politically likely, private schools funded with vouchers. So far, while thousands of charter schools (and a few voucher programs) have been established across the country today, they are located almost exclusively in poor inner-city neighborhoods to give Megagap schoolchildren an alternative to their local public schools. This has been done in part to insulate charter schools from the accusation by diehard opponents that they achieve student performance gains by "cherry-picking"—i.e., enrolling less troubled children than the public schools with which they are being compared. But the more salient reason is the mistaken belief that there seems to be no need.

Offering district students the option of attending a charter school is predicated on the failure of local public schools to meet desired academic standards. Yet, given the mediocre expectations of most mainstream schools, *their* students seem to be doing just fine and don't appear to need such an option.

The main argument of this chapter, however, is that mainstream students are not doing "just fine." Therefore, it is past time to stop seeing charter schools—or other school choice initiatives —as a panacea just for Megagap children, where they have not always been effective in any case, and start deploying them in mainstream communities, where they could easily electrify academic achievement. If the specifications for new mainstream charters were carefully spelled out along the lines of the measures reviewed in this chapter (and proven to be effective in Massachusetts and elsewhere), there is a much higher probability that they would be thoroughly implemented as intended by such charter schools than they would be in the regular district schools. And, as charter school proponents are quick to point out, if these schools failed to make significant gains, their charters could be revoked.

SUMMING UP

Taking aggressive steps to close America's Mainstream learning gap is the surest way of making the United States once again the world's best-educated nation—and it also happens to be by far the easiest. For six decades now, like Sisyphus condemned for eternity to pushing a boulder uphill, American civic and educational leaders have devoted the lion's share of their educational reform efforts to closing the country's educational Megagap. This is an eminently worthwhile objective but one we have not been very successful in reaching so far—and we might meet with better results by following the path outlined in chapter 3. In the meantime, the effort has distracted reformers from tackling (or even acknowledging) the

Mainstream gap that, as Massachusetts has proven in less than two decades, can be definitively closed with a few, not very expensive, sharp redirections in education policy.

To reiterate briefly, the central idea in this chapter is that students everywhere will learn only as much as they are expected to, so raising expectations leads inevitably to higher outcomes. That this is so is readily apparent in the great variation among American states in the academic performance of their students on nationally standardized tests—holding constant the key demographic variables of race and class. We can get the majority of schoolchildren who are not otherwise disadvantaged by poverty or other handicaps to learn more by such proven steps as:

1. Following a more rigorous curriculum in all key subjects and in every grade.

2. Putting in place a regimen of testing and school accountability.

3. Recruiting more capable and appropriately trained teachers.

4. Requiring high school graduation exit exams aligned with college expectations.

5. Offering mainstream students a choice of schools.

All of these reforms can be implemented without increasing school system budgets; some, like school choice, might actually reduce them. Adding merit pay to this repertoire might cost more, but despite its embrace by many education reformers, its effectiveness is as yet unproven. I believe the other reforms should be tried first.

Won't raising the academic performance of mainstream students widen the achievement disparities between them and more disadvantaged students, namely the Megagap? Ideally, no. As chapter 3 indicates, we can go a long way toward tackling the roots of the Megagap through expanded—and effective—preschool and extended learning time. If we can make this happen, and if it succeeds in its objective of substantially leveling the academic playing field early in the game, Megagap schoolchildren will benefit as much or more from these measures as those in the Mainstream. However, even if this does not happen as quickly or completely as we might hope, it is still no reason to keep all the rest of America's schoolchildren from reaching their scholastic potential.

Making College Pay Off

In the United States and every other advanced society today, the share of the population with some level of post-secondary education (college, in ordinary parlance) is one of the primary indicators of the country's human-capital development—and therefore of its "smartness." Here, as in every other aspect of formal education, America got there first. Despite having to endure the new world's frontier hardships, despite suffering from a scarcity of resources, despite having only a minuscule number of fellow citizens prepared for college, the earliest American settlers in the seventeenth and eighteenth centuries chose to establish universities among their first institutions: Harvard in 1636, William and Mary in 1693, Yale in 1701, Princeton in 1746, and a host of other still-functioning places between 1750 and 1800. U.S. higher education made a quantum leap forward—in numbers of colleges and students enrolled—after passage of the Morrill Act in 1862 (sponsored by Vermont congressman Justin Morrill and enthusiastically signed into law by Abraham Lincoln). Another quantum leap in college attendance was triggered by passage of the G.I. Bill (formally known as the Servicemen's Readjustment Act) after World War II. These seminal and highly original pieces of legislation, along with a host of less prominent national and state policies adopted over the last century and a half, have made it possible for Americans in every decade after the Civil War—until the near present—to go to college at many times the rate of even the richest countries of Europe, or the other comparable former English colonies: Canada, Australia, New Zealand.

The Morrill Act, enacted at a time when only the very rich in Europe sent only their most academically oriented male children to college, quite explicitly aimed to create across the country an American network of higher-education institutions for the masses. These were designed, in typical American pragmatic fashion, to give any eligible young American possessing the equivalent of a secondary education advanced training in agriculture, home economics, engineering, and other practical professions. The mechanism was a significant land grant (of 30,000 acres, times the number of members in its congressional delegation) to any state that launched a public university open to all of its academically eligible citizens, at no or nominal charge. The states were expected to sell the land and use the proceeds as a permanent endowment. In just about every state today, the main public university (as well as Cornell in New York and MIT in Massachusetts) is a Morrill Act descendant.

The G.I. Bill, one of the most productive human-capital investments in American history, was enacted in 1944 both to reward ex-G.I.s for their service in the war and to keep them from flooding the postwar job market (memories of the Depression were still fresh, and most civic leaders were terrified of the possible resumption of high levels of unemployment). In one fell swoop, the G.I. Bill enabled hundreds of thousands of young men (and some women), who never would have done so otherwise, to go to college, largely at the taxpayer's expense. It had the further effect of dramatically expanding the number and size of U.S. academic institutions, public and private. My alma mater, Syracuse University, to take a typical example, doubled its enrollment after 1948. Another key federal initiative that fueled a surge in college-going in the latter decades of the last century was the enactment of need-based financial aid by way of Pell Grants (named after its sponsor, Senator Claiborne Pell of Rhode Island) and low-interest loans.

In these actions, as well as in the rhetoric of politicians and the civic elite, Americans have consistently demonstrated their determination that the United States should have the best-educated adult labor force in the world—which necessarily meant having *the world's highest percentage of college (broadly understood) graduates.* If the trends of the last few decades persist, however, this will no longer be the case, because among the world's advanced economies we are falling further behind with every passing year, especially when it comes to the emerging generation of young adults (age thirty to thirty-four), as seen in table 5.1. Some of this erosion is due to rapid post-secondary gains in other countries over the last few decades, but a more important reason is that our progress in this sphere—impressive for four decades after World War II— has essentially come to a standstill.

IS COLLEGE NECESSARY?

With clear-eyed determination and strategic investments, the United States can reverse these trends and regain its status as having the world's best-educated population, but first the case must be made for doing so. Today, most Americans think a college education is essential for career success, a belief that is backed up in practice as two-thirds of all U.S. high school graduates enter college, and 90 percent would like to. Yet a significant strain of contrarian thinking questions this drift toward near-universal higher education.[1] The most common arguments the contrarians make

....

Table 5.1

Percent of College Completers by Age and Country, 1970–2010 (ranked by 2010 status—ages 30–34)

Country	1970 All 25+	1970 30–34	1990 All 25+	1990 30–34	2010 All 25+	2010 30–34
Japan	3.0	6.8	14.0	27.9	23.9	40.0
Australia	14.0	18.0	17.2	16.8	22.4	37.7
Great Britain	4.9	7.5	7.0	8.1	14.4	30.6
Canada	8.4	10.7	14.6	18.1	21.1	26.6
Sweden	4.8	7.5	12.5	17.2	16.7	23.8
Ireland	3.0	4.8	9.6	14.0	20.3	22.4
Netherlands	4.7	5.7	10.8	15.2	16.5	22.2
United States	**12.4**	**18.8**	**25.3**	**30.7**	**20.0**	**21.7**
France	2.8	4.3	6.2	8.4	10.6	19.1
Germany	2.0	2.6	8.6	10.3	12.8	11.7

Source: OECD StatExtracts, Education and Training.

are that the national labor market doesn't need any more college graduates (with the collateral assertion that large numbers of currently employed college graduates are working at jobs that don't require a college education), and, most damningly, that no more than a third of the American college-age cohort is even capable of doing college-level work.

Whether the U.S. economy needs more college-educated workers is a complicated issue, but threading through the available data, one can unambiguously conclude that on this point the contrarians are wrong. The U.S. Bureau of Labor Statistics (BLS, a division of the Department of Labor) issues periodic reports on the occupational and industrial composition of the American labor market—and the education necessary to fill those jobs—now and over the next decade. These studies are quite fine-grained, looking at every major occupational and industrial category, comparing wages, worker demand, and ostensible minimum educational requirements. On the basis of the BLS's highly conservative analysis, it appears that the current college attainment rates and the demands of the job market are pretty well aligned. However, a closer look at the data (table 5.2) reveals that the majority of occupations that are projected to *grow* over the next decade and beyond—as well as those with the highest pay—do require some (or even a lot of) post-secondary education. The range of high-need career opportunities is both broad and diverse—from familiar occupations in medicine and dentistry to all manner of exotic specializations in technical, entertainment, personal service, and design fields. The common denominators defining the careers of the future are that they require more than a high school education, they pay well, and, most interestingly, they are almost impossible to outsource overseas. Even allowing for some hyperbole, the consensus estimate of jobs needing higher education in the coming decades ranges from 60 to 67 percent.[2]

In almost all occupations, beyond formal education requirements, there is also a need for supplemental training and years of experience. Nearly two-thirds of all career preparation actually takes place in the workplace, through employer-sponsored training and learning on the job. However, far from showing that this makes formal post-secondary education superfluous, the data indicate that the willingness of employers to hire workers in the first place (the prerequisite for gaining experience) *and* to invest in their training is precisely proportional to the amount of formal education the workers already have under their belt.

But the strongest case for having more Americans go to (and complete) college isn't just that the U.S. labor market demands it. The most important benefits of a college education accrue to college graduates themselves. As indicated in table 5.3, they earn

Table 5.2

Emerging Occupational Demand by Education Required, 2010–20

Occupational category	New jobs (millions)	% of total	Education required	Median annual pay ($)
High qualifications	5,990	29.3	Four-year college/ Graduate school	
Management	615.8	3.0	Baccalaureate/ Graduate	91,440
Computer and mathematical	778.3	3.8	Graduate	73,720
Business and financial	1,172.5	5.7	Baccalaureate/ Graduate	60,670
Healthcare practitioners	2,019.7	9.9	Baccalaureate/ Professional	58,490
Education and training	1,403.7	6.9	Baccalaureate +	45,690
Intermediate qualifications	6,448.6	31.5	Two-year college +	
Installation, maintenance, and repair	800.1	3.9	Associate/ On-the-job training	40,120
Office/administrative support	2,335.7	11.4	Associate +	30,710
Healthcare support	1,443.7	7.1	Associate/ On-the-job training	24,760
Sales and related	1,869.1	9.1	Associate/ On-the-job training	24,370
Low qualifications	3,073.7	15.0	High school or less	
Building/Grounds maintenance	664	3.2	High school or less	22,490
Personal care and service	1,336.7	6.5	High school or less	20,640
Farming/Fishing/Forestry	(19.5)	(0.1)	High school or less	19,630
Food preparation and serving	1,092.5	5.3	High school or less	18,770
Total all occupations	20,468.9	75.6	High school or less	33,840

Source: U.S. Bureau of Labor Statistics.

more, they live longer, they are more apt to get and stay married, and they are far more likely to see their children completing college—reinforcing a highly virtuous intergenerational cycle. Indeed, currently the best apparent predictor of higher levels of personal and household quality of life, as measured by any number of indicators (including those that measure the welfare of children), is the amount of education attained, with evidence of a strong threshold effect tied to college completion.

It has been argued that this relationship is merely one of correlation rather than causation, implying that the personal attributes that lead to getting a college education are the same ones making success more likely in all aspects of life. This argument can be challenged inferentially by noting that college attendance (and graduation) is currently so tightly tied to parental socioeconomic status, *and cognitive ability is not*, that we can safely assume that most bright, ambitious young adults on the middle and lower rungs of the socioeconomic ladder could succeed in college and later life—*if their high schools prepared them academically for college and they could afford to go*. Further confirming the individual benefits of a college

Table 5.3

Indicators of Personal Benefit for College Graduates, 2012

Education level	Median income ($)	% Unemployed	% Married	% Divorced/ Never married	Life expectancy at age 25
Professional	90,220	2.1	72.7	22.0	–
Baccalaureate	55,432	4.5	64.4	29.5	54.7
Associate	40,820	6.2	60.5	31.5	52.2
High school	33,904	8.3	55.9	31.0	50.6
Less than high school	24,492	12.4	46.3	34.9	47.9

Source: U.S. Bureau of the Census.

education are numerous longitudinal studies comparing lifetime outcomes of college graduates from less-advantaged families with demographically and socially matched, but less-educated, peers.[3]

THE AMERICAN HIGHER-EDUCATION PARADIGM: NOMINAL UNIFORMITY/FUNCTIONAL DIVERSITY

At the same time, in developing policies to reposition Americans in the forefront of higher-education attainment, we do need to recognize the constraints posed by the normal distribution of cognitive ability and motivation in the adult population and by the particular skill needs of the "knowledge economy" labor market. Not all young adults are equally "intelligent" (at least as measured by IQ scores), and not all are equally motivated to go the full educational distance. As for the labor market, even in a knowledge economy, a great many jobs require specialized skills training rather than an advanced arts and sciences education, and a large number of jobs depend more on innate talents, good work habits, and other personal attributes than on anything that can be learned in school.

It is the United States' good fortune that the institutional configuration of American education—both elementary/secondary and post-secondary—is better adapted to address these constraints than educational systems in Europe or Asia. Typically, in other countries schoolchildren are sorted at an early age by academic and cognitive ability, and then channeled into divergent academic and career tracks. The "gifted" are prepared for college, usually in academically rigorous pre-collegiate high schools; those of intermediate ability are primed for specialized vocational training in general high schools; and the rest are given a minimal high school experience and expected to go directly to work as teenagers, or perhaps enter apprenticeships.[4] While this framework seems to make sense intuitively (and even the United States had a considerably less rigid version of this before the 1970s, as noted in chapter 2), it reinforces socioeconomic class stratification and responds poorly to the emerging skill needs of a market economy, violating two fundamental American values: social egalitarianism and economic dynamism.

In contrast, American school districts engage in a minimal amount of tracking before high school, and in high school largely leave it to students to choose courses geared to their own academic and career interests, within state-mandated curricular boundaries. As it happens, the overwhelming majority of American high school students today do aim to go to "college," but what is referred to as college can take many different forms. The largely positive aspects of this arrangement are that it minimizes premature socioeconomic stratification, gives teenage students plenty of opportunity to think through their academic and career options, and, thanks to the wide variety of collegiate institutions that compose the U.S. higher-education sector, is extremely adaptive to the knowledge and skill requirements of an ever-changing labor market.

One of the primary reasons that the American higher-education system is so adaptable is that in its universal nomenclature it fudges underlying cognitive and socioeconomic differences among American "college" students, while its fairly fine-grained differentiation of missions and curricula accommodates the highly varied needs of contemporary American industries and occupations. Not only are there more institutions of higher education per capita in the United States than in any other country, they are far more varied than anywhere else: in academic focus, in sponsorship, and in selectivity (table 5.4). As a result, most American high school graduates can find places somewhere in their region that fit their career objectives and academic aptitudes. At the same time, this spectrum of institutions ably prepares its graduates for just about every industry and occupation in the contemporary American economy. By maintaining this highly varied repertoire of higher-education offerings under the umbrella of "college" or "university," we take the edge off the most invidious class distinctions among college-going young Americans and foster more social mobility and interpersonal social mixing than takes place in countries where traditional educational hierarchies (and nomenclature) prevail.

Today, the United States has more than 4,700 institutions of higher education, in three broad sectors: public—almost always state operated (35 percent), private nonprofit (35 percent), and private for-profit (30 percent). Within each of these sectors there is enormous differentiation. The state-operated sector includes major research universities (like the University of California at Berkeley or the University of Michigan), baccalaureate colleges that offer some professional and academic master's programs, community colleges, and, in some places, technical colleges. The private nonprofit sector includes elite research universities (like Harvard or Stanford), small elite liberal arts colleges (like Swarthmore or Colgate), religiously affiliated universities and colleges (like Notre

Table 5.4

Institutional Diversity of American Higher Education, 2011–12

Institution type	Public Number	Public Enrollment	Private Number	Private Enrollment	For-profit Number	For-profit Enrollment
Top research universities	73		34		–	–
Other doctorate granting	101	1,421,400	73	1,208,300	–	–
Master degree granting	270		364			301,400
					733	
Baccalaureate granting	191	6,626,300	517	2,679,000		1,257,700
Associate degree granting	967		100		671	397,700
		7,062,500		39,900		
Specialized technical	47		565			

Source: National Center for Education Statistics.

Dame or Holy Cross), and less selective universities and colleges (the majority). The for-profit sector (the newest and still controversial addition to the pack) includes reputable regional collegiate networks with academic specializations in business and information technology (like Strayer University), national networks of varied academic quality and focus (like the University of Phoenix or Capella), and quite a few disreputable fly-by-nights.

DOING A BETTER JOB

While in broad outline the American educational system design is refreshingly democratic and adaptable, it suffers from serious flaws in its execution. The most glaring problems lie not in the higher-education system itself, but in the deficiency of American high schools. As noted in chapter 4, even students bound for the more selective institutions suffer from notable gaps in their education, and many of the rest are woefully underprepared for college-level work—even at community colleges and second- and third-tier baccalaureate institutions. As a result, only half of all college-enrolled students ever earn a diploma and colleges devote inordinate resources to (largely unsuccessful) efforts at "remediation"— teaching material that should have been mastered in high school.

But not all the blame can be placed on the prior preparation of college students. When it comes to the academic heart of the higher-education enterprise, undergraduate and graduate student instruction, too many American colleges and universities give it short shrift. For the most part, they do take professional and technical education (engineering, architecture, medicine, accounting, nursing, etc.) seriously and, under the watchful eyes of specialized program accreditors, they train their graduates well. That can also be said of those institutions with recognized programs in the fine and performing arts (painting, sculpture, music, theater). Where most schools—even the elite ones—fall down is in the effort they put into instruction in the liberal arts and sciences and, for entirely different reasons discussed in chapter 4, teacher education. The blunt truth is that, in all but small, selective liberal arts colleges, making sure that most undergraduates get a rigorous general education is not a high priority. This has long been an open secret among higher-education professionals, but only recently—and belatedly—has it gained the attention of the general public with the publication of a hard-hitting book by Richard Arum and Josipa Roksa, *Academically Adrift: Limited Learning on College Campuses.*[5]

Elite research universities—both public and private—recruit, tenure, and promote their full-time faculty based almost entirely on the volume and quality of their research, leaving most undergraduate teaching to inexperienced Ph.D. students. When their eminent faculty members do teach, it is in very large classes (over one hundred, and sometimes as many as one thousand, students), with Ph.D. assistants assigned to smaller discussion sections. Community colleges, which bear the lion's share of the burden of trying to bring underprepared high school graduates to college-level proficiency, because of severely constrained budgets depend heavily on part-time faculty for most of their teaching. The for-profit sector also deploys mainly part-time faculty, in this case to maximize profits. The only higher-education institutions that hire and retain full-time faculty primarily to teach, and also try to keep class sizes reasonable, are small private liberal arts colleges and mid-sized state colleges, most of the latter descended from nineteenth-century "normal schools." But even in these places, with the exception of small, elite liberal arts colleges, undergraduate teaching suffers. Being for the most part unselective institutions, they water down the content of their arts and sciences courses to accommodate academically mediocre students and, to keep costs down, they impose heavy teaching loads on their professors, largely offsetting the benefits of having small classes and a predominantly full-time faculty.

Blaming this state of affairs on the "low productivity" of college teaching, a vocation that has probably not changed appreciably in a thousand years, the most fashionable remedy gaining currency today is to put an increasing share of college courses online—that is, taught asynchronously on the Internet. The extent to which this is viable, or even desirable, remains to be seen. But let me just interject at this point that as a university administrator for a number of years who has overseen the education of more than 300,000 undergraduates annually as well as the entire online course enterprise of the university, I do not see online instruction as a panacea—or even a scalable option. Fixing undergraduate teaching and learning, the tried-and-true "low-tech" way, is actually not that difficult—or even expensive.

Just as in high school (where, incidentally, no one talks of moving to online instruction), the key to effective teaching and learning in college must rest on high academic standards, rigorous curricula, test-based student evaluation and promotion, and faculty who are demonstrably proficient in their subjects and have enough time to personally meet their students and to thoroughly evaluate their work. As in K–12 education, the best evidence that unsatisfactory student performance is not a hard-wired demographic or cognitive given can be found in the enormous variation among states—and specific institutions—even when all other explanatory variables are held constant. In other words, if the same kinds of students do much better in some places (i.e., states/colleges) than they do in others, it must be the places that account for the difference.

THE MYTH AND REALITY OF COLLEGE AFFORDABILITY

By any standard, completing a college education, even at today's high tuition rates, is a value proposition for the graduate and for society. That said, the way in which an American college education is financed today is something of a mess. America's colleges and universities, especially in the private nonprofit sector, spend more than they need to and are notoriously opaque and disingenuous in how they reveal and justify what they do spend. Students and their families go too heavily into debt to pay for college even at public institutions. And, as will be reviewed later in this chapter, the largest category of financial assistance—federal student aid— is poorly allocated with respect to both lightening student burdens and raising college academic standards.

Among the leading complaints directed at American higher education today is its presumed "unaffordability" and, by extension, the burden that its cost places on college students' families (if they are the ones paying it), state governments (which underwrite about half the cost at state colleges and universities), or the federal government (through its student financial aid in the form of need-based grants and subsidized loans). The recent recession has only further exacerbated the problem of college affordability. States are now so fiscally stretched that they are sharply cutting back direct tax-levy support and raising tuition at state colleges; the federal government is scaling back its financial aid programs; and families battered by unemployment, home foreclosures, and shrinking stock portfolios are in no position to take up the slack.

One of the most unquestioned assumptions surrounding the issue of college affordability is that it is the inevitable result of the way in which a college education is being delivered today: courses (many of them with small enrollments) set in physical classrooms, taught by well-paid faculty, on leafy campuses with myriad desirable but not necessarily essential ancillary facilities such as student unions, fitness centers, museums, and stadiums. This entire arrangement, it is widely believed, is anachronistic and must unavoidably result in a high outlay per student, to be borne at private schools by students' families and at public ones by the states. Given this diagnosis, the fashionable remedy is, first, to sever the link between college instruction and the college environment (we don't need the campus anymore) and, second, to deliver much or all instruction online.

Many Americans, especially those who are working, raising families, or otherwise strapped for time, might benefit from a non-campus-based college experience, but there is a lot more to college than classroom instruction, which is why we will still want as many students as possible getting their education in a campus setting. And, while online instruction has a place in a college education, in terms of educational benefit it can never entirely replace taking courses with a live instructor, surrounded by live classmates, in a traditional physical classroom.

Just as almost no one tilling the vast K–12 education reform garden suggests doing away with our traditional elementary and secondary school facilities, there is no need today to do away with our traditional college campuses. In fact, these places are in many ways among the most glorious of American institutions, and the envy of the rest of the world. Nevertheless we need to definitely rethink what goes on in them and how they are financed. If the key question being raised these days is whether we can still afford—at least on a mass scale—the traditional campus-based college experience, my answer is a resounding yes—so long as we undertake certain reforms in the underlying structure of collegiate financing.

Let's start with the generally unrecognized fact that, at a typical American campus, an *undergraduate* college education of good quality is not necessarily all that expensive. Tuition price inflation has its origins in the private, nonprofit sector through the ripple effects of too many affluent high school graduates trying to gain admission to America's highest prestige institutions (e.g., the Ivy League, selective small colleges such as Swarthmore, Amherst, Colgate, or Oberlin, and leading technical institutes like MIT). Flooded with more applicants than freshman openings, the response on the part of such institutions has been to ration their seats in the first instance by selectivity and in the second by price.

The resulting tuition windfall is then spent on underwriting faculty research and certain high-cost professional specializations; massive cross-subsidization of needier (but presumably equally talented) students; wasteful indifference to the cost of personnel and supplies; and building construction sprees. Tuition at these elite institutions, rising at a rate well above prevailing inflation, then becomes a benchmark for the rest of the private higher-education sector, and indirectly even for religiously affiliated and subsidized state universities.

As a former administrator of the State University of New York, the United States' largest unified system of higher education, which has sixty-four campuses ranging from community and technical colleges to small liberal arts colleges and respected research universities (and 35 percent of Cornell), I know what it costs to deliver a quality college education. According to a recent, highly detailed analysis of revenues and expenses at every SUNY campus and its benchmarked national peers, we find, for example, that at the State University's most highly regarded undergraduate school, SUNY Geneseo (which is ranked among America's best colleges, and where students receive an exemplary education delivered by well-credentialed full-time faculty, in small classes, on a highly attractive, amenity-laden, well-maintained campus), the total yearly per-student cost—excluding room and board, but including hidden fringe benefits and debt service—comes to $15,777. Its benchmarked peers across the United States, with comparable standards and amenities, spend $16,379. In contrast, average tuition (not including room and board) at private nonprofit colleges today ranges from $25,600 (in the South) to $36,800 (in New England). That spread of $10,000 to $20,000 is both enormous and unnecessary. Apologists for the private colleges will claim that, after cross-subsidization, needier students pay hardly more than they do at the state schools, but in the meantime the tab for this surcharge is picked up by the federal government (in financial aid) and the hapless families of full-pay students. In any case, whatever the pros and cons of cross-subsidization, at give or take $15,000 a year, college today is nowhere near as costly as it is made out to be. The corollary of this observation is that we needn't sacrifice the many benefits of a traditional campus-based experience for the next generation of American college students on the altar of "affordability."

WHAT NEEDS TO CHANGE

The American higher-education system, despite much hand-wringing, is still in pretty good shape and, by many standards, better than that in any other country. Unlike its lower-education (i.e., K–12) sibling, it is not a government monopoly; as noted earlier, unlike its global counterparts, its institutions are more numerous and more varied, making the system as a whole marvelously adaptive to the wide range of cognitive abilities and occupational interests of its students—without resorting to the kind of invidious stratification seen overseas. In addition, its facilities are more modern, better equipped, and better maintained than those in any other country.

That said, for adult Americans to continue to be the best (college) educated people in the world, the U.S. higher-education system must change. There are four generic problems facing the preponderance of American colleges and universities. Most of them have been festering for decades, but are getting worse as college enrollment has expanded and student selectivity has declined. Colleges admit too many unprepared students; they invest too little in undergraduate instruction; they are too cavalier about graduation rates; and their financing is so erratic that millions of qualified high school graduates don't even go to college, and those who do are overly burdened with debt.

Among these problems, perhaps the most easily corrected by unilateral college action is the misalignment between the academic preparation needed to succeed in college—even in narrow technical and professional programs (like computer science or nursing)—and the instructional standards of American high schools. Let me emphasize once again, this is a problem not just for graduates of struggling inner-city high schools, but also for a majority of those coming out of schools in middle-income suburbs. As noted earlier, practically the only actions taken by all but the most elite American colleges to deal with this problem is to invest heavily in "remedial" courses, under the hopeful assumption that one or two semesters of catch-up English and math courses can compensate for four years of high school failure. Not surprisingly, the hope is unjustified, and less than a quarter of all students taking such courses ever make it out of the remedial purgatory ready to continue successfully in the regular curriculum. We now have more than four decades of failed experience with the remediation paradigm, yet, in the name of broadened college "access," we continue to waste vast resources—institutional, public, and personal—on this flawed concept.

What should be done instead is to more thoroughly align high school curricula and instruction with college expectations. Despite the voluminous lip service paid to this objective, it is rarely achieved in practice. The only way that it might be achieved is to directly involve colleges in the high school instructional experience in several concrete ways. The first order of business should be for the colleges to get directly involved in determining what is to be covered in high school courses. To some extent this idea is already embedded in the Common Core state standards reviewed in chapters 2 and 4, but this initiative is still in its infancy. The American collegiate establishment, represented by eight key organizations,[6] must weigh in on this project to ensure both that the standards are adequate and that they are being implemented on the ground.

The other effective action that colleges could take is to not admit students who graduate from high school without a proven "college-ready" academic diploma. As indicated in chapter 4, even with a majority of American high school graduates taking high school exit exams, few really screen out the unprepared. My recommendation earlier was that all states should mandate rigorous exit exams, and only give academic diplomas to those sufficiently prepared for college. Until this happens, the best course would be for colleges to rely on the national SAT or ACT entrance exams, and not admit any students falling below the college-ready threshold (about 1575 on the combined SAT and 18 in English and 22 in math on the ACT). During my tenure as provost of the SUNY system, we encouraged many of our less selective colleges to raise admissions standards in just this way. The campuses that did so—about a dozen of the thirty baccalaureate-granting SUNY institutions—saw sharply higher graduation rates as a result.[7]

One of the inevitable consequences of higher admission standards at baccalaureate institutions is to divert the non-college-ready high school graduates to the community colleges—as happened about fifteen years ago in the City University of New York (CUNY)—and to saddle them with the burden of remediation. Community colleges, by custom generally and by law in some states, are committed to being "open access," meaning they take all comers, prepared or unprepared alike. The unsurprising result has been that community colleges devote inordinate resources to remediation—with no greater success than that of baccalaureate schools—and have truly abysmal graduation rates (11 to 42 percent, averaging in the low 20s, as seen in table 5.5). Getting community colleges to become more selective may be a lost cause, but even confining remediation to this sector, as CUNY has done, would represent a partial victory and enable America's baccalaureate institutions to become much more academically successful. And perhaps, once they cornered the nation's remediation market, community colleges in many states would have a much stronger incentive to work with their local high schools to raise the level of college preparation.

Table 5.5

College Graduation and Retention Rates in Selected States, 2009–10

State	Graduation rate (all colleges)		Freshman-to-sophomore retention rate		
	6 Years (baccalaureate)	3 Years (associate)	Public baccalaureate	Private baccalaureate	Public associate
Massachusetts	69.2	20.2	79.4	86.0	53.6
Rhode Island	66.2	12.4	78.0	83.5	54.1
Connecticut	65.9	11.7	83.5	81.7	54.3
Pennsylvania	65.7	36.9	81.4	83.9	51.6
Maryland	64.1	21.8	80.8	84.5	54.6
All states	55.5	29.2	78.4	79.4	53.0
Arkansas	41.2	23.5	69.4	74.1	52.0
Louisiana	40.7	28.8	72.0	78.2	51.3
New Mexico	39.4	20.1	71.5	73.6	49.4
Nevada	35.8	42.7	75.3	58.0	52.8
Alaska	26.9	13.3	68.7	62.1	23.5

Source: The National Center for Higher Education Management Systems, 2013.

Another major failing of American colleges today, as noted earlier, has been the shortchanging of undergraduate instruction, especially for the most critically important freshman and sophomore years. This dereliction takes two forms. The one that has gotten the greatest attention from conservative higher-education advocates is the problem of "general education," which refers to the liberal arts and sciences foundation that all college graduates, regardless of eventual career orientation, are expected to have. As it stands today, with notably few exceptions, too many American baccalaureate institutions—including the most selective—are supremely indifferent about which pre-major liberal arts and sciences courses freshmen and sophomores elect to take and almost as indifferent to the (entirely faculty-determined) content of such courses. There are two likely reasons for this indifference. First, an overwhelming priority is given by students and college administrators alike to the career preparation courses taught in the later undergraduate years—these constitute the primary rationale for students choosing to go to college, they are the greatest revenue generators for the institutions, and they are closely overseen by external disciplinary or professional evaluators. Second, the organized faculty fiercely guard their prerogative of being the only ones to decide what is being taught. (Interestingly, faculty nevertheless meekly acquiesce on curricular matters when they are imposed by outside disciplinary and professional accreditors.) It is difficult to "prove," but it is reasonable to suppose that a strong general education foundation is highly beneficial in promoting a greater mastery of complex material in the later career-oriented coursework, a greater maturity in decision-making as a working professional, and a greater understanding of all aspects of life: cultural, scientific, and civic.

The first two years of undergraduate coursework are shortchanged more fundamentally by the paucity of instructional resources devoted to them. Well-endowed private universities and the best of the public ones divert resources away from early undergraduate instruction to allow their senior faculty to engage in serious research (on which both the faculty's and the institution's reputation depends), and to pay for it. Less research-driven baccalaureate colleges and community colleges skimp on lower-level instruction because they need to conserve their resources to pay for the more expensive upper-level and professional coursework on which *their* reputation rests. The way in which in almost all American colleges and universities square this resource circle is to cheat their freshmen and sophomores by placing them in oversized course sections and assigning poorly paid "adjunct" faculty and graduate students to teach them. Given how important the first two years of college are, an issue exacerbated by inadequate preparation for college work, this state of affairs is nothing short of scandalous. Nor can the problem be solved, as noted earlier, by resorting to online instruction—whether in massive open online courses or conventionally. In any case, also as noted earlier, most American colleges and universities have enough revenue to give freshmen and sophomores small classes taught by qualified full-time faculty—if they put their minds to it.

Crowning the insufficient attention paid by American colleges to the quality of the undergraduate academic experience is their relative indifference as to whether their students make it to the finishing line in a timely fashion—or even at all. Again, a variety of factors are in play. Having chosen to be less selective in admissions, most baccalaureate colleges anticipate a less-than-complete graduation rate, and congratulate themselves when they exceed their mathematically calculated "expected graduation rate." Given their open-admissions mission, almost all community colleges have very low graduation-rate expectations to begin with and adamantly reject this as a qualitative criterion. To be fair, some colleges and statewide higher-education systems take pains to preemptively advise their students online about taking necessary courses and try to ensure that all courses necessary for gradua-tion are being offered. But outside the insular world of academic institutions, with its fatalism and excuse-making about graduation rates, parents, politicians, and thoughtful higher-education leaders are rightly concerned.

Finally, perhaps the most serious dereliction in American higher education is the fact that millions of talented young Ameri-cans who would benefit from a college education don't go to college at all, or go to an inferior institution, or fail to graduate when they do go—a problem that is much too closely correlated with family social class and income. Further, most American college students, regardless of talent or family income, now leave school excessively burdened with student loan debt, which casts a deep financial shadow on their post-collegiate careers as they pay it off, or on fed-eral financial aid programs when they don't. This problem is exac-erbated as colleges in the private, nonprofit sector keep raising tu-ition levels beyond the rate of general inflation and divert resources to cross-subsidize favored students or to fund faculty research.

A "MAGIC BULLET" TO MOTIVATE HIGHER-EDUCATION REFORM

All of these deficits in higher education can potentially be attacked through a single policy lever, one already under government juris-diction: federal financial aid. A broad outline of how this might be accomplished is offered in the recommendations of Britain's Browne Commission to the United Kingdom parliament in its 2010 report, *Securing a Sustainable Future for Higher Education*.[8]

The Browne Commission report lays out the design for a pro-gram of national financial assistance with these specific goals: to make it possible for all college-ready Britons to go to college by broadening access to higher education; to do this in a way that does not excessively burden college graduates with debt; and to place British institutions of higher education on a sound financial footing. The primary mechanism is giving all qualified high school graduates access to low-interest loans to pay for college, with repayment tied to earnings—so that financially strapped young college graduates with low-paying (or no) jobs are not forced to choose between penury or forfeiture. At the same time, the report envisions that this will make students bear a much larger share of the cost of higher education (which has been nearly free until recently), making British colleges less dependent on annual tax-levy appropriations (which haven't kept up with inflation).

Much of what the Browne Commission envisions is already in place in the United States. Unlike Britain, we have a very elaborate and well-funded system of financial aid for college students, which is primarily federal (see table 5.6) with varying levels of assistance

Table 5.6

U.S. College Federal Aid by Category, 2010–11

Program	Outlay ($million)	Number of recipients (thousands)	Average loan/grant ($)	Eligibility criteria
Perkins (low interest)	970	442	$1,852	Low–moderate income
Stafford (low interest)	39,700	9,300	3,658	Low–moderate income
Stafford (unsubsidized)	46,100	8,800	4,094	Any income
Pell Grants	34,800	8,094	3,706	Lowest income
Educational Opportunity Grants	760	1,600	669	Lowest income
Work-study supplements	1,200	733	1,700	Moderate income
Loans to graduate students	17,100	884	11,784	Family independent
Loans to student parents		350	19,133	Dependent student
TOTAL	**140,630**	**30,203**		

Source: National Association of Student Financial Aid Administrators, 2012.

provided by the states. What is missing, however, are some key features of the proposed British model: making access to financial aid exceedingly simple and equitable—without cumbersome (and often unfair) family means-testing; charging very low rates of interest; and tying repayment to earnings rather than, as is currently the case, to a fixed repayment schedule (which can be deferred, but at great future cost). Something else is missing in both the British proposal and the American reality: attention to quality and overcoming the deficits of higher education enumerated earlier.

Here is what I propose—call it Browne Commission, Americanized and enhanced:

1. Any American high school graduate—with an academic diploma (per the recommendation made in this chapter and chapter 4) will be eligible for a low-interest college loan for as much as the full cost of an undergraduate education. Loans would be extended for up to five years for students enrolled in four-year baccalaureate programs; up to six years for those enrolled in five-year programs (like architecture and engineering); and up to three years for community college students. Requiring applicants to have an academic diploma will ensure that they are ready for college-level work. Setting time limits on the availability of loans will motivate timely completion.

2. All applicants will be eligible for loans large enough to cover full tuition and fees at a public undergraduate college, net of typical levels of state support. Those who choose to declare that they are financially independent from their family will be eligible for loans large enough to also cover living expenses for the duration of their tuition coverage. Family-independent applicants would not be subject to means-testing or family income documentation. The idea here is to encourage college students to be seen as independent

adults (regardless of age), neither advantaged nor handicapped by family circumstances; and to encourage students to study full-time and not be distracted or delayed by the need to work.

3. The maximum value of a loan would be set at 50 percent of the full prevailing average cost of educating undergraduates at *U.S. public colleges (inclusive of personnel benefits and capital facilities but exclusive of research and graduate education).* Most U.S. states currently underwrite about half of the full cost; federal aid should not result in reduced state efforts. Ideally, the aid ceiling will motivate private institutions and more expensive public universities to practice cost discipline and make subsidization of scholarships and research more transparent.

4. Interest rates would be set at the government's cost of borrowing: long-term treasury bonds (currently 2.90 percent) or what the government charges banks (federal funds rate, currently 0.25 percent)—plus administrative costs. *There is no reason for the government to make a profit on student loans, nor should banks be treated more leniently than college students.* The government's "profit" will be realized in higher future tax revenues generated by the higher human capital created.

5. Repayment details: To concentrate the minds of students and college administrators on college completion, any student who graduates in good standing (the equivalent of a 3.0—i.e., B—grade point average or better) will have up to 50 percent of their loan forgiven. All remaining loan amounts—both for those in the loan forgiveness program and for those ineligible because of non-completion—could be repaid through the federal income-tax system, in proportion to annual income. The loan forgiveness program would be financed by the

funding currently allocated to Pell and other direct grants. The idea is that under this proposal all students, including the most disadvantaged, would be able to attend college, to affordably repay their loan debt, and, if they managed to graduate, to benefit from a grant at least as valuable as what is available to them today.

6. College quality: Loans would be approved only for attendance at qualified institutions. Qualifications would include, as they do now, regional accreditation, but also graduation rates, class sizes, percentage of full-time faculty, and student performance on nationally normed exams (taking a leaf from national K–12 aid strings). This would have the effect of making all American institutions of higher education more attentive than they currently are to the quality and resources devoted to undergraduate instruction.

This set of proposals can be quite easily aligned with current federal expenditures, with some of the financial parameters shown in table 5.7. Last year, all federal aid to college students totaled over $140 billion. Of this, nearly $104 billion was in the form of loans, at various rates of interest and directed at various categories of student eligibility. The rest, nearly $37 billion, was in the form of grants, again under various eligibility criteria but with the majority aimed at low-income students. Let's begin by looking at using federal loans to increase fair access to a college education, along the lines of proposals 1 and 2. The aggregate current federal outlay of $104 billion is large enough—without any increase in the total amount of disbursed—to enable every qualified American high school graduate, at any level of family income, to receive a very low-interest loan to cover the entire cost of four or five years of tuition (at a public university—or a private one with a scholarship), and for those declaring family independence to underwrite

....

Table 5.7

Current and Proposed Formats for U.S. College Financial Aid

Degree level	Annual new loans	Estimated annual cost ($millions)	
		Loans (full-term)	Loan forgiveness
Associate	942,327	14,135	7,067
Baccalaureate	1,715,913	51,477	25,739
Master	730,635	877	438
Doctorate	163,765	6,141	3,071
Total	**3,552,640**	**72,630**	**36,315**
Current Outlay		**103,870**	**36,760**

Sources: National Center for Education Statistics, Bureau of Labor Statistics, and National Association of Student Financial Aid Administrators.

living costs for the same period. With respect to the loan forgiveness proposal, justified by the need both to motivate students and college administrations to focus on graduation and to reduce post-collegiate debt burdens, this could be funded with current federal grant appropriations, even with graduation rates projected to rise because of the program.

SUMMING UP

American higher education remains the model for the world, with more and better institutions, a more richly varied mix of institutions in terms of mission and access, and, for most of its history, serving more of the country's citizens than post-secondary systems anywhere else. That said, America's higher-education complex is not without some serious faults, but these can be remedied fairly easily—if we have the will. Too many able and motivated high school graduates who would benefit from college aren't going, either because they can't afford it or because no one in their family or local schools has encouraged them. At the same time, too many unprepared students are going—and then drop out before they earn a degree. Currently the financing of college is an incoherent mess, burdensome to students and their families, even as it fails to provide most institutions with the resources they require to offer a high-quality education to all their students—which often results in shortchanging undergraduate instruction.

Despite the serious nature of these problems, I do not recommend any heavy-handed federal intrusion into collegiate affairs. Clearly in this arena "one size does not fit all," because our colleges and universities are so diverse, even the public ones, and because they operate under so many different auspices: public, private nonprofit, private for-profit, religious, and secular—and we should cherish and nurture this diversity. But the federal government already plays an overwhelmingly important role in being the primary financier of students' tuition and thus, indirectly, of campus revenue. It can easily leverage this role to overcome some of the most serious deficiencies in the status quo: increasing access to college for millions of qualified but disadvantaged high school graduates; making college more affordable and collegiate debt burdens less onerous; promoting sharply higher rates of college completion; and motivating campuses to significantly ramp up the quality of undergraduate instruction.

The High-Technology Workplace

Most discussions of human capital—and the determinants of a smart society—begin with education, and rightly so. There is now universal agreement that education is the indispensable prerequisite for unlocking the human-capital potential of each individual; by extension, the greater the amount of education possessed by a society's citizens, the smarter the country becomes. Hence, the space devoted to education in the previous five chapters.

However, when plans are laid to raise human capital it is often forgotten that education—no matter how extensive—is not enough. As noted in chapter 1, the full development of both individual and society's human capital depends on how it is put to use, and that in turn depends on what happens in the workplace. The next two chapters will be devoted to this issue: the current chapter focuses on the importance of smart, technologically advanced workplaces, and how we can make more of America's workplaces even smarter; chapter 7 will focus on how the country's workplaces—and the country's workers—can benefit from greater individual and aggregate work effort.

How the United States came to having the world's most technologically advanced workplace is absolutely central to the story of how it became the world's smartest society. Workplace technology provided American workers with the *physical* capital—the machinery and now the computers—that made them the most productive in the world, and this in turn has been responsible for driving the economic growth of the United States over the past century as well as for generating the world-class standard of living that Americans now enjoy (figure 6.1).

In every era we can find examples of highly educated societies where their education-based human capital has gone to waste because it wasn't properly harnessed in smart workplaces. For much of the last millennium that was true of China, a country that long valued education and made it accessible to a far larger share of its population than the Europeans did. Today, we can look to Russia and much of the Islamic world as places where they are not seeing a return on their investments in education because of insufficiently smart workplaces.

THE CAUSAL CHAIN

So what does it take to have a smart workplace? The most important ingredient is advanced technology—advanced, that is, by the standards of the time. That in turn depends on being at the frontier of science, because all technology is grounded in scientific discovery. Throughout the nineteenth and early twentieth centuries, the path from the contemporary scientific frontier to technology in the workplace ran through pioneers of invention who, while basing their work on the best scientific research of the time, operated independently or were employed by industrial corporations. In the nineteenth century we had communications breakthroughs

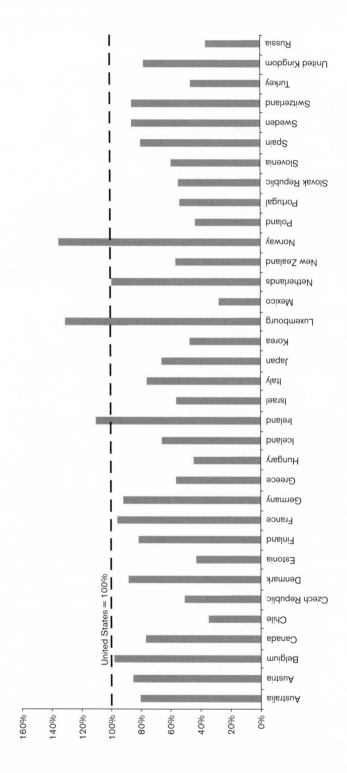

Fig. 6.1 American Labor Productivity Is among the Highest in the Developed World, 2011

Source: OECD, Productivity measured as GDP per hour worked as a percentage of the United States in 2011.

like the telegraph (Samuel Morse, 1835) and the telephone (Alexander Graham Bell, 1876); the development of photography (George Eastman, 1888); new labor-saving machinery with the mechanical reaper (Cyrus McCormick, 1831), the sewing machine (Elias Howe, 1846), and the typewriter (Christopher Sholes, 1868); and the most game-changing technology of all, usable electricity through the invention of the lightbulb (Thomas Edison, 1879) and the generation of alternating current (Nikola Tesla, 1887). By the late nineteenth and early twentieth centuries, inventions were increasingly the domain of rising corporations like Edison's, the forerunner of General Electric, and auto magnates like Henry Ford.

In the era since World War II, however, the scientific realm has become so advanced and the technology to be gleaned from it so complex that further progress requires a substantial investment in scientific research, both basic and applied. A lot of this research can be financed by private industry but, for reasons gone into later in this chapter, much of it also depends on government funding. Regardless of the funding source, any expenditure on science research is worth the outlay many times over.

Thus, cutting-edge scientific research is *the indispensable prerequisite for the development of technologically smart workplaces.* More research generates scientific discoveries that lead first to new research-based consumer-product applications for which workplaces are needed and second to new production technologies to make these products as inexpensively as possible. Linking the world of science and the world of production are patents, government-issued protections of the intellectual capital embedded in applied science, filed either by scientists who are able to translate their research into functional applications or by intermediaries who can do so. Thus more patents mean more new inventions—new or better machines, new electronics, new medicines, new or more efficient forms of transportation—available to the consumer and generating work for the producer. This means that the volume of new domestic patents represents perhaps the best metric for monitoring the robustness of the research-to-technology pathway.

Even given this formulation, why does the science have to be conducted in the United States? After all, in a global scientific universe—and with a global patent system (up to a point)—can't American inventors and entrepreneurs draw on scientific discoveries made anywhere in the world? In theory, yes, but in actual fact, no. It can easily be shown that, especially in a fast-paced, technologically competitive global environment, the countries that achieve the most rapid and successful transitions from science to technology to production are those where the science originates.[1] Further, American science is now such a large component of the worldwide total—and acts as such a critical feeder and spur to the research efforts of other countries—that without our research investments there would be a dearth of research to draw on from abroad.

There is no question that the United States today still leads the world in research funding in absolute terms: an estimated $415 billion will have been spent on research and development (R&D) domestically in 2011;[2] that's more than twice the amount spent by China, the second biggest R&D funder. Yet, taking into account the size of the United States' economy, its status as the world's leader in science research may be in jeopardy (table 6.1).

As can be seen in figure 6.2, South Korea, Japan, and Germany have outperformed the United States in respect to the size of their economies, and China, which spent practically nothing on research twenty years ago, is rapidly gaining on us. Put simply, if the United States is to remain at the global scientific frontier, the volume of American research must grow faster than the American economy—yet it isn't.

Table 6.1

Total R&D Expenditures by Leading Countries and the European Union

Country/Region	1985		1995		2005		2011	
	$millions	% GDP	$millions	% GDP	$millions	% GDP	$millions	% GDP
United States	**115,219**	**2.8**	**184,077**	**2.5**	**325,936**	**2.6**	**415,193**	**2.7**
European Union	–	–	138,143	2.2	230,521	2.4	320,456	2.7
China	–	–	10,512	0.6	71,055	1.3	208,172	1.7
Japan	42,616	2.7	82,468	2.9	128,695	3.3	146,537	3.3
Germany	25,574	2.4	40,129	2.2	64,299	2.5	93,055	2.8
South Korea	–	–	13,305	2.3	30,618	2.8	59,890	3.9
France	15,789	2.2	27,410	2.3	39,236	2.1	51,891	2.2
Great Britain	14,846	2.2	21,854	1.9	34,081	1.7	39,627	1.7
Canada	5,692	1.4	11,307	1.7	23,090	2.0	24,289	1.7

Source: OECD, Main Science and Technology Indicators.

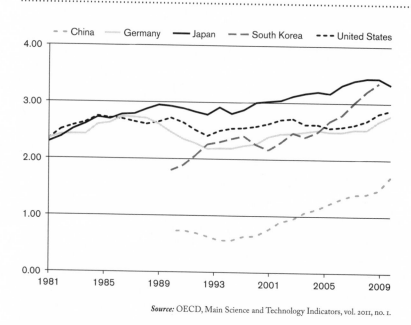

Source: OECD, Main Science and Technology Indicators, vol. 2011, no. 1.

Fig. 6.2 R&D Output by Country as Percent of GDP

GROWING RESEARCH—AND WHO SHOULD PAY FOR IT

The pace of American technological advance—a critical aspect of its human-capital tripod and a key determinant of our high standard of living—depends on an accelerating volume of American research discoveries, and that in turn requires increased investment in America's scientists and research laboratories. This raises two related issues: determining the optimal level of research funding, and how the burden should be shared between government and the private sector—mainly American corporations, but also including private foundations and universities drawing on non-governmental resources.

Throughout this book, we are exploring ways to raise American human capital—to make America smarter—that do not significantly expand the scope or cost of government. That said, there

159

are some areas where small but strategic government investments can make a game-changing difference, and research investment is one of them. The overall share of the U.S. government's support for research has actually fallen over the last four decades, and the private share has grown. Nevertheless, there is a natural limit to how much—and what—research private-sector firms can or should pay for, based on the likely commercial benefit they will gain from the expenditure.

All else being equal, most economists would assert, the free market leads to the most efficient allocation of resources. Government involvement, whether through taxation, subsidy, or other means, can lead to misallocation of scarce resources, pushing society away from an optimal equilibrium. However, there are circumstances where even the most pro-market economists agree that government intervention of some kind might be warranted, and that is when the purely private provision of a good (or service) is compromised by the generation of what economists call "positive or negative externalities." A negative externality, simply put, occurs when the costs of a particular activity or product are borne by those removed from the production process. A positive externality generates benefits to members of society who don't contribute to the costs of production. Those benefiting are often referred to as "free riders."

Clearly in the positive externality, free-riding category is scientific research—particularly basic research—which at a significant scale generates massive social benefits beyond any that a company making such an investment could recapture in revenues accruing from the sale or licensing of products or patents. Economist Adam Jaffe of Brandeis University noted in 1996 that the social benefits of scientific research are between 50 and 100 percent greater than the immediate private benefits.[3] Large swaths of research can be characterized this way, such as the biological discoveries that led to lifesaving heart medications, or the underlying physics research behind the engineering of productivity-enhancing new machines and electronic appliances.

Perhaps the best example of this is the development of the Internet, also known as the World Wide Web. Often referred to as the "grandfather" of the Internet, the Advanced Research Projects Agency Network (ARPANet) was a defense project envisioned as a way of giving researchers across the country access to a nationwide network of high-powered computers. In 1969, the first electronic messages were sent through ARPANet; by 1990 the National Science Foundation Network (NSFNet) had replaced it; and the fully commercialized Internet as we know it today was finally operational in 1995. The long-term benefits of the Internet are immense but also largely intangible. Communication, commerce, politics— all spheres of life have been tremendously affected by this innovation that started as a Defense Department project a little over forty years ago. The cost? Numbers vary, but ARPANet had about $26 million allocated to information processing research in 1970.[4] Was it worth it? Perhaps that's a question best answered by the 2 billion Internet users around the world. Would the private sector have invested in a project to help academics communicate? Probably (and rightfully) not. There would have been little financial incentive to do so. Yet its value to all Americans (and the rest of the world) in dollars and functionality has been truly incalculable.

THE OVERALL STATE OF U.S. SCIENTIFIC RESEARCH AND DEVELOPMENT

In the early decades after World War II, scientific research in the United States grew exponentially, driven primarily by government spending. In 1970, for instance, government agencies accounted for $61 billion out of a total of $108 billion in national R&D spending (in constant 2005 dollars). By 1980, the relative research expenditure shares of government and the private sector had become about equal. And in 2010, the last year for which complete data are available, out of a total U.S. research expenditure of $366 billion (also in constant 2005 dollars), only 31 percent came from direct federal appropriations, much of it allocated to designated research agencies like the National Institutes of Health and the National

Science Foundation.[5] Most of the remaining research expenditures originated in the private sector, with nonprofit foundations and state governments filling in the remainder. As shown in figure 6.3, this illustrates an important—and by and large desirable—trend in American support for scientific research; it is no longer dependent solely on government funding, but increasingly includes a significant investment by the private sector and, to a lesser extent, nonprofit organizations.

While the U.S. government *pays* for much American R&D—directly through appropriations for federal research agencies, and indirectly through favorable tax treatment of corporate research—almost all American research is actually *conducted* by nonfederal, usually nongovernmental, organizations. Private corporations are the biggest players, accounting in 2010 for $251 billion (constant 2005 dollars) in research expenditures, 88 percent of which was self-funded. Almost all of the rest takes place in American universities, constituting about 15 percent of all research in a typical year, and most of that depends on federal research grants (figure 6.4).

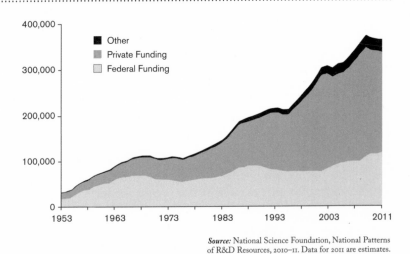

Source: National Science Foundation, National Patterns of R&D Resources, 2010–11. Data for 2011 are estimates.

Fig. 6.3 Total R&D Funding (in constant 2005 $millions)

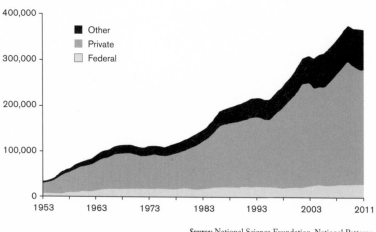

Source: National Science Foundation, National Patterns of R&D Resources, 2010–11. Data for 2011 are estimates.

Note: Federally funded research centers are categorized in "other."

Fig. 6.4 R&D Performers (in constant 2005 $millions)

It is important to note, however, that the private sector's large role in financing R&D is focused primarily on *patentable research*—a new mechanism of action for a potential drug, for example. The kind of research that leads directly to a patent is narrowly focused and generates fairly immediate returns to its inventors—whether through licensing or through manufacturing and selling the product. Such patentable inventions, however, don't develop in a vacuum. They are almost always grounded on some stratum of underlying scientific research, generally referred to as "basic" or "pure" research, without which patentable ideas could never develop. Indeed, a study by Martin Meyer, a business professor at the University of Sussex, found a significant (though often indirect) pathway from basic research to patents.[6] Given this linkage, it is important to understand how basic research originates.

Narrowing in on basic research as a subset of total U.S. research spending, the lion's share is paid for by the federal government. Of the nearly $70 billion (in constant 2005 dollars) spent on basic research in 2010, more than half came from federal government

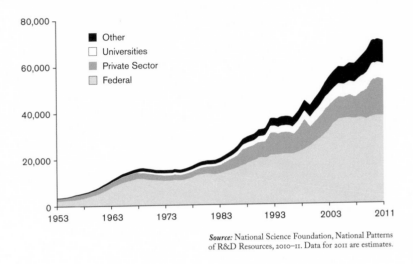

Source: National Science Foundation, National Patterns of R&D Resources, 2010–11. Data for 2011 are estimates.

Fig. 6.5 Basic Research Funding (in constant 2005 $millions)

appropriations, with the rest accounted for by universities (using nonfederal funds), the private sector, and sources like nonprofit foundations and state governments (figure 6.5). Looking at this in another way, around 60 percent of all federal government research spending is devoted to basic research. And it should be, because no private sponsors of such research could ever justify the expenditure in terms of any profitable or even prestige-enhancing payback.

For one thing, basic research discoveries—profitable or not— are usually unpatentable. In a 2010 opinion, a federal appeals court bluntly stated that "[p]atents are not awarded for academic theories, no matter how groundbreaking or necessary to the later patentable inventions of others."[7]

The goal of a patent is to encourage and promote innovation by protecting the inventor's intellectual property and rewarding him for his ingenuity. To achieve that goal, patents must be broad enough to make infringement unprofitable, but specific enough not to restrict other innovation. The fact that many basic research discoveries are not patentable puts a fine point on the free-rider problem noted earlier. We are faced with the dilemma that while the social benefits from investment in basic research are tangible and real we cannot expect any nongovernmental entity to undertake it. Because there are few, if any, immediate economic benefits from basic research, the corporate sector understandably underinvests in it. As for the nonprofit sector—foundations and universities—even the largest U.S. foundations have limited resources and a diverse array of funding targets, and universities (as noted in chapter 5) are constrained with respect to how much they can cross-subsidize research with tuition revenue.

This, then, is the fundamental rationale for the federal government to step in to fill the void. Make no mistake, federal support of basic research is absolutely critical, because in its absence no other institution is in a position to support it, and without basic research, the pace of all applied research discovery—and the technology that it breeds—will wither. Still, there is one issue that must be addressed if we are counting on federal funds to support basic research, and that is which research possibilities, among a vast array, should receive support, and in what proportion.

Happily this issue is resolved through two features of the federal research allocation protocol that determine where the research is undertaken, and what is to be studied. First, as noted above, most federally funded basic research is in fact conducted by universities, and second, research grants to universities are competitive, based on grant applications reviewed by external disciplinary panels of highly distinguished scientists. In 2009, universities conducted more than half of all basic research in the United States—over \$30 billion worth. All other sectors—whether business, government, or nonprofit—didn't come close to matching the volume of basic research conducted at universities (figure 6.6).

Looking at the specific federal agencies that actually disburse the funds, six agencies account for the preponderance of all research grants: the National Institutes of Health (NIH), the National Science Foundation (NSF), the Department of Defense,

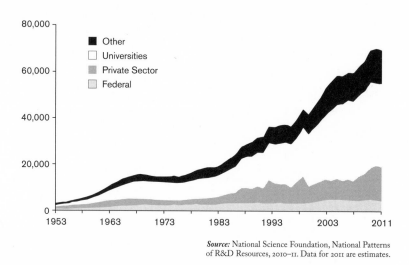

Source: National Science Foundation, National Patterns of R&D Resources, 2010–11. Data for 2011 are estimates.

Fig. 6.6 Basic Research Performers (in constant 2005 $millions)

the National Aeronautics and Space Administration (NASA), the Department of Energy, and the Department of Agriculture.

The NIH, by a large margin, provides the majority of all federal funds dedicated to academic basic research, roughly $9.8 billion (in constant 2005 dollars) in 2012.[8] This is a reflection of both the centrality of biomedical science on the frontier of basic research, and its popularity with politicians because of its obvious potential in leading to better health-care interventions. With its focus on medical research across a broad spectrum—ranging from cancer treatments to human genome research—the NIH has, to its credit, successfully resisted politicization. Indeed, the NIH's successes include research with incalculable benefits like the Human Genome Project, led in large part by Francis Collins, now director of the NIH. Findings from such research have helped pave the way for the development of a host of new, lifesaving medicines—

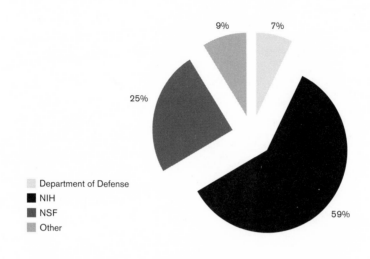

Source: National Science Foundation, Survey of
Federal Funds for Research and Development, 2012.

Fig. 6.7   Federal Funding of Academic Basic Research by Agency

something that would have been beyond the profit-driven calculus
of even the most far-sighted pharmaceutical corporation.

Collectively, the "big three" federal agencies that contribute to
academic basic research—the NIH, the NSF, and the Department
of Defense—account for a full 91 percent of the federal government's commitment to such research, about $13 billion (in constant
2005 dollars) of 2012's $14.3 billion total. Other agencies like the
Department of Energy, NASA, and the Department of Agriculture contribute the remaining $1.3 billion (figure 6.7).

WHAT KIND OF RESEARCH IS TAKING PLACE?

Just as the sources of research support have changed in recent
decades, so have the research targets. A little over a decade ago, in
2000, the sector contributing the most in terms of scientific research
was computer manufacturing—and the pharmaceutical industry

Table 6.2

Top Three For-Profit Industries by R&D Share (percent)

	2000	2009
Pharmaceutical	10.6	18.3
Computer manufacturing	21.2	21.4
Transportation manufacturing	12.2	10.7

Sources: Bureau of Economic Analysis 2010 R&D Satellite Accounts; National Science Foundation/ National Center for Science and Engineering Statistics, Business R&D and Innovation Survey, 2008 and 2009.

was in a distant third place (table 6.2). Roughly a decade and two recessions later, the pharmaceutical industry has made tremendous gains in its share of overall research spending, catching up with the computer manufacturing sector and making up nearly a fifth of private-sector R&D. Meanwhile, the computer industry's share has remained relatively the same, indicating a strong, stable industry, but one that may not be investing as much money in research in the future. Transportation research (including electricity-powered motor vehicles) has dropped from second to third place.

It is easy to understand why the pharmaceutical sector is so research-intensive. Its main products are medicines and medical devices. While manufacturing a medical device is marginally more difficult than manufacturing a pill, in both cases the major cost is not in the production phase; rather, it is in the work of laboratory scientists and engineers as they seek clues in basic science discoveries that can be translated into new—and presumably effective—drugs or devices. Breakthroughs in efficacious and marketable new medical devices (like artificial hearts or hip replacements) build on the latest research in biomechanics as well as on extensive trials in animals and humans; the development of new medicines depends on finding molecular compounds that have the potential to treat specific ailments—and deciding which ailments to target. In both cases the process requires going through thousands of leads—dead ends—to find a successful one and it is invariably very expensive. It would be even more expensive if the pharmaceutical companies weren't able to rely on government-funded basic research—usually conducted at universities—to help develop the theories and methods later applied in manufacturing successful biomedical products.

At the end of the research phase is the holy grail of patent protection, along with the need to generate enough of a payback in the sale of new treatments before the company's patent protection lapses. The very long and costly process of FDA-monitored controlled trials on prospective patients is also built into the pharmaceutical enterprise's research bill. This description is not offered as a rationale for government subsidization of the pharmaceutical industry—government policy should be industry-neutral. This merely offers an explanation for why pharmaceutical research has grown so much, and why more than half of the NIH's research budget goes to fund university-conducted basic biomedical research.

Despite the importance of research critical to the pharmaceutical, computer, and transportation industries, these are not by any stretch of the imagination the only fields where basic research funding is needed. A guiding principle in underwriting basic research is that we cannot second-guess where science will take us, nor can we "order" science to solve specific societal problems. For example, the broad area of energy is of enormous importance today: there is great scientific interest in new and enhanced sources of energy (beyond the overhyped fields of solar and wind energy); how energy can be harnessed for use in transportation, industry, space conditioning, and machinery; the environmental impact of generating and using energy; and many other scientific questions. But the answers will not necessarily come only from research sponsored by the Department of Energy, or projects with "energy" in their titles. That was one of the flaws in the "green energy" research agenda of the American Recovery and Reinvestment Act, which led to the Solyndra Corporation debacle (a manufacturer of solar panels that went bankrupt despite millions of dollars in federal subsidies). With robust funding of *basic* research in physics, chemistry, even biology, scientists will stumble on discoveries that, without ever having been anticipated as energy-relevant, can transform energy science and the energy industry.

The same can be said for countless other twenty-first-century concerns: a sustainable environment; the impact of climate and migration (of both people and wildlife) on agriculture; or new potential prototypes of shelter and urbanization. The only way we can cross these exciting frontiers critical to our long-range survival is to invest heavily in science—across the various disciplines and subdisciplines—and see where it takes us. It is also important to understand that for the United States to fully benefit from crossing these frontiers, the research must be conducted here—not in China, Japan, India, Europe, or, for that matter, Canada or Brazil.

THE GOAL: GROWING DOMESTIC PATENTS

If all of the many advances in the American research landscape are to succeed in stimulating innovation, it is crucial that researchers and inventors are enabled to take full economic advantage of their capabilities and be appropriately rewarded. This, in turn, depends on robust maintenance of the United States' strong system of intellectual property rights. The primary vehicle for protecting intellectual property generated by research is the patent. Under ideal circumstances, increased domestic research output would lead to increased domestic patents; for most purposes, America's annual volume of patents—and the rate of growth of that volume—is the best measure of its pace of technological innovation and the payoff from its investments in research. The good news is that the U.S. Patent and Trademark Office (USPTO), with a total of 503,582 patent applications in 2011, *almost* leads the world in patent volume, just behind China but ahead of Japan and the European Union (table 6.3). The several strands of bad news, however, are that a growing share of U.S. patents granted are now filed by foreigners, the rate of growth in U.S. patents is falling, and the volume of U.S. patents for civilian industrial products (as opposed to defense-related items) is meager and declining relative to international competitors.[9]

Ideally, patents backed by a strong judicial system should guarantee patent holders full discretion over who can manufacture their invention, and ensure that infringers be required to compensate them appropriately. The basic economic reasoning here is that with the proper protections, inventors will have strong incentives both to invent and to take their inventions to market, secure in the guarantee that their intellectual capital will be protected. The innovative firms that are born as a result—and the products they make—generate enormous human-capital benefits, creating the jobs that harness America's human capital and the extraordinary productivity with which the country's work is done.

But the link between research productivity and patent generation cannot be taken for granted. America's strong legal tradition of protecting property rights—including intellectual property—is central in this regard, and makes the proper functioning of the U.S. patent system a critical issue. Because property rights are the foundation of the American lead in innovation, we need to look at the institution created to defend and operationalize those rights—the U.S. Patent and Trademark Office. The USPTO is actually one of America's oldest federal agencies, established in 1790 to support the injunction of Article I, Section 8 of the U.S. Constitution: "To promote the Progress of Science and useful Arts."

The USPTO's mission is twofold: first, it serves as an arbiter for all patent applications in the United States. It is effectively the gatekeeper of innovation, as all inventors must eventually submit their patent applications in order to protect their inventions. The

Table 6.3

Patent Volume by Country and Resident/Non-Resident Filers, 1980–2011

Country/Region	1980		1990		2000		2011	
	Resident	% World	Resident	% World	Resident	% World	Resident	% World
World resident			687,680	100.0	874,600	100.0	1,358,600	100.0
World non-resident			309,821	100.0	501,500	100.0	786,800	100.0
U.S. resident	**62,098**	—	**90,643**	**13.2**	**164,795**	**18.8**	**247,750**	**18.2**
U.S. non-resident	**42,231**	—	**80,520**	**26.0**	**131,100**	**26.1**	**255,832**	**32.5**
E.U. resident	279,743	—	210,135	30.6	203,208	23.2	215,220	15.8
E.U. non-resident	135,013	—	58,816	19.0	117,525	23.4	117,567	14.9
Japan resident	165,730	—	332,952	48.4	384,201	43.9	287,580	21.2
Japan non-resident	25,290	—	27,752	9.0	59,118	11.8	55,030	7.0
China resident	0	—	5,832	0.8	25,346	2.9	415,829	30.6
China non-resident	0	—	4,305	1.4	26,560	5.3	110,583	14.1

Source: World Intellectual Property Organization (WIPO), *World Intellectual Property Indicators*, 2012.

second part of the USPTO's mission is more nuanced: it actively advances intellectual property rights in a variety of ways, not only by advising the president, the Department of Commerce, and other agencies on intellectual property issues but also by working with international patent agencies to develop cooperation agreements that harmonize patent laws across international boundaries.

The USPTO plays a critical role in support of American technical innovation and overall it does a pretty good job. Nevertheless, it has accumulated a significant backlog in excess of 600,000 unexamined patents, a serious—and entirely unnecessary—impediment to speeding up the flow of domestic patents. The USPTO is aware of the problem and has promised to reduce its inventory of unexamined patents to about half by 2015. There is good reason to hope that the USPTO will be successful in meeting its goal: since October 2011, it has reduced the unexamined patent backlog by about 15 percent, and, if this trend can be maintained, there is no reason why 50 percent by 2015 isn't feasible. But frankly, even a 50 percent reduction is far too modest an objective; ideally the marker should be set at no backlog at all.

To its credit, but also at the heart of the backlog problem, the USPTO is perhaps one of the leanest of all government agencies, coming in at a net cost of *zero* to the federal budget. The Patent Office lives entirely on industry fees that it charges for patent filings, priority examination requests, and various other services. Moreover, the Fiscal Year (FY) 2014 budget request for the USPTO was a mere $3.07 billion—around less than 0.001 percent of the total federal budget. Given the critical role the Patent Office plays, these are pennies compared to the benefits of having a strong intellectual property champion. In addition, the USPTO is involved in a massive global initiative called the Patent Prosecution Highway, an international compact that will allow a patent applicant with claims patentable in any country subject to the agreement to be put on a fast track for patent issuance in every other signatory country. This reduces the barriers to innovation and gives inventors the opportunity to expand to foreign markets.

With all the good things the USPTO does, leaving it inadequately funded seems perverse. In a small dose of beneficial reform, Congress has passed the America Invents Act of 2012, which includes a provision for the USPTO to keep surplus industry fees in a reserve fund for future use. But this may not be enough. Policy makers should consider adding a modest increment of funding to the Patent Office from general revenues. A small sum of money (say, $100 million) could be allotted to the Patent Office with the requirement that it be used only to help clear the unexamined patent backlog or speed up existing patent examinations; this is the same approach taken by the FDA, which uses industry fees to consider new drug applications more efficiently and reduce the time between submission and decision. At almost no cost to the federal budget (and less than the government-subsidized loans given to bankrupt green ventures), this would be money well spent.

Some, however, argue that the patent system as it operates today in fact hinders innovation. The Electronic Frontier Foundation, an anti-copyright advocacy group, has a Web page dedicated to this very idea, arguing that "[p]atents may have been created to help encourage innovation, but instead they regularly hinder it."[10] The main problem today appears to be "patent trolling" (discussed later in this chapter), but patent filings and grants can also lead to industries cartelizing and creating unfair monopolies that restrict, rather than promote, innovation.

While there is room to reform the American patent system in numerous ways, we shouldn't throw the baby out with the bathwater. The American industries today that are the chief battleground for patent wars are those tied to information technology—the world of computer hardware and software—including the growing domain of mobile devices and applications. Despite the raging

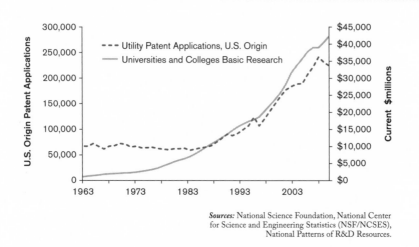

Sources: National Science Foundation, National Center for Science and Engineering Statistics (NSF/NCSES), National Patterns of R&D Resources.

Fig. 6.8 Bayh-Dole Stimulated R&D and Patent Applications

patent conflicts in this sector, the latest empirical evidence shows that firms in these industries are nevertheless doing very well, directly and indirectly accounting for some 40 million jobs in the American economy and about 35 percent of GDP. These industries also pay well compared to the rest of the economy—about 42 percent better than other sectors.[11]

One area where enlightened government policy has promoted innovation-stimulating patents is the Bayh-Dole Act, passed in 1980, which allowed *universities* to patent their research. Driving this measure was the assumption that universities would respond to such an incentive by pumping more of their own (or externally raised) resources into funding their scientists and laboratories. The initiative has clearly lived up to its expectations; just a few short years after its passage, the basic research expenditures of universities have grown exponentially, and so have overall domestic utility patent applications (figure 6.8).[12]

AN AGENDA FOR RAPID TECHNOLOGICAL PROGRESS

The entire premise of this chapter is that, after education, one of the most important factors in American human-capital development—and the indispensable determinant of its world-beating standard of living—is having the world's smartest workplaces. That requires that the United States must always be at the global technological frontier, which cannot happen unless the United States is also at the global scientific discovery frontier. And that depends on two things: world-leading investment in scientific research—both basic and applied—and a healthy patent system that processes all legitimate patent applications quickly and protects the work of legitimate scientists, engineers, and inventors from the depredations of patent infringers and patent trolls.

The good news is that, as of today, the United States still has an unmatched advantage in scientific research. We do more of it and do it more efficiently than anywhere else in the world, leading to the rapid adoption of science-driven technological innovations that continue to make American workers among the most productive in the world (and, not incidentally, make men and women of the American armed services the world's most effective military force). But this isn't a position to be taken for granted. Direct and indirect government support for science and technology is crucial to maintaining this status, and without appropriate policy adjustments, America's lead will be usurped by a growing number of competitors in the European Union and Asia, where China is now becoming the most formidable.

Recommendations for federal government promotion of American technological leadership include:

Allocate Government Funding Strategically Simply spending more money or creating new government bureaucracies is unlikely to address the complicated dynamics underlying our weakening lead in scientific research. Rather, a successful science and technology strategy calls for targeted increases in certain categories of spending. However, even if funding is better targeted, ramping up America's research enterprise—both private and public—will require more money, most of it supplied by the federal government. Categorically, out of all of the thousands of programs funded by the federal government, most far more costly, none rivals research funding in terms of the "bang for the buck" accruing to the national benefit.

Subsidize Where It Is Needed Government expenditures are most effective—and sometimes essential—in pursuits where the private sector, for economic or institutional reasons, is less motivated to invest. Basic research belongs in this category because, as noted earlier, private firms cannot justify expenditures in this area because they have little prospect of a direct return on their investment. Thus, if we want basic research conducted in the United States, federal government support is the only way we are going to get it.

Eliminate the Patent Backlog While the U.S. Patent and Trademark Office is certainly a model of cost-effectiveness compared to most other federal agencies, there is considerable room for improvement. One important target for the Patent Office is reducing its backlog of unexamined patents; though there's been significant progress made on that front, a veritable mountain of patents still remains unexamined. A simple solution? Allow the Patent Office some minor amount of discretionary funding above what it collects in applicant fees. This funding should be earmarked for hiring additional patent examiners. Alternatively, a "reward" system could be established for the Patent Office for every goal it meets on time (with appropriate oversight by the Government Accountability Office).

End Patent Trolling The most urgent of the other reforms of the U.S. Patent Office is to address the problem of patent trolls. In short, patent trolls—also known as patent assertion entities—focus on buying and prosecuting patents against firms that have often started using a particular technology after developing it on their own. Most of these suits are frivolous and, indeed, some 92 percent of them fail.[13] However, most companies tend to settle these suits rather than going to court because of the high costs of patent litigation. Patent trolling places a costly roadblock in the path of many promising start-ups and wastes billions of dollars that might otherwise be invested in developing new technologies.

The best way to thwart patent trolls would be to raise the cost of frivolous patent lawsuits. One approach—informally known as "loser pays"—would require that the loser of a patent suit pay the legal fees and administrative costs borne by the victor. Because most of these suits that are actually tried end up failing, the incentive for defendant companies to settle arises from the cost of legal fees rather than a fear of losing the suit. Requiring the loser to cover these fees would help eliminate the incentive to settle.

Another approach, as proposed in a recent bill by Senator Charles Schumer, would allow the USPTO to investigate and invalidate the kinds of dubious patents that are often acquired by patent trolls to blackmail technology start-up firms. Doing so would make it less valuable for patent trolls to accumulate large numbers of patents, but would also increase the quality of American patents—a win-win.

Ramp Up Private-Sector Research Incentives The existing tax incentives for private-sector research are lodged in the Research and Experimentation tax credit against a firm's corporate tax liability—originally a temporary provision enacted in 1981 but renewed fourteen times since then. The nonrefundable credit allows businesses to deduct a certain amount of their qualified research expenditures. Because of its temporary nature—it expires after short intervals, requiring Congress to repeatedly reenact it—companies may be hesitant to invest in research, for fear that the ever-present political gridlock in Washington makes periodic—and timely—renewal of the credit far from certain.

There is absolutely no reason not to make the credit permanent, as well as making it less complex and more generous. Under current rules the credit can be maddeningly difficult to calculate, as noted in a recent Brookings Institution report.[14] More seriously, the relative value of the credit—as compared to similar tax treatment in other countries—has significantly eroded over the years. Simplifying and increasing the size of the credit—from 14 to 20 percent—would cost a modest $6 to $8 billion annually.[15] But the direct economic benefit in terms of increased GDP is estimated to be at least $66 billion annually, along with thousands of new jobs created and new patents filed each year.[16]

Making the research tax credit permanent would protect one of the single most beneficial corporate tax incentives from the politics of annual budgetary maneuvering and make the research investment environment for innovative companies far more predictable—certainly something that legislators across the political spectrum should be able to agree on.

Ramp Up Support for Basic Research Funding Federal government support for basic research in 2012 was about $31 billion, accounting for the lion's share of all U.S. basic research expenditures (for reasons outlined earlier). Four agencies account for most of this spending: the National Institutes of Health (NIH), 65 percent; the National Science Foundation (NSF), 15 percent; the national laboratories of the Department of Energy, 10 percent; and the Defense Advanced Research Projects Agency of the Department of Defense, 7 percent. As a percentage of GDP, current federal outlays for basic research amount to 0.19 percent.[17] Given the size of the American economy this isn't a small sum, but we can certainly afford to spend more. The most reasonable basis for determining the level of federal support for basic research, both to assure its adequacy and to stay ahead of our more aggressive international competitors (like China), is to tie it to the growth of U.S. GDP. This would put in place a virtuous cycle: research investments cause GDP to grow; GDP growth results in increased research investment, and so on. Such a rule would also insulate this critical federal outlay from fiscal politics (like the 2011 Budget Control Act sequester cuts) and, hopefully, the exigencies of the business cycle.

My recommendation is that Congress specify a ten-year basic-research-as-a-percent-of-GDP target of, say, 0.4 percent—effectively doubling basic research's current share of the economy, but an extremely modest sum nevertheless. The basic research budgets of the NIH, NSF, and other relevant federal agencies would be given five-year budgets tied to this criterion, enabling them to set research priorities and making it easier for those seeking research grants to lay the groundwork for their applications. Since most basic research is actually conducted at universities and private research laboratories, a predictable funding stream would enable those involved to plan ahead in hiring the requisite research personnel and building the necessary research facilities.

Ending Idleness
as We Know It

Chapters 2 through 5 reviewed how human capital is initially acquired through education, from preschool to college. Chapter 6 focused on how this human capital is applied in the workplace—leveraged by the quality of workplace technology—to create economic value, what is generally referred to as productivity. Overall national productivity also depends, however, on the proportion of the adult population that is working. When healthy, working-age adults are *not working*, their potential productivity comes to nothing. Since education and workplace technology both require costly societal investments (nowhere more so than in the United States), unnecessary idleness, among other negatives, amounts to a big waste of societal human capital. For the United States to realize the full benefit of its investments in education and technology, Americans must work, and the more they work, the better. This may seem to be an intuitively obvious point, yet many of the current labor market policies that affect whether Americans work or not take us in just the opposite direction. This chapter takes a look at why so many Americans are not working, what they and the country lose by it, and how we might get them back to work.

We are fortunate to have the wind at our back. As will be shown further on, Americans possess an intense, culturally entrenched work ethic that leads them to work longer and harder than workers in other advanced economies. For most of our history, government policies have reinforced it. Now, however, many Americans—especially men—are working a lot less than they used to and, more to the point, less than they might *want* to—given the opportunity and the incentives. The percentage of men over age twenty who are working has gone from over 84 percent in 1950 to under 68 percent today.[1] Some of the drop can be explained by men in their early twenties still going to college, and the overall employment rate has not dropped by as much because more women have gone to work. But the bottom line is that all those Americans who are not working, but who would like to and are able to, represent a vast loss of potential national human capital—amounting to a corresponding loss of national income and economic output.

Most of the decline can't be blamed on the decisions of American workers. In addition to the massive job losses caused by the recent recession and by business cycle downturns more generally, Americans' unambiguously positive work ethic has been systematically undermined over the last five decades by a variety of shortsighted government policies, some the unforeseen legacy of welfare state programs that were adopted long ago, others the product of political pressure from organized labor, and, more recently, some in response to recurrent budgetary or economic downturns. The growing relaxation of disability pay eligibility criteria; the design of the unemployment insurance program; the facilitation of premature retirement; these and other dynamics have led us down a path where, increasingly, individuals are paid *not* to work—indeed, we've started to incentivize idleness. Reasserting America's singular work ethic and getting to true "full employment" will require a comprehensive rethinking of official government labor market policy into one that recognizes that work as much as education builds and harnesses human capital; that in a smart society all adults should be enabled to work as much as they want to or can; that reconfigures work-related safety net entitlements, and promotes work opportunities across the economy.

THE CONTEXT: AMERICANS' DEVOTION TO WORK

First, the good news. Much has been written about Americans' intense adherence to the Protestant work ethic, drawing on Max Weber's formulation of the concept in the early twentieth century. There is solid evidence that Americans' uniquely positive attitude toward work remains one of the United States' most powerful comparative economic advantages. A study published in the *Journal of Economic Perspectives* ascribes roughly a quarter of America's productivity lead over other advanced economies to the fact that its workers work longer and harder than those in most other rich nations.[2]

Behind Americans' greater work effort[3] is their greater love of work. In 2005, the International Social Survey Programme documented workers' attitudes toward work in the world's most advanced economies, probing two basic themes: whether they worked out of enjoyment or necessity, and whether they would accept less-than-ideal working conditions. On the former point, perhaps the most revealing question asked workers if they agreed that a job was only a way to earn money. Workers in the United States overwhelmingly (60 percent) disagreed, compared to 55 percent in Germany, 53 percent in France, 51 percent in Britain, 42 percent in Japan, and 36 percent in Korea. In a similar vein, asked if they would work even if they did not need the money, 64 percent of American workers said yes, roughly comparable to respondents from Japan and Korea but well ahead of workers in

Canada (59 percent), France (58 percent), or Britain (56 percent). When asked if they were satisfied in their jobs, only in the United States did a majority of workers say yes (56 percent), compared to 49 percent in Germany, 44 percent in Canada, 43 percent in Britain, 32 percent in Japan, and only 20 percent in Korea.[4]

Among those not already working, only in the United States did a solid majority (54 percent) say they were eager to get a job, as opposed to 41 percent of the French, 36 percent of Canadians, 31 percent of Germans, and 30 percent of the British and Japanese. Asked if they were willing to learn new skills to get a job, 87 percent of Americans answered affirmatively, putting them ahead of workers in every surveyed country other than Germany (89 percent), and far ahead of the ostensibly conscientious Asians (Korea, 70 percent; Japan, 58 percent). If necessary, 60 percent of American workers expressed a willingness to work for less pay, something only 55 percent of Germans, 41 percent of Canadians, 30 percent of the French, or 29 percent of the Japanese agreed to. As for working only part-time if that was all that was available, 78 percent of Americans said they would, sharply outscoring Canadians (65 percent), the British (62 percent), the French (58 percent), or the Japanese (a mere 34 percent). The ultimate work ethic test is the willingness to work at more than one job, something engaged in by 25 percent of all American workers but only 12 percent of Germans, 10 percent of the French, and 6 percent of the Japanese.[5]

Americans' superior work ethic is out of step not only with contemporary workers in other countries but also with human predilections since the dawn of civilization. Taking a long historical perspective, humans have always wanted to work as little as possible. Anthropologists tell us that Paleolithic and Neolithic societies were definitely work-averse; our prehistoric Paleolithic hunter-gatherer ancestors worked only enough to feed themselves and spent most of their days enjoying leisure.[6] Their Neolithic-age farmer successors worked somewhat more because farming is so labor intensive, but even they did only as much as needed to subsist, and of course took time off during much of the year between the period when they gathered their crops and the next planting season.[7] Obviously, much was accomplished during the great civilizations of the post-historic age (Egypt, Rome, Persia), but that work was mainly assigned to slaves or other members of the lower social orders; the decision-making classes that ran things worked as little as possible. After their fall, during the first Christian millennium, work was disparaged by the church because it got in the way of religious devotion and led inevitably to excessive attachment to material things.[8]

The long-ingrained cavalier human attitude toward work only began to change after the Protestant Reformation of the sixteenth century and the onset of the eponymous work ethic so famously delineated by Max Weber.[9] Under Protestant (mainly Calvinist) theology, those who achieved material success—almost always due to the extent and efficiency of their work effort—came to be viewed as being in a state of grace and thus the only ones predestined to be welcomed into heaven. For the first time, work was valued in and of itself, and as a result Europe in the post-Reformation period saw tremendous economic growth and the rapid development of modern-day capitalist economies.

Although the Protestant work ethic was born in Europe, it reached its greatest flower in North America—more specifically in the United States (which from the time of American independence to the present day has surpassed Canada in this regard). European persecution pushed large numbers of Calvinists and other Protestants to seek religious freedom (and greener pastures) in the New World, bringing their values with them. While these values were initially held by people who were actual Protestants (of a great variety of denominations), they quickly became an integral part of the American national value system. Beyond religion rewarding it, hard work paid off. America was a land of boundless opportunity, offering vast tracts of free or cheap land to those willing to farm it; vast consumer markets for aggressive entrepreneurs; and vast job opportunities to the formerly unemployed if they were willing to intensively apply their brawn—and brains—to the work at hand. Most of the Irish and other immigrants who flocked to the United States in the nineteenth century were in fact Catholic, yet they quickly assimilated to the stringent work ethic of their native-born American predecessors. The pattern continued with all subsequent immigrants, regardless of their prior religion or national origin: the Chinese who built the western segment of the Transcontinental Railroad, Japanese immigrant farmers in California, the waves of turn-of-the-last-century immigrants from eastern and southern Europe. This is just as true of the most recent arrivals to the United States—Hispanic, Caribbean, and Asian immigrants of the last half century. A survey conducted in 2004 by Deborah Schildkraut of Tufts University found that both immigrants and native-born Americans believe that "the work ethic . . . is an essential component of being American,"[10] underscoring that while religion was certainly important in initially establishing Americans' attitudes toward work, the work ethic has since become firmly embedded in the national culture.

HOW MUCH MORE DO AMERICANS WORK?

It is easy to show that Americans' apparent love of working is matched by their actual labor-market behavior as measured by various statistics. Let's begin by looking simply at time spent at work. Taking the high-income countries of Europe as a benchmark, we find that American workers, on average, work more hours per week and more weeks per year than their European counterparts (table 7.1). Figure 7.1 makes the same point by comparing the percentage of the workforce among major OECD countries putting in more than forty hours a week.

Table 7.1

Time Spent at Work in Selected OECD Countries, 2004

Country	Annual hours	Hours per week	Weeks per year
United States	1820	39.4	46.2
Spain	1642	38.9	42.2
Ireland	1586	36.3	43.7
Great Britain	1547	38.2	40.5
Italy	1533	37.4	41.0
Germany	1482	36.5	40.6
France	1466	36.2	40.5
Denmark	1412	36.3	38.9
Netherlands	1349	38.1	38.4
Sweden	1349	38.1	35.4

Source: OECD StatExtracts.

Americans also tend to start working at an earlier age, and keep working longer, than residents of other countries. In 2011, for instance, 25.8 percent of all Americans between the ages of fifteen and nineteen had jobs; the European Union average for this age group was 17.1 percent; and that for France was 10.6 percent. Among OECD countries, only in the United States was more than a minuscule share of those older than seventy-five working, 7 percent in 2011; the European Union average was 1.3 percent; that for Canada was 3.6 percent.[11] While currently more older Americans work than their age peers abroad, as we discuss later in this chapter, even more might want to if they were offered the right incentives.[12] And thanks to Americans' superior work effort (and state-of-the-art technology), during the hours they are on the job, American workers get more done than workers in other countries, as figure 6.1 in the previous chapter illustrates.

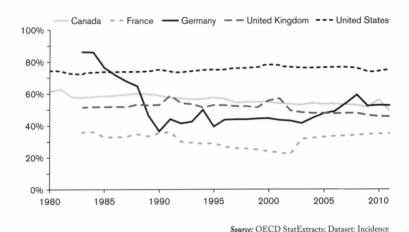

Source: OECD StatExtracts; Dataset: Incidence
of employment by usual weekly hours worked.

FIG. 7.1 Percent of Labor Force Working
40 Hours or More in Select OECD Countries

Americans' natural inclination to prefer work over leisure doesn't even stop at *paid* work. As table 7.2 shows, Americans do more volunteering than the citizens of most other developed (i.e., OECD) countries.

People in the United States volunteer four times as much as those in the United Kingdom and eight times as much as those in France. This may reflect Americans' conviction that not every societal need should be left to government, but it also demonstrates their enjoyment and valuation of work. While volunteering may not necessarily build skills or require high levels of human capital—running a recreation program for inner-city children, serving as a volunteer fire fighter, or giving out food at a soup kitchen aren't particularly human-capital-intensive skills—it still involves trading off considerable leisure time to work for no pay.

Table 7.2

Time Spent Volunteering in Selected OECD Countries, 2012

United States	8 minutes per day
Germany	7 minutes per day
OECD average	4 minutes per day
United Kingdom	2 minutes per day
France	1 minute per day

Source: OECD Better Life Index; Community topic:
http://www.oecdbetterlifeindex.org/topics/community/.

LESSONS FROM EUROPE

While the robustness of the American work ethic can largely be explained by our history, it is puzzling that in Europe, the cradle of the Protestant work ethic, work effort is so much lower than in the United States. One explanation, with a direct bearing on the theme of this chapter, can be found in a 2005 paper for the National Bureau of Economic Research (NBER) by Alberto Alesina, Edward Glaeser, and Bruce Sacerdote.[13] Shortly after World War II, Europeans by and large worked as many hours as Americans, but as they recovered from the war and rebuilt their economies, their work effort plummeted. The authors attribute this to government policies adopted in Europe's richer countries, generally as part and parcel of their welfare-state culture. These policies fall under four general categories:

1. Curtailment of working time, negotiated (through collective bargaining) or mandated, taking the form of long vacations, a plethora of official holidays (table 7.3), and shortened workweeks

2. Generous stipends for the unemployed and pensions for the retired (coupled with retirement eligibility set at an early age)

3. A high statutory minimum wage (figure 7.2)

4. High marginal income-tax rates to pay for generous welfare state benefits (table 7.4)

Why the Europeans enacted such anti-work policies is not necessarily relevant, except with respect to one key contention in the NBER paper: the apparent correlation of such policies with the extent of unionization. Unions everywhere in the world were born out of a desire to counter worker exploitation; to that end they used collective bargaining and political muscle to end child labor, protect job security with procedural safeguards, improve working conditions, and, of course, gain more pay. Along the way, however, in both Europe and the United States, a growing share of the worker benefits they negotiated (or had government impose) have involved *getting paid for working less*. Because the influence of unions, with both employers and government, depends on levels of unionization, they have had much greater success in promoting work-less policies in Europe, where unionization is high, than in

Table 7.3

Paid Days Off in Selected OECD Countries, 2003

Country	Total days off	Holidays	Mandated vacation	Other vacation
Italy	39.5	16	20	3.5
Germany	39	16	20	3
France	35	16	25	6
United States	**19.5**	**12**	**0**	**7.5**

Source: OECD StatExtracts.

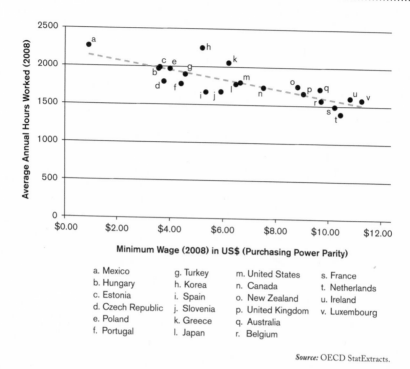

Fig. 7.2 Minimum Wage and Variation in Hours Worked in Select OECD Countries, 2008

a. Mexico
b. Hungary
c. Estonia
d. Czech Republic
e. Poland
f. Portugal

g. Turkey
h. Korea
i. Spain
j. Slovenia
k. Greece
l. Japan

m. United States
n. Canada
o. New Zealand
p. United Kingdom
q. Australia
r. Belgium

s. France
t. Netherlands
u. Ireland
v. Luxembourg

Source: OECD StatExtracts.

the United States, where it is not. In 2004, for instance, 18 percent of Americans in the labor force were represented by collective bargaining agreements; in Europe, typical percentages of unionized workers include Austria, 98 percent; France, 92 percent; Germany, 90 percent; the Netherlands, 71 percent; and Britain, 47 percent.[14] Within the United States, where levels of unionization vary widely by state, work-curtailing state policies are also proportional to the extent of union influence.[15]

Critics on the left repeatedly excoriate the United States' historically lower—and falling—levels of unionization, viewing it as chiefly responsible for stagnant worker incomes and the country's highly skewed income distribution. But the indictment is misplaced. The truth is that in the United States (or Europe, for that

191

Table 7.4

Welfare State Variables in Selected Countries, 1999

Country/Region	Minimum wage as % of average wages	Tax revenue as % of GDP	Social benefits as % of revenue
France	50	50.4	20.1
Germany	55	44.5	20.5
Sweden	52	57.9	21.1
Great Britain	40	40.4	15.7
European Union	53	45.4	18.1
United States	**39**	**31.0**	**11.0**

Source: Alberto Alesina, Edward Glaeser, and Bruce Sacerdote, "Work and Leisure in the U.S. and Europe: Why So Different?," Working Paper 11278 (Cambridge, Mass.: National Bureau of Economic Research, April 2005), http://www.nber.org/papers/w11278.pdf.

matter) no amount of union pressure, either directly on employers or indirectly through politics, can make employers pay workers more than they are worth in productivity—at least not for long. All it can do is ask (or force through legislation) employers to extract fewer hours of work from each worker, or to use fewer workers; employers then make up the shortfall by mechanizing, outsourcing, or scaling back benefits and pay raises. Unions (and European politicians) may not realize it when they pursue such policies, but what they are doing is making the overall workforce poorer, and squandering vast amounts of human capital.

MATCHING AMERICA'S WORK EFFORT POLICIES
TO ITS WORK ETHIC VALUES

As our rich European peers have gradually scaled back the amount of time they work as their welfare states have grown (with a resulting drop in European productivity), we've retained our effort-focused mentality. Nevertheless, the United States has not entirely escaped enacting policies and programs that, mirroring those of

Europe, underwrite idleness; they are just not as comprehensive, generous, and destructive of work effort—yet. In the pages that follow, I will review the main ones, and then suggest ways in which they might be reformed to promote work in place of idleness. But first, I want to address some shibboleths that often keep us from aiming for greater employment, those that feed the belief among policy makers, unions, and even the general public that there aren't enough jobs for everyone who might want to work, and that the unemployed are doing the rest of us a favor.

LABOR MARKET FALLACIES

Organized labor and left-leaning politicians often pursue policies that reduce labor participation in the conviction that national employment is a zero-sum game. From the earliest days of the Industrial Revolution to the present day, people not well-versed in economics—which unfortunately includes large numbers of public officials—have believed that the number of workers needed in their economic region was essentially fixed, and that employment for some must come at the expense of unemployment for others. This belief, labeled "the fixed lump of labor fallacy," has been thoroughly repudiated by economists who unequivocally assert that the need for workers in any region grows in direct proportion to its population, something borne out through centuries of experience in the United States and across the world. Unfortunately, governments (like France's today) and labor unions (almost everywhere) are still in thrall to the fallacy, leading them to needlessly—indeed, harmfully—enact policies to keep people from working as much as they might.

Another equally mistaken but currently more fashionable view alleges that higher levels of employment, and work effort generally, are no longer possible because the United States is in the grip of a new—and growing—"structural" economic and labor market dynamic. The argument goes that the rapidly changing in-

dustrial structure of the global economy, the international mobility of labor and goods, and the premium placed on unique skills
will make most ordinary workers, in America or elsewhere, either
obsolete or low-paid. Under these conditions, the only valuable
workers will be those who are cheap or those who are brilliant—
who "add value" in the words of Thomas Friedman—and the rest
are doomed.[16]

If Friedman and others[17] who advance this thesis are saying
that Americans will be more employable and better paid if they
acquire higher-order human capital (mainly through more and
better education) and approach their work with dedication and
creativity, then they are right. But many economic "structuralists"
go way beyond this point when they claim the global job market
is now so crowded, so rich in talent, and so internationally inter-
changeable, that only those with extraordinary gifts can make it,
and the rest are relegated to inferior (or no) jobs and low (or no)
pay. The implied corollary is that without revolutionary upgrades
in education and zealous self-improvement, Americans can never
get back to the full employment levels and decent pay they enjoyed
just five years ago; that even a baccalaureate will not be enough to
get a good, or maybe any, job. This exaggerated view of both the
American job market and the human-capital needs of the twenty-
first century is dead wrong. The American economy will always be
able to absorb its labor force, regardless of its size; the only true
limitation on total national employment is total national willingness to work. Obviously, the better educated workers are, the better their job prospects and their pay, points made throughout this
book. But to say that otherwise, Americans won't be able to find
good jobs at good pay is patently absurd.

Why? First, a general point: there is no limit to human material needs or wants, and in an affluent society like the United
States, these can and will be satisfied. Throughout history, labor
has become more efficient and trade has expanded without causing

greater unemployment (except during recessions, an entirely unrelated phenomenon); rather, any workers displaced by technology or trade get jobs producing the next wave of goods and services, using prevailing labor-saving technology. In the current American context, it is easy to see many fields where more workers will be needed. To cite just a few: One of the fastest-growing industries today is health care. While some of its work can be mechanized, most of it is both hands-on and tied to the location of patients; thus, we will need an army of health-care professionals in the decades ahead: doctors, dentists, physical therapists, laboratory and imaging technicians, nurses, and those who merely make patients comfortable and keep health facilities clean. Then there are the fast-growing professional fields that require both highly specialized skills and continual in-person interface with clients; a wide variety of design practices in architecture, landscape architecture, interior decoration, restaurant, retail, and theater design; a broad array of highly specialized legal and financial services (including tax preparation) made necessary by ever-growing societal laws and rules. In our highly mechanized and computerized consumer economy, increasing numbers of essential things break and need to be continually maintained; so we will need a wide variety of skilled technicians to service our growing roster of complex products and equipment. There is no need to belabor the point (pun intended), but let me assure the reader that there will never be a shortage of jobs in the United States, most of them decently paid, or anywhere else, for that matter, where economies are well managed.

GETTING AMERICANS BACK TO WORK

One category of job-killing policies endemic in Europe—but also popular with American labor unions and the left generally—has had only a marginal impact on employment in the United States. These are federal, state, and local regulations that distort the economics of job markets by setting minimum wages and imposing onerous collective-bargaining rules. In some American states, these regulations may be stringent enough to restrain employment there, but because of interstate competition, their effect nationally is to geographically shift overall employment rather than to curtail it. Of course, federal government policies also play a role in this arena. It mandates a national minimum wage, currently $7.25, which President Obama has proposed raising to $10.10 by 2015. Congress is unlikely to let it go that high, and historically the federal minimum wage has tracked the bottom of the wage scale, limiting the degree of labor market wage distortion. Through the National Labor Relations Board, the federal government also sets basic national collective-bargaining parameters. Here, too, the overall impact has generally been restrained, especially in recent decades, mainly because of the country's low level of unionization. All of this could change, of course, but for now this particular bane of European countries is not a serious problem in the United States.

What is a matter of concern are two pervasive sets of policies that are quite effective in keeping Americans from working. These can be grouped under two broad headings: first, programs that provide income to people *of working age* who are not working, specifically long-term (often permanent) stipends for the disabled and short-term stipends for the unemployed; and second, programs that facilitate premature retirement for those healthy enough and otherwise willing to work, specifically Social Security old-age pensions, Medicare, and state and local public employee pensions. In both cases, some relatively simple reforms might trigger a quantum increase in the level of both labor participation (wanting to work) and employment (holding a job).

THE POSTER POLICY THAT GOT SOME AMERICANS BACK TO WORK

In considering how these policies might be altered to promote work rather than idleness, we can profitably borrow from one of the most successful domestic policy transformations of the last half century—the reform of "welfare" in 1996 with the passage of the Personal Responsibility and Work Opportunity Reconciliation Act of 1996 (PRWORA). What used to be called "welfare"— support for indigent families and individuals—was not so long ago a vast idleness-promoting program, but since 1996 it has been so thoroughly recast that it is now a model to emulate rather than a problem. At the time that PRWORA was adopted, the U.S. welfare caseload covered 12.6 million individuals and 4.5 million families. By 2012, only sixteen years later, the caseload has fallen to 4.0 million individuals and 1.7 million families, reductions of over 68 and 62 percent respectively![18]

Like other programs that underwrite idleness, pre-reform welfare, then called Aid to Families with Dependent Children (AFDC), was predicated on the idea that its beneficiaries—generally unmarried single mothers with children—were incapable of working, either because of their child-care responsibilities or, more fundamentally, their lack of job skills. AFDC, a program heavily underwritten with federal grants but administered by the states, had its roots in the New Deal and was designed to provide income support for widowed mothers who, given contemporary mores and the extent of joblessness, were not expected to work. Even then, the law was controversial; many argued that it encouraged indolence and created disincentives to work. By the 1970s, few of AFDC's beneficiaries were widows, and a growing chorus of critics faulted it for promoting out-of-wedlock childbearing, paternal abandonment, and permanent dependency. Calls to reform AFDC resonated across the ideological and partisan spectrum, most forcefully articulated by the late Senator Daniel Patrick Moynihan, and New York's commissioner of social services, Blanche Bernstein. But what ultimately tipped the balance in favor of action—as with Harriet Beecher Stowe's *Uncle Tom's Cabin* and slavery, Rachel Carson's *Silent Spring* and environmentalism, or Ralph Nader's *Unsafe at Any Speed* and consumer safety—was a book: Charles Murray's *Losing Ground*, underwritten by the Manhattan Institute and published in 1984. The publication of *Losing Ground*, more than any other event, set in motion—a decade later—the bipartisan welfare-reform initiative enacted by Congress in 1996 with the support of the Clinton administration.

The most important provision of PRWORA mandates that states put a five-year limit on cash assistance to welfare families and limit unconditional welfare benefits to twenty-four months, after which recipients are required to work or be on the path to getting work. The law further required states to demonstrate that, by 2002, 50 percent of their 1996 caseload was working, with the minimum work effort (for single parents) specified at thirty hours per week. While the states could fudge this point somewhat, the law defined work as entailing a *job*—rather than job training or education. To make the transition to work more palatable, and to mitigate any possible harm to children—the majority of those actually being supported by welfare—the states could use their federal grants to subsidize child care. For the same reason, after they began working, former cash assistance recipients could continue to receive Medicaid and food stamp benefits for a number of years if their pay still made them income-eligible.

If welfare reform is to be a model for restoring work incentives in other corners of the American welfare state, as will be discussed later in this chapter, it is useful to understand how the states actually managed to move millions of poor, usually unskilled women (and some men) off of dependency and into the workforce. To begin with, they had no choice; if they didn't succeed they would lose federal funding, and this powerfully concentrated their minds on reaching the mandated targets. More fascinating is how they accomplished this. What most states ended up doing—most notably New York, where welfare rolls fell even faster than in the country as a whole—was to engage welfare-to-work contractors and to condition the contracts on successful job placement (de-

fined as remaining in a job for at least a year). Many of the successful contractors were private for-profit firms, like the spectacu-
larly successful America Works, others were nonprofit, and some,
like the State University of New York (my employer), were public.
The singular success of these contractors stands in sharp relief to
the dismal record of decades of publicly funded job-training programs, many of which are still operating.

When all else failed, many states and localities took the work
requirement even further. In New York City, welfare recipients
who continued to be unemployed (because they never entered a
welfare-to-work program, or the program couldn't find them a
job) were required to work in unpaid jobs under the city's Work
Experience Program. The goal was simple: keep people working,
no matter what.

Most studies of welfare reform have reached positive conclusions as to its overall efficacy—in achieving its work goals, in its
impact on family and child poverty, even in the attitudes of former
welfare recipients.[19] The lesson here is that getting nonworking
adults back to work—even the hardest cases—can be done.

GETTING OTHER AMERICANS BACK TO WORK

At its peak, welfare (meaning AFDC) was America's largest program providing income for households headed by nonworking
adults. It no longer is; that distinction now goes to the programs
for disability insurance and unemployment insurance. The rationale for both of these programs is in many ways similar to that
for welfare: the individuals involved "can't" work, in the first instance because they are ostensibly too "disabled" to work, in the
second because they lost their jobs (through no fault of their own)
and can't find new ones. Both justifications, on the surface, appear
to be quite compelling. But scratch the surface, and we find that
not all legitimate disabilities (discounting outright fraud) prevent
a person from holding *any* job; nor need it be impossible for all

those who lost their job to find *any* new one, even during a recession. Remember, most of the three million or so adults who moved from welfare to work between 1996 and today were even more difficult to place in jobs than either the disabled or the momentarily jobless: they had never worked, they had few job skills, and they had gotten thoroughly used to their dependency. In the pages that follow, I review the dynamics of disability and unemployment insurance to explore the possibility that here, too, we might achieve breakthroughs in moving from idleness to work. If we can, it would be another great American human-capital victory—another way the United States can become a smarter society.

Disabled Workers Although everyone associates Social Security (officially titled Old-Age, Survivors, and Disability Insurance—OASDI) with old-age retirement benefits, a significant portion of the program, labeled disability insurance (DI), makes payments to workers who claim they are too disabled to work any longer. This program is distinct from OASDI's Supplemental Security Income (SSI) program, which makes grants to the permanently mentally or physically disabled. While on paper the eligibility criteria for receiving benefits under the DI program are quite stringent, and a

Table 7.5
Growth in Disability Rolls

Year	U.S. workforce (thousands)	Disabled rolls (thousands)	Disabled as % of workforce
1970	71,006	1,493	2.1
1980	90,528	2,859	3.2
1990	109,487	3,011	2.8
2000	131,881	5,042	3.8
2007	137,645	7,099	5.2
2011	131,497	8,576	6.5

Source: Social Security Administration, Beneficiary Data.

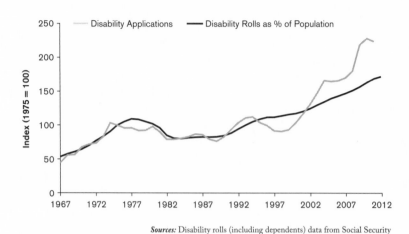

Sources: Disability rolls (including dependents) data from Social Security Administration's "Beneficiary Data." Award data from http://www.ssa.gov/oact/STATS/table6c7.html; Population data from the Census Bureau.

Fig. 7.3 Increase in Disability Rolls since 1967

host of provisions are designed to get DI beneficiaries back to work, the exponential growth in the numbers of beneficiaries and payouts over the last four decades belies their effectiveness. Between 1970 and 2011, the U.S. labor force grew by 85 percent. During that same period, the disabled rolls grew by 474 percent! Put another way: in 1970, the disabled worker rolls accounted for 2.1 percent of all workers, but by 2011, the 8.6 million who were ostensibly disabled represented over 6.5 percent of the total workforce—more than the numbers of unemployed in typical non-recession years (table 7.5 and figure 7.3). This explosive growth occurred in the face of great strides in workplace safety (the Occupational Safety and Health Act was passed in 1970, and has been rigorously enforced since then), a massive shift in jobs from strenuous and dangerous occupations to the predominantly milder work being done today, and generally improving adult health. Most alarmingly, disability enrollment has accelerated over just the last thirteen years; in 2000, the ratio of disabled to all workers was still 3.8 percent.

Clearly, something quite unwholesome is going on. The most frequently offered explanation for the recent surge of applications—which lies behind the growth in the disability rolls—is the depth of the 2008–2010 recession. Yet even in 2007, before the onset of the recession and when the unemployment rate averaged only 4.5 percent, disability awards had risen to 5.2 percent of the workforce, nearly double their level in 1990. Even aside from the obvious fact that the recession itself could not have increased workplace disability (it could only have motivated newly unemployed workers to seek disability payments), the growth of awards over the last few decades—and its acceleration in the last few years—can be ascribed to only one dynamic: a dramatic increase in disability applications, many of them fraudulent—or at least dubious—abetted by compliant doctors and other references, and approved by careless or sympathetic DI intake workers. Even more damning, it is quite evident that the numerous provisions of DI law imposed by Congress to screen out unjustified claims and to make DI recipients return to work are not being enforced; they have, effectively, become a dead letter.

There can be no doubt, notwithstanding the sensible-sounding text of DI law, that the barriers to receiving disability payments have been substantially lowered, something confirmed in the literature on Social Security disability. In a 2006 paper, researchers explained that:

> The 1984 liberalization of Disability Insurance vastly increased the complexity and subjectivity of disability screening (Social Security Advisory Board, 2001). Prior to 1984 (as discussed earlier), determinations of disability focused primarily on medical criteria and gave limited credence to non-verifiable symptoms such as pain and mental disorders. The revamped process is much more subjective, requiring the Social Security Administration to evaluate an applicant's workplace function

and the extent of pain or mental illness, to determine the ve-
racity of supporting evidence provided by the claimant, and to
give primary weight to that evidence unless it is at odds with
other information.[20]

And as the criteria for receiving disability have been loosened, applications for disability—and, concurrently, the disability rolls—
have exploded.

How bad is this state of affairs? First, the cost. In 2012, total
disability payments came to $140 billion, $31 billion more than the
DI trust fund took in and higher than the annual budget of every
U.S. state. There is also a significant additional cost not reflected
in the DI statistics: disabled workers are covered under Medicare
twenty-four months after qualifying for disability, which most
likely increases the total federal disability-related outlay by 50 percent. So, paring back the disability rolls to their historic average
could save anywhere between $86 to $136 billion per year, more
than enough to fund every human-capital investment recommended in this book.

Certainly, many applicants have legitimate disabilities: mental
illnesses or serious physical impairments that make it impossible
to work. But a great many—the majority, actually—suffer from
less acute ailments, like back pain or arthritis, that shouldn't prevent them from working; nevertheless, the relaxed disability standards put in place in 1984 and the loose standards of disability
claims examiners result in successful awards. A recent paper in the
American Economic Review demonstrated conclusively that many
disability applicants suffered from relatively minor ailments that
did not necessarily preclude working; that, regardless of their disability or its severity, most older applicants' claims (over 73 percent) were accepted; and that the impact of the program on labor
force behavior was substantial, lowering long-term employment
rates of the applicant population by over 28 percent.[21]

While this book is about human capital, not about welfare state fraud or even national budgetary stability, when it comes to the explosive growth of the disability rolls, these issues are firmly intertwined. Workers not suffering from real work-impairing ailments who use the DI program as a combination of unemployment insurance and early retirement benefit are not only cheating American taxpayers (and the truly disabled) but also squandering vast amounts of human capital.

So what can be done? If it were politically feasible, the best approach might be to borrow two ideas from welfare reform: setting specific numeric targets for reducing disability rolls (maybe tied to historic rates of disability), and encouraging the engagement of welfare-to-work contractors, with payment contingent on successful job placements. Barring that, the Social Security Administration can more strictly enforce the eligibility criteria already on the books. To curtail abuses by the not-really-disabled, for example, the agency could be authorized to conduct independent medical evaluations of disability insurance claims to root out those that are unwarranted.[22]

Less controversially, we might borrow reform ideas from a most unlikely source: countries at the heart of the European welfare state. Denmark, determined to find employment for its disabled workers, gets employers to put disabled workers into "flex jobs" that are compatible with their disability.[23] This is quite similar in intent to a recent, but largely unimplemented, change in American disability law: the Ticket to Work and Work Incentives Improvement Act adopted in 1999. Another Scandinavian welfare state, Norway, is pioneering the issuance of "partial disability" payments for those who go back to work, setting the size of benefits on a sliding scale based on the level of disability. For instance, someone receiving disability payments for back pain may be required to work a minimum number of hours per week in order to continue to qualify for the payments. The disability payments themselves are also income-adjusted—someone with a managerial job requiring little physical activity but with a high pay grade receives lower disability payments than a manual laborer. These kinds of reforms keep more individuals in the workforce, and they raise the cost of not working, since refusal to work results in the loss of both salary and disability benefits. (On the other hand, they might also increase the number of disability applicants who would pursue dual benefits available from both disability and work.) Finally, to the extent that some applicants seek disability status to. gain access to health insurance, passage of the Patient Protection and Affordable Care Act of 2010 (also known as "Obamacare") removes that incentive.

Better enforcement of current disability laws, coupled with the adoption of some reforms, can quickly stem the growth of disability rolls and restore much idle human capital to the American economy.

Unemployment Insurance The other major American public program providing income to working-age adults who are not working is unemployment insurance (UI), jointly administered by the U.S. Department of Labor and the states (under federal guidelines). The program is financed through employer payroll taxes (with a few states requiring minimum employee contributions as well) and provides up to twenty-six weeks of benefits based on a fifty-two-week earning cycle (subject to each state's maximum allowed payments). As a result of the recent recession, however, federal legislation has allowed the duration of benefits to be extended substantially, based on state unemployment rates; at the peak of the recession, unemployment benefits were paid up to ninety-nine weeks in the highest unemployment states.[24] Indeed, the recent growth in unemployment benefits has been several times greater than during previous peaks (figure 7.4).

It is hard to quarrel with the underlying rationale for unem-

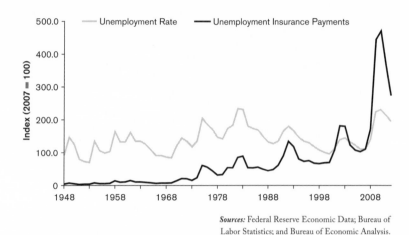

Sources: Federal Reserve Economic Data; Bureau of
Labor Statistics; and Bureau of Economic Analysis.

Fig. 7.4 Unemployment Insurance Payments Compared to Unemployment Rate

ployment insurance as an indispensable piece of the American safety net; when workers lose their jobs—through no fault of their own, as stipulated in unemployment insurance law—they should not become indigent. And when the entire American economy is in recession, especially the kind of economic meltdown we experienced between 2008 and 2010, the existence of unemployment insurance can be a godsend both in providing an income cushion for laid-off workers and in braking the downward economic spiral by sustaining some level of continued consumption.

Nevertheless, many economists claim that the very existence of unemployment stipends creates labor market distortions, and the more generous the benefits, the greater the distortion. Unemployment insurance, along with companion benefits like food stamps and Medicaid, can raise workers' "reservation wage" (the minimum wage they would accept), making them pickier in taking an available job if it doesn't pay enough, or making them complacent about looking for work even after the economy recovers. Such distortions are likely to be magnified when, as we saw between

2008 and 2012, workers become dependent on unemployment benefits for longer periods. The empirical studies on these points lead to mixed conclusions. University of Chicago economist Casey Mulligan alleges the recent extension of unemployment insurance (and the expansion in social benefits like food stamps) has contributed significantly to the sluggish jobs recovery.[25] In the same vein, a recent paper by two Stanford University graduate economics students finds that people receiving unemployment benefits tend to search for work much less frequently than those without benefits but, within a few weeks of benefits expiring, they ramp up their job search efforts.[26] Other research by Jesse Rothstein of the Brookings Institution, however, estimates that extensions of unemployment insurance contributed only marginally to increasing the unemployment rate in 2011.[27]

From a human-capital point of view, the most serious problem with unemployment insurance as it currently operates in the United States is that it effectively subsidizes idleness; maybe unwanted or unavoidable idleness, but idleness nonetheless. It is most harmful in the case of long-term unemployment. It is well documented that the longer a person is unemployed, the less "employable" they become in the future—human capital degrades over time without use. The challenge is to take the funds that government now spends underwriting idleness to subsidize work instead.

The goal, then, should be to transition the existing unemployment insurance program to a *reemployment* program. Let's look at the money involved. The estimated annual unemployment insurance outlay for 2013, for the federal and state governments combined, is $74.4 billion. With approximately 9 million former workers receiving payments, the average award per recipient is $294 a week, the equivalent of $15,300 annually. Assuming no change in the amount the United States currently spends on the program, the question becomes whether these funds can be used to subsidize work instead of idleness.

Several approaches are being tried or have been suggested. Between 2003 and 2005, Germany undertook a major revamping of unemployment policy (the so-called Hartz reforms, named after Peter Hartz, the chairman of the commission that recommended them) designed explicitly to subsidize work rather than idleness. Its two key features were, first, to require all applicants for unemployment assistance to make strenuous efforts to find work—utilizing private employment placement firms (as in the U.S. welfare-to-work initiative); and, second, to take the money it used to spend on unemployment benefits to subsidize firms to maintain their employment rolls, or to take on new workers, even in periods of slack demand. As a result, even during the ongoing European recession that has caused unemployment to rise sharply in neighboring countries, Germany's unemployment rate (after a brief uptick in 2008–2009) has steadily fallen; it is 5.4 percent today, more than two points below ours.

An American version of this approach might combine stringent work-search requirements with several kinds of employer subsidies *paid for out of unemployment insurance revenues*. For instance, at a given level of unemployment (say, 7.5 percent) employers could be eligible for "re-employment" tax credits or, alternatively, the employer share of payroll taxes could be waived for those who take on new workers.[28] It might even be worth considering a "government-as-employer-of-last-resort" policy (very much like New York City's curtailing of welfare through its Work Experience Program), assigning the unemployed to state and national AmeriCorps jobs. For those unemployed requiring job training, the largely useless federal training programs[29] should be scrapped, and their funds turned over to the states in block grants that could be used to underwrite community college tuition or contracts with welfare-to-work organizations.

DELAYING RETIREMENT: SOCIAL SECURITY

There is another large contingent of nonworking Americans to-day: those receiving retirement benefits under the U.S. Social Security old-age pension program who, nevertheless, might be both willing and able to work under the right conditions. Reiterating the fundamental premise of this chapter, a surefire way to grow American human capital is to increase labor participation; in that quest, this group should be a prime target. The challenge here is to get as many healthy older Americans as possible to delay their retirement.

The scale of enrollment and pension benefits under Social Security is enormous, dwarfing every other American safety-net initiative many times over. Almost all American workers, 161 million today, or 94 percent, are covered, and 37 million are now receiving benefits; the average annual benefit is $15,144 per year, costing the system more than $646 billion yearly.[30] The system is funded by payroll taxes levied on all American workers and their employers over the course of their working life. In 2013, the combined tax amounts to 12.4 percent of wages, split equally between employer and employee contributions. In theory, this money is held in a "trust fund" out of which benefits are paid. However, unlike a true insurance annuity, which generates payouts based on the investment return on each member's accumulated contributions, Social Security simply pays out current benefits—for both old-age pensions and disability insurance stipends—from current contributions. (A separate benefit within the disability category, SSI, is not based on lifetime earnings, but a requirement is meeting the low-income threshold.)

As not only the largest, but also the earliest piece of the American social safety net, the Social Security pension program has been an enormous success. Designed to provide income support for workers after they retire, the program has succeeded in slashing the poverty rate of the elderly. Arguably, Social Security is still the most effective element of the American welfare state. Yet it does have two serious flaws. What most concerns lawmakers today is its fiscal solvency as the demographic tsunami of baby boomers reaches retirement age. What most concerns me is that the program has encouraged millions of perfectly able-bodied "young elderly" Americans (those between sixty-two and seventy years of age) to stop working, even when they might have enjoyed and financially benefited from staying at their jobs (or finding new ones).

The simplest way to get potential retirees to keep working is to make it pay off financially. The way Social Security benefits are calculated today, that doesn't happen. Without being too tedious, here is a brief primer on how old-age benefits are calculated.

Social Security takes the average of the thirty-five highest earning years of a person's work life, and indexes them to average wages in the economy. These "indexed wages" are then run through a formula that determines each person's benefit, but with a firm dollar cap to limit the benefits of high lifetime earners (making the benefit structure progressive). This gives the typical retiree a pension roughly equal to 69 percent of their highest pre-retirement annual income.[31] Because of indexing, the "replacement rate" (the percentage of prior income replaced by Social Security) is inversely correlated with income—the higher the lifetime income, the lower the replacement rate.

Currently, the only incentive to delay receiving old-age benefits under the program is known as the delayed retirement credit.[32] For those born in 1943 or later, each year they delay retirement increases their annual benefits by 8 percent, but with no additional increases after age seventy. Until the age of sixty-nine, this is "actuarially fair" in that the pension income foregone is roughly equal to the higher payments received after retirement (assuming typical life expectancies). Those who choose to delay retirement past seventy, however, seriously lose out, both because benefit increases are capped, and because they are still hit with the payroll tax. A 2009 study by former Principal Deputy Commissioner of the Social Security Administration Andrew Biggs (now a scholar at the American Enterprise Institute) found that the typical "internal rate of return" for each extra year a potential retiree worked (the value of benefit increases minus additional taxes paid, expressed as an annual interest rate) is actually negative.[33]

As noted earlier, there would be a great human-capital gain if more seniors delayed their retirement. So, how many seniors are we talking about, and how many years of retirement postponement is feasible? Realistically, the main target demographic is the cohort that today is between sixty and sixty-four years old, numbering 17.9 million; maybe we could also entice some of the sixty-five- to seventy-four-year-olds as well; that group numbers 22.5 million. Currently, over 50 percent of those sixty-five or under retire; if that share was reduced to 40 percent, that would mean 1.8 million additional workers. By age seventy-five, over 92 percent of Americans are retired, but between sixty-five and seventy-five, we might be able to entice another 5 percent to work; that would come to another 1.1 million added to the workforce. Of course, all of this is premised on these seniors *wanting* to work. Among all those over sixty-five who *are* working, over 75 percent say they enjoy it, and not just for the income. From survey data one can also infer that approximately 15 percent of those who are not working might like to—roughly in line with the hypothetical estimates suggested above.[34]

If we really want healthy seniors to work longer, what we need to do is to change the parameters of the benefit formula. This might be a win-win for both retirees and the finances of the Social Security Trust Fund. A modest increase in the delayed retirement credit, say to 10 percent, coupled with elimination of the age seventy cap on benefit increases, should provide a strong incentive for those elderly who have jobs (or can easily find them) and who enjoy them (a large number, according to surveys) to keep on working. During the additional working years, the system gains financially in two ways: not having to pay out benefits and collecting the payroll taxes. Even if the payroll tax were waived, as some have proposed, the federal government (outside of Social Security) still benefits because of the additional income-tax revenue that is generated. Studies that have looked at various ways of enriching delayed retirement benefits indicate that such reforms could increase labor force participation of people near retirement by around 8 percent for men and 5 percent for women.[35]

Beyond introducing such a straightforward and uncontroversial reform, the simplest—but undoubtedly most politically fraught—measure would be to scale back the option of "early retirement" at age sixty-two. There is really no justification for it today. The provision was enacted (in 1956 for women and 1961 for men) out of concern that many people of that age might not be physically capable of working until the full retirement age (then sixty-five, currently sixty-seven). Yet it isn't clear that this sort of accommodation is still necessary. Since its enactment, life expectancy has risen, on average, by four years; the percentage of those between fifty and sixty-four years of age reporting fair to poor health has fallen to 16 percent, 8 percentage points less than thirty years ago; and the number of physically demanding jobs held by men has fallen from 47 percent in 1982 to 19 percent today.[36] A reasonable reform of the early-retirement threshold would be to treat it somewhat like disability; only those who can document that their health or working conditions call for it would be allowed to retire at sixty-two. With this no longer being a universal option, a compassionate compromise might permit those who really must retire prematurely to receive full (above age sixty-five) pension benefits, rather than the scaled-back amount that is currently in force.

DELAYING RETIREMENT: STATE AND LOCAL WORKERS

There is another large group of Americans who are encouraged to retire at an even much younger age than those on Social Security. That is the growing army of state and local public employees who are not only entitled to extremely generous pensions but also permitted to claim them at ages well below the national retirement norm. As of 2011, 19.4 million workers were enrolled in state and local pension systems, along with 8.6 million current retirees. The provisions of these pension systems vary considerably among different states and localities, but they do share two common design features: they are "defined-benefit" plans (guaranteeing a certain dollar level of pension payout, usually as a percentage of the employees' highest earnings), and they permit retirement after a specified number of years of service, generally around twenty-five to thirty years. Since many of these workers begin their service in their twenties, this permits them to retire as early as age fifty. They also share another characteristic: they can no longer be afforded. They are—literally, in some cases—bankrupting the places that offer them, and diverting public revenues that might otherwise be used to provide current public services, like good schools and adequate public safety.

Nevertheless, my concern here is not the fiscal plight of the jurisdictions that foolishly agreed to these pension benefits, but the waste of human capital they entail. There is a policy fix, however, that can remedy both problems—that can both motivate state and local employees to work to the normal retirement age and stabilize state and local government budgets. That is moving from a policy of defined benefit to "defined-contribution" pensions. Defined-contribution pension plans—which, incidentally, cover most American college faculty (including those in state universities)—work somewhat like 401K plans. A retirement account is established for each covered worker with a fixed rate of contributions made monthly (usually shared by employer and employee);

payouts are determined by the size of the account at the time of retirement and how the funds are invested. Most defined-contribution plans, while giving their subscribers some investment leeway, are carefully designed to minimize investment risk.

The beauty of these plans is that everyone wins: to the extent that employers contribute, they do so on a pay-as-you-go basis, with no overhang of liability for past retirees, assuring fiscal stability. Employees win because they can change jobs without jeopardizing their vested benefits and accumulate a sizable retirement nest egg that they can live on as an annuity, or use for other purposes (like buying a retirement home, paying for their grandchildren's college education, or as a bequest to their heirs). But the most important benefit from a human-capital standpoint is that the longer they work, the fatter their account becomes, and thus the larger their retirement income will be.

Despite the unassailable logic behind defined-contribution pensions, which are the norm for most private employees and most college faculty, they are strenuously resisted by public employee unions, even if they were only to apply to new hires. Nevertheless, as an increasing number of American states and localities face fiscal Armageddon paying their former employees' pensions, and as some—like Riverside, California, and Central Falls, Rhode Island—escape this burden by going bankrupt, defined-benefit pension plans will become obsolete, and defined-contribution ones will take their place. Even more than its promotion of sensible public finance, by encouraging millions of the affected workers to work longer, this will engender another confirmation of America's work ethic and another boon for America's stock of human capital.

SUMMING UP

This chapter has highlighted the fact that only when they are working, are Americans actually utilizing their hard-earned human capital. The corollary is that one of the most direct ways of *increasing* American human capital is to have more Americans working. This obvious point is often lost in the welter of public policies that affect whether people work or not. While the United States has one of the highest human-capital stocks in the developed world, at least in part because Americans work more than the citizens of other countries, this particular comparative advantage may not persist for much longer. We have a number of policies, all part of the national "safety net" and most directly or indirectly under the jurisdiction of the federal government, that pay people not to work. They may be compassionate, and their rationales may be plausible, but our disability, unemployment insurance, and old-age pension programs are mostly structured in ways that discourage employment and motivate potential workers to rely on public stipends instead. The prevailing assumption is that the design of these programs is immutable; that it is unreasonable to expect any of their beneficiaries to work. That assumption has been questioned here, along with suggestions on how, with reasonable reforms, all might be recast so that millions more Americans can rejoin the workforce—to their benefit and the country's. Reforming these programs, with the goal of maximizing the incentives to work, is crucial to maintaining America's competitive edge.

CHAPTER EIGHT ....

Importing
Smart Americans

....

As shown in the previous chapters, in building a smart society, one rich in human capital, the United States was one of the first countries in the world to give all its children access to education; to enable large numbers of its young adults to attend college; to apply the latest technology in its farms, factories, and shops; and to foster a culture that generously rewarded high work effort and skill. Yet another way that the United States has led the world in building human capital—the subject of this chapter—is its warm welcome to immigrants and its success in making them, in every way, fully assimilated Americans.

Taking in immigrants has always been among the most important ways the United States added to its human capital, a fact insufficiently appreciated, not only by anti-immigrant nativists, but even by many of those who say they favor greater investment in human capital. As the United States has grown and prospered, immigrants have been absolutely indispensable in settling the country, tilling its farms, manning its factories and offices, policing its streets, teaching in its schools, and preaching in its churches. Immigrants have built America's major industries, designed its utility infrastructure, made and acted in its movies, contributed to its literature and fine arts, led the way in scientific and techno-logical discoveries, and often governed the country, holding every political and judicial office except the presidency.

It is not just the scale of its immigration that makes the United States unique. Immigration has taken place throughout human history in every corner of the globe, and continues to do so today. What differs widely is how well immigrants are integrated into the life of the countries they settle in—and it is in this singu-lar aspect that the United States *is* unique. The conceptual foun-dation, the social "glue" as it were, of almost every other country in the world (with very few exceptions) is a common ethnic and/or religious heritage. Invariably, most migrants to most coun-tries do *not* share the ethnic or religious heritage of the natives they are joining. And everywhere that has spelled trouble, so much so that it has canceled out much of the human-capital benefit that immigration might otherwise bring. Nevertheless, because *our* social glue is a heritage of civic values, enshrined in our history and founding documents, *every* new wave of immigrants—even the most disparate—has with time been successfully assimilated, and thus significantly enriched America's stock of human capital.

Undeniably, the United States has not been spared bouts of rampant nativism or instances of anti-immigrant bigotry in places where new immigrants were most heavily concentrated, especially when immigration volume was high or the immigrants were suf-ficiently different from the earlier settlers. As discussed later in the chapter, the most serious of these nativist episodes occurred at the turn of the last century and led to the adoption of restrictive im-migration laws in the 1920s. Nevertheless, the country has always been able to get past these lapses in its pro-immigration heritage, and immigrants of every wave have come to see themselves, and be accepted as, Americans. Nativism's most regrettable legacy was the restrictive legislation it triggered, but even that came to be significantly liberalized with the passage of time. Thus, immigration has proven to be an unalloyed boon for the smart society of the United States, an absolutely essential leg of its human-capital tripod.

IMMIGRATION DIVERSITY AND ASSIMILATION

Except for true Native Americans, the United States has indeed always been, as Americans proudly assert, a "nation of immigrants." What is insufficiently appreciated is how continuous the pace and diverse the mix of immigration has been. In characterizing diversity it is important to consider that this is always in the eyes of those already here—themselves of course immigrants or their descendants. Most Americans today probably believe that Americans of English ancestry—the legendary WASPs (white Anglo-Saxon Protestants)—were dominant until the end of the nineteenth century, when the waves of eastern and southern Europeans arrived. In fact, true WASPs (as opposed to northern European whites generally) lost their demographic ascendency well before 1850 (the earliest accurate census of the foreign-born) as a result of large waves of immigration from Roman Catholic Ireland and from Germany. By 1850, when the U.S. population included over 2.2 million foreign-born residents (9.7 percent of the total), over three times as many had been born in Ireland, and twice as many had been born in Germany than had arrived from England. By 1890, even Scandinavians significantly outnumbered the English. Today these may seem to be small ethnic distinctions, but in the nineteenth century such affiliations of national origin and religion loomed as divisively in Europe as any ethnic differences roiling the world today. So ethnic diversity—by the standards of the time—has been a feature of U.S. life from the very beginning. By the end of the nineteenth century, the United States experienced a quantum increase in immigration and an even more varied mix from the viewpoint of that time (tables 8.1 and 8.2).

The key to the success of American immigration, given its diversity, has been its remarkable record of assimilation. In popular usage, most people define *assimilation* as meaning that immigrants largely abandon their ethnic cultural folkways and take on *the behaviors* of the natives they are joining; in other words, that they become largely indistinguishable, except perhaps in skin color or other physical features. This, over time, may happen almost everywhere that immigrants settle, but it is not really assimilation—it is *acculturation* and it has proven to be absolutely no barrier to anti-immigrant prejudice or interethnic conflict and polarization. America has been fortunate to achieve *true* assimilation (often with limited acculturation) predicated on immigrants signing onto America's bedrock values and, in turn, Americans accepting immigrants as full members of the national family while taking a tolerant view of their cultural idiosyncrasies.

Table 8.1

Pace of Immigration, 1820–2011

Year	New immigrants	As % of population
1820	8,385	0.09
1850	369,980	1.60
1880	457,257	0.91
1910	1,041,570	1.13
1940	70,756	0.05
1970	373,326	0.18
1990	1,535,872	0.62
2000	841,002	0.30
2011	1,062,040	0.34

Source: U.S. Department of Homeland Security, Yearbook of Immigration Statistics.

As I wrote in 1997:

American assimilation owes its power to four unique aspects of American society: 1) the liberal, universalist ideas embedded in the U.S. Constitution; 2) . . . an economy built on market

Table 8.2

Foreign-Born Population by Nation of Origin

Nation of birth	1850	1880	1910	1930	1960	1990	2011
					Nation of birth as % of foreign-born		
England	12.4	9.9	6.5	5.7	5.4	2.4	–
Ireland	42.8	27.8	10.0	5.2	3.5	0.9	–
Germany	26.0	29.4	17.1	11.3	10.2	3.6	–
Scandinavia	0.8	6.6	10.2	8.9	5.4	1.1	–
Italy	0.2	0.7	9.9	12.6	12.9	2.9	–
Poland/Russia	0.1	0.5	8.8	8.1	7.1	1.7	–
China	0.0	1.6	0.4	0.3	1.0	2.7	5.6
Other Asia	0.0	0.0	1.0	1.6	4.0	22.5	22.7
Mexico	0.6	1.0	1.6	4.5	5.9	21.7	29.3
Other Latin America	0.3	0.3	0.4	1.1	3.4	20.8	23.8
Total foreign-born (thousands)	2,244	6,680	13,516	14,204	9,738	19,767	39,956

Source: U.S. Bureau of the Census.

capitalism; 3) the density and redundancy of organizational life—governmental, political, religious, social, economic, and philanthropic; and 4) a persistent, society-wide [commitment to] modernity and progress. Each factor by itself is assimilationist. Together, they make assimilation irresistible.

. . . By allowing all immigrants to become citizens after a brief residence and a painless apprenticeship, the United States has offered them formal membership in the American community. Finally, as the practical embodiment of universally cherished, if often breached, principles of civic idealism embodied in the "American Idea," the U.S. political system has served as a compelling philosophical rallying point for all Americans.[1]

This subjective assessment of America's success in assimilating its immigrants is supported empirically by some recent studies. Jacob Vigdor, a leading scholar of assimilation, has developed an index of assimilation, by immigrant nationality and country, based on three indicators: economic, civic, and cultural (equivalent to acculturation). In a 2007 study, looking at assimilation trends from 1980 to 2007, he found that most immigrants who entered the United States during this period displayed extremely high rates of assimilation, with some variation depending on their nationality or indicator.[2] Looking at another gauge of assimilation, the rate of naturalization for immigrant cohorts from 1900 to 2007, Vigdor shows that, for most nationalities, after twenty years three-quarters of all immigrants become citizens, a very high number.[3] In another study, using a different methodology, Vigdor compares assimilation levels among a number of European countries, the United States, and Canada. Except for Canada (whose immigration policy is reviewed later in this chapter) and Portugal, the United States scored highest in Vigdor's International Assimilation Index.

However, America's singular assimilation track record should not be taken for granted. The twin pillars on which it has rested are the rigor with which the country's constitutional framework has outlawed all discrimination based on ethnic distinctions, and the strong expectation on the part of most Americans, native and foreign-born alike, that immigrants should and will assimilate. Both of these pillars are being undermined by a currently fashionable but misguided ethos of "multiculturalism" that fosters ethnic particularism (in the name of "protecting heritages") and that is indifferent—even hostile—to the notion of assimilation.

One of the associated casualties of multiculturalism has been indifference to immigrants' English-language proficiency. How well adult immigrants speak English depends primarily on prior English instruction in their home country (which can be specified as part of immigration policy), but the proficiency of their *children* depends on what happens in America's schools. Therefore it is critically important that they are rapidly immersed in English in school (through ESL if needed), and not isolated and held back in the "bilingual" instruction programs so popular with multiculturalists.

THE HISTORY OF AMERICAN IMMIGRATION
For most of American history, from the time of Columbus until 1882, immigration to the United States (and before Independence, the American colonies) was totally unrestricted. Furthermore, with the passage of the Naturalization Act of 1790, all who came could quickly become U.S. citizens, with all the constitutionally guaranteed rights and privileges of the native-born. The first specific restriction on immigration (aside from nineteenth-century laws that permitted the deportation of criminals, "lunatics," and other "undesirables") was the Chinese Exclusion Act of 1882. This legislation, triggered by popular hysteria in California after the

importation of Chinese laborers to build the western leg of the Transcontinental Railroad, suspended Chinese immigration for ten years, kept those Chinese already in the country from becoming citizens, and authorized the deportation of any who entered the United States illegally.

With the arrival of Chinese railroad workers and millions of eastern and southern Europeans at the end of the nineteenth and the early decades of the twentieth century, more comprehensive restrictions on immigration entered the picture. The Immigration Act of 1891 created a Bureau of Immigration in the Treasury Department—a precursor to the later enforcement of immigration quotas. The Naturalization Act of 1906 moved immigration oversight to the Department of Commerce and tightened naturalization requirements, including making knowledge of English a condition for achieving citizenship. The movement to further limit immigration—especially of the newer or more exotic nationalities—gained increasing force after 1900, and by the 1920s achieved its goals of putting a numerical ceiling on overall immigration volume and introducing an overtly discriminatory "national origins" quota system heavily biased in favor of northern European nationalities, which was driven by racist notions that mainly targeted groups that today are unambiguously classified as "white."

These principles were embodied in three pieces of legislation enacted in the 1920s. The Emergency Quota Act of 1921 capped immigration at 350,000 annually, setting a quota for each non–Western Hemisphere country of 3 percent of the people with that ancestry living in the United States in 1910. Immigration from Canada, Latin America, and the Caribbean was exempt from these limits. The National Origins Act of 1924 was more restrictive. It reduced the overall cap to 165,000, and lowered the per-country ceiling to 2 percent from each nationality—with no Western Hemisphere exemption. The 1924 law was modified in 1929, restoring the exemption for immigrants from the Americas, but requiring all immigrants to obtain visas from an American consulate in their country before they entered the United States. Restrictionist immigration laws remained in force for another three-and-a-half decades.

It took a few years for these laws to have their full impact, but by 1932, new immigration had come to a virtual halt: those potential immigrants who would have liked to come to the United States were disqualified; the English, Scottish, Scandinavians, and Canadians who would have been allowed were by now comfortable in their homelands. And in a particularly outrageous interpretation of the immigration laws, a very numerous cohort of Germans who desperately sought to enter, and would have been permitted to do so under the quota system, were barred because they were Jewish.[4]

As it turned out, the immigration laws of the 1920s and their implementation in the 1930s were a disaster. They violated the national smart-society blueprint on which American prosperity and social harmony had rested for centuries; they deprived the United States of a generation of industrious and often brilliant new citizens; and, without question, they seriously exacerbated the economic collapse of the Great Depression.[5] There is a clear object lesson in this experience. When America abandons its immigration heritage, the third leg of its human-capital tripod, it rapidly becomes a less smart society, and ends up paying a great price in all manner of economic and social hardship.

After World War II, the country saw the last hurrah of virulent immigration restrictionism (coupled with racism) with the passage of the Immigration and Nationality Act of 1952 (the McCarran-Walter Act), which further limited the national quotas to one-sixth of one percent (of those in the United States in 1920). A little more than a decade later, however, America's historic optimism regarding immigration—and tolerance of ethnic diversity—was at least partially restored with adoption of the Hart-Celler Act in 1965 (sponsored by Senator Philip Hart of Michigan and Representative Emanuel Celler of New York), which dropped the national origins quota system in favor of regional quota ceilings—170,000 per year from the Eastern Hemisphere (with a 20,000 per country limit) and 120,000 for the Western Hemisphere.

Over the five decades after Hart-Celler's adoption, the United States has seen the greatest surge of immigration since the turn of the last century (table 8.3). In 2010, the foreign-born

Table 8.3

U.S. Population by Nativity (U.S. or foreign), 1850–2000

Year	Total	Native-born	Percent	Foreign-born	Percent
2010	308,745,538	268,363,964	86.9	40,381,574	13.1
2000	281,421,906	250,314,017	88.9	31,107,889	11.1
1990	248,709,873	228,942,557	92.1	19,767,316	7.9
1980	226,545,805	212,465,899	93.8	14,079,906	6.2
1970	203,210,158	193,590,856	95.3	9,619,302	4.7
1960	179,325,671	169,587,580	94.6	9,738,091	5.4
1950	150,216,110	139,868,715	93.1	10,347,395	6.9
1940	131,669,275	120,074,379	91.2	11,594,896	8.8
1930	122,775,046	108,570,897	88.4	14,204,149	11.6
1920	105,710,620	91,789,928	86.8	13,920,692	13.2
1910	91,972,266	78,456,380	85.3	13,515,886	14.7
1900	75,994,575	65,653,299	86.4	10,341,276	13.6
1890	62,622,250	53,372,703	85.2	9,249,547	14.8
1880	50,155,783	43,475,840	86.7	6,679,943	13.3
1870	38,558,371	32,991,142	85.6	5,567,229	14.4
1860	31,443,321	27,304,624	86.8	4,138,697	13.2
1850*	23,191,876	20,947,274	90.3	2,244,602	9.7

Source: U.S. Bureau of the Census.

*Data do not include the national origins of slaves.

population as a share of the total was over 13 percent, the highest level since 1920. This great immigrant influx has, for the most part, been enormously beneficial. It has clearly profited the American economy across many industries, and it has enriched the country's social fabric, culture, arts, and even its cuisine. Most strikingly, the new immigrants have dramatically revitalized the cities in which they settled. (Conversely, the cities bypassed by immigration have languished.)

Nevertheless, in one respect the new framework abandoned one restrictive criterion (national/ethnic origin) only to impose another, giving overwhelming preference to family members of citizens and legal immigrants. Just as the design of the earlier limits deprived the United States of millions of talented immigrants, so has the design of Hart-Celler and its successor laws. Ironically, the family preferences of these laws—in combination with another of their features, geographic ceilings—have also prevented millions of poor Mexicans and Central Americans from entering the United States legally—so they have come illegally instead.

That problem became the central focus of the Immigration Reform and Control Act (IRCA) of 1986, sponsored by Senator Alan Simpson of Wyoming and Representative Romano Mazzoli of Kentucky. This legislation was designed to address illegal immigration by granting amnesty to existing illegal immigrants while curtailing the influx of future ones through penalties on employers who "knowingly" hired them. While the amnesty did bring three million or so existing illegal immigrants out of the shadows, IRCA did little to reform the immigration system more substantively, and the failure to enforce its employer penalties haunts the development of enlightened immigration policy to this day. Although it established temporary visas for seasonal agricultural workers, the law's most serious deficiency was that it did not liberalize the rules for new *legal* immigration—a serious impediment for the American labor market, and virtually a prescription for new illegal immigrants entering the country and for employers hiring them despite the sanctions.

Immigration law today is largely determined by the provisions of the Immigration Act of 1990 (with some minor modifications enacted since then). That legislation substantially raised overall annual immigration quotas, setting them at 700,000 for 1991–92, and 675,000 thereafter. It established four broad categories under which immigrants can be admitted. Under the general rubric of "family reunification," the law allows in immediate relatives of American citizens (with no set annual visa limit) and other relatives of citizens and lawful permanent residents with annual visa caps; under employment-based quotas, it admits high-skilled (H-1B) and low-skilled (H-2B) immigrants sponsored by potential employers, as well as "priority workers," professionals, and entrepreneurs; it provides for victims of persecution in modest quotas for refugees and asylum seekers; and under the heading of "other humanitarian" considerations, it offers a Diversity Visa lottery for individuals outside of all the other visa categories.

Aside from these admission categories and visa quotas, the law sets per-country ceilings that limit the number of immigrants from any one nation to 7 percent of the total, or roughly 50,000. The diversity quota itself is subject to a 7 percent per-country cap, meaning the quota for any country can't exceed 3,500. The detailed rules of current immigration law are summarized in the appendix, and actual current admissions under each category are shown in table 8.4.

Since 2007, Congress and the president (first George W. Bush, now Barack Obama) have been wrestling with legislation to comprehensively recast American immigration policy. All of the reform ideas swirling around Washington center on three themes: securing the border (i.e., keeping new illegal immigrants from entering the United States), legalizing the status of the 11 million or so illegal immigrants already here, and expanding or altering the quotas for admission of new immigrants. The specific design of these proposals and their impact on America's human capital will be discussed later in this chapter.

As table 8.4 shows, current immigration rules—still based on quotas set in the 1990 legislation—are overwhelmingly skewed toward family reunification. Theoretically, annual immigration volume is still subject to the ceiling of 675,000 set in 1990, but because immediate family members of American citizens and asylum seekers are not counted toward the cap, the actual number of

Table 8.4

Allocation of U.S. Immigration Visas by Class of Admission, 2007–11

Visa category	Total	Percent
All Family-based	**3,532,569**	**65.5**
Immediate relatives/citizens	2,448,529	45.4
Other relatives (family sponsored)	1,084,040	20.1
Unmarried adult children	127,293	2.4
Immediate relatives/LPRs	488,880	9.1
Married adult children/citizens	136,335	2.5
Adult siblings/citizens	331,532	6.1
All Employment-based*	**755,059**	**14.0**
Priority workers	170,605	3.2
Professionals	280,537	5.2
Skilled workers	251,309	4.7
Special immigrants	40,934	0.8
Employment creators	11,674	0.2
Refugees/asylum seekers	**784,656**	**14.5**
Diversity Lottery	**231,633**	**4.3**
TOTAL	**5,395,024**	**100.0**

Source: U.S. Department of Homeland Security, Citizen and Immigration Services.

*Number includes employees and their family members.

annual immigrants is slightly over a million, and has been (with some yearly fluctuations) for the last decade. Between 2007 and 2011, over 65 percent of all visas—688,000—were allocated on the basis of family connections, either for immediate family members of citizens (spouses, young children, or parents), or under the group of "family preference" categories set aside for immediate relatives of legal aliens and less close relatives of citizens. Even so, because of overall and per-country caps, there is still a multiyear backlog of eligible applicants. As of May 2013, for certain classes of Mexican immigrants, the waiting time to obtain a visa is estimated to be over *twenty years*,[6] a product of the per-country quota limits.

Meanwhile, the quota for individuals coming to *work* in America—employment-based immigration—is the least-favored visa category, accounting for 14 percent of all arrivals from 2007 to 2011. It peaked at 22 percent of the total in 2005, but has since fallen to around 13 percent in 2011. Even refugees and asylum seekers do better, accounting for 14.5 percent of legal entrants over the same period. Finally, as a sop to millions of otherwise ineligible applicants, 50,000 visas are issued under a Diversity Visa lottery (commonly referred to as the "Green Card lottery").

THE GOAL OF AMERICAN IMMIGRATION POLICY IS . . . ?

In 1883, Emma Lazarus famously wrote the sonnet "The New Colossus," part of which (italicized below) is inscribed at the base of the Statue of Liberty:

Not like the brazen giant of Greek fame,
With conquering limbs astride from land to land;
Here at our sea-washed, sunset gates shall stand
A mighty woman with a torch, whose flame
Is the imprisoned lightning, and her name
Mother of Exiles. From her beacon-hand
Glows world-wide welcome; her mild eyes command

The air-bridged harbor that twin cities frame.
"Keep, ancient lands, your storied pomp!" cries she
With silent lips. *"Give me your tired, your poor,*
Your huddled masses yearning to breathe free,
The wretched refuse of your teeming shore.
Send these, the homeless, tempest-tossed to me,
I lift my lamp beside the golden door!"

The poem and its evocative inscription suggest that the most compelling rationale for American immigration is to offer refuge to all those unhappy in their homelands who want to come. This may have been the reality, but certainly not the intention, of U.S. immigration policy—or more accurately non-policy—back in the days when entry into the country was unrestricted. With open borders, the United States had no immigration policy, or a need for one. We assumed that immigrants, wherever they came from and for whatever reason they came, would both work out and fit in—and they did. Even then, given the enormous cost of crossing the ocean, it was only the strongest and smartest of potential émigrés who made it to the American shores, so that the United States in fact attracted the world's best and brightest immigrants without even trying.

However, once we began seriously setting limits on numbers of immigrants in the early twentieth century, we also had to establish criteria as to whom to admit. The earliest criteria, as outlined earlier, based as they were on ethnic prejudice, were both outrageous and, from a human-capital perspective, counterproductive. Yet we have never fully laid out any coherent *alternative* admissions criteria. In the name of compassion—and in response to a vocal political constituency—current immigration law heavily favors admitting relatives of American citizens and legal residents in what is euphemistically referred to as "family reunification." To the extent that all immigration generates some human-capital benefit, it also does so under this policy. And current law does make a few explicit concessions to human-capital considerations and labor market needs at opposite ends of the skills spectrum: allowing in a limited number of extremely low-skilled workers, primarily to work in agriculture and other low-wage occupations, and an equally limited number of highly skilled immigrants to work in advanced technology industries. In the midst of this, current law makes a modest bow in the direction of Emma Lazarus by way of small quotas for refugees from persecution and the lucky winners of a visa lottery.

American immigration policy—especially with respect to quotas and preferences—needn't be so incoherent. While immigration almost always raises the stock of American human capital, regardless of the backgrounds of specific immigrants, the *extent* to which that happens is dependent on the contours of immigration policy. There are at least six admissions criteria to consider.

Education and Skills Admitting immigrants who already have substantial education and/or training is probably the fastest and surest way to raise America's stock of human capital. Making those investments at home—the subject of chapters 2 through 5—while absolutely essential, is costly and often problematical. Schooling takes anywhere from twelve to twenty-plus years; it costs anywhere from $10,000 to $25,000 per person per year in the United States today, and is not always successful. Therefore, given the enormous embedded value of education and training, the more of it a potential immigrant brings, the greater the human capital that is being "imported." There is another bonus in admitting better-educated immigrants. Their *children* are more likely to become well-educated or skilled; children's success in school and beyond is more closely correlated to parents' education than any other single variable. The bottom line: educational and skills attainment should be the dominant admissions criterion, ideally accounting for the majority of all new immigrants. One way to start, already rooted in various congressional proposals, is to give Green Cards to every foreign student graduating from an American college or university. What else might we look for?

Fluency in English Fluency in English makes employment and success on the job more likely. It accelerates assimilation. It helps in bringing up children. It speeds the path to citizenship and participation in civic affairs. It should be made an immigration admissions criterion.

Work Experience Chapters 6 and 7 stressed the importance of human-capital development in the workplace, and one of the ways that workplaces do this is through the on-the-job-training and experience they give their workers. So allowing in immigrants who already have substantial work experience makes sense.

Willingness to Work at Jobs That Native-Born Americans No Longer Want to Do One of the most frequently cited rationales for allowing immigration, not only in the United States, but everywhere in the world, is the need for workers to do undesirable jobs. It looms large for menial agricultural work like crop picking, animal slaughtering, landscape gardening, household cleaning and child care, cleaning in general—the list is endless. The rationale for bringing in immigrants to take these kinds of jobs seems compelling, but there are also serious downsides to consider. Such immigrants usually can't speak English, have greater difficulty functioning in the community, take more time to assimilate (or never do), and may become indigent. Often overlooked is what happens to many of their children. Living as they do in poor neighborhoods (even if they can afford something better, because they want to send money to relatives back home) and influenced by delinquent peers, their children may do badly in school, get in trouble outside of school, experiment with drugs, or become teenage mothers. A common pattern is that these children quickly assimilate to the worst behaviors of their American friends and just as quickly lose their parents' strong work ethic.

How do we square this circle? We think we need low-skilled immigrants to take the economy's most undesirable jobs; yet the associated problems cancel out much of the human-capital benefit. We need to reexamine the underlying premise. A high-human-capital economy with an educated and skilled labor force can get its low-end work done in a number of ways. The most desirable adaptation is to have it done by machines. America has been doing that for two centuries, from the farm machinery of the nineteenth century that eliminated over 90 percent of the most tedious farm labor to the washing machines, vacuum cleaners, and dishwashers that ended the engagement of full-time household help. Not all low-end jobs can be eliminated this way, but many—if not a majority—can, especially when it comes to farm work. For most of the remaining jobs that can't be mechanized, there is another alternative—pay more. The conventional wisdom that American workers won't take menial or unpleasant jobs is largely untrue; they just won't take them at rock-bottom wages. Most low-end jobs can and will be done by native-born workers if they pay enough. So what does this mean for immigration policy? Keep quotas for low-end workers to a minimum.

Family Ties in the United States Family ties are the dominant criterion in current immigration policy. This preference undoubtedly makes immigrants and their American relatives happy, a not unimportant humane—and political—consideration. Perhaps it also speeds immigrants' social and psychological adjustment, eases their financial transition, and facilitates their access to housing, social services, and job references. But its human-capital benefit is random and uncertain, depending on each immigrant's background. So it is a valid immigration policy consideration but shouldn't, as it is currently, be paramount. As to numbers, unless we decide to increase overall immigration beyond the million or so that we currently admit, the family reunification quotas will have to be scaled back.

Refugees and Asylum Seekers Remembering Emma Lazarus, what should we do for those who face political persecution or severe hardship in their home countries? As a moral obligation and part of our commitment in international conventions, we must continue to admit refugees and asylum seekers; there may even be a human-capital benefit, because many of these immigrants are well educated or talented. The relatively modest quotas in place today are just about right.

Finally, we should reconsider the process by which immigrants are admitted. Ever since the introduction of immigration restrictions and quotas, almost all potential immigrants have had to be "sponsored" by either families or employers (see the appendix). We may want to seriously consider going back to a system of "self-sponsorship," whereby immigrant applicants can petition for admission directly under one of the visa categories without relying on relatives or businesses—just as students apply to be admitted to a college. This was certainly the case when immigration was unrestricted, and it is a prominent feature of Canada's successful immigration law, described below. One of the stated reasons for requiring sponsorship has been to prevent indigence, since sponsors must guarantee some level of financial support for their applicants. However, indigence should not be a concern in admitting educated, skilled, or experienced immigrants, so they at least should be allowed to apply directly, without an intermediary. Even in the other categories, self-sponsorship might be permitted because there is little evidence that sponsors have ever actually provided much of a financial backstop for poorer immigrants. Aside from simplifying the process, self-sponsorship reinforces the notion of immigrant initiative rather than dependency.

WHAT TO DO ABOUT ILLEGAL IMMIGRATION

The IRCA legislation of 1986 was supposed to end the problem of illegal immigration once and for all with two strands of policy: legalizing the status of most illegal immigrants present at the time, about 3 million, and imposing stringent sanctions on employers if they hired undocumented workers. Clearly, the legislation failed in its objective; today the United States is estimated to be home to 10 to 12 million illegal immigrants, about half of them adult workers, the rest nonworking dependents and children.

Failure can be attributed mainly to the inability or unwillingness of the federal government to keep employers from hiring illegal immigrants. The harsh truth is that many employers, and the business community generally, never had any intention of observing the law, and from the time of the law's adoption until quite recently, the government didn't care. In the early pre-Internet period, enforcement was difficult in any case, because there was no easy way to identify violators. In the last two decades, however, the online data systems of the Social Security Administration and the Department of Homeland Security have made it possible to catch at least two-thirds of all unauthorized hires.[7] Even feeble attempts to do this, however, have been met with howls of protest from business and immigrant advocacy groups.

After three decades of complacency, the issue of how to deal with illegal immigration—past, present, and future—has come to dominate the entire immigration policy debate. Clearly, having millions of illegal immigrants remain essentially "stateless," without civil rights and in constant fear of deportation, cannot continue indefinitely. Hispanic advocacy groups, churches, and businesses dependent on immigrant labor have long fought to give illegal immigrants a path to legal status and eventual citizenship. On the other side are millions of Americans who are outraged by the presence of illegal immigrants, either out of nativist sentiment or because they believe we should not condone law-breaking. They call legalization "amnesty" (which is indeed how it was characterized in IRCA); instead they want illegal immigrants deported, or, if that is not feasible, kept in their present limbo.

Trying to break this impasse, in an update of the IRCA formulation, a 2007 bipartisan immigration reform initiative in the U.S. Senate, sponsored by Senators McCain, Kyl, and Kennedy and supported by President George W. Bush, proposed a path to legalization of most currently illegal residents, together with stringent measures to curtail future illegal entry, including more rigorous employee verification measures and stiffer employer sanctions. The legalization provision, however, was the bill's downfall. As I am writing, legislation similar in outline to the 2007 bill—but with more stringent border security measures—has once again been taken up by the Senate, and this time passed. Its fate in the House of Representatives is as yet unclear.

If American immigration policy is to be effectively reformed it must address the issue of illegal immigration in both its key dimensions. Future illegal immigration must be substantially curbed, even if it might never be stopped altogether. Even more important, the current illegal population must be put on a path to legalization. Both are key human-capital concerns. From a human-capital perspective, future illegal entrants should be barred because they have the lowest human-capital endowments and turning a blind eye to their entry makes a mockery of legal immigration quotas. But also from a human-capital perspective, if we pull this population out of its legal limbo, adults working illegally can become more productive and free to better themselves, and their children (about half of the total illegal population) will more easily acquire education and skills. This latter point goes to the heart of our attempts to raise American human capital through higher education (discussed in chapter 5). While currently a great many undocumented young Americans are going to college or acquiring specialized training despite their immigration status, there can be no question that the number doing so would explode if the cloud of illegality were lifted. In addition, sheer humanity and our democratic heritage demand that we can't let millions of fellow Americans live among us without any rights.

LEARNING FROM OUR NORTHERN NEIGHBOR

If we want to see an immigration policy explicitly geared to maximizing human capital, we need only look over our northern border to find a place that pretty much gets it right.

Canada, which more self-consciously bases its immigration policy on human-capital considerations, has instituted an immigration admissions system very different from that of the United States (figure 8.1). Of the 736,000 immigrants entering that country from 2007 to 2009 (a larger immigrant cohort, relatively, than that of the United States), 60 percent were admitted because of superior education or skills, 27 percent based on family ties, and 10 percent because they faced persecution. Canada's immigration admission criteria—what they call "independent" immigration—are based on a merit point system, aspects of which were incorporated in the U.S. Senate's stillborn 2007 initiative. Under Canada's rules, to be admitted an immigrant must compile at least 67 points, which can be accumulated on the basis of education (25), work experience (21), employer sponsorship (10), knowledge of English or French (English only: 16, French only: 8, both 24), at least two years of Canadian college, or marriage to an educated spouse (10 each).[8]

Canada's policy differs from ours in another critical way: under the point system, immigrants are not dependent on having

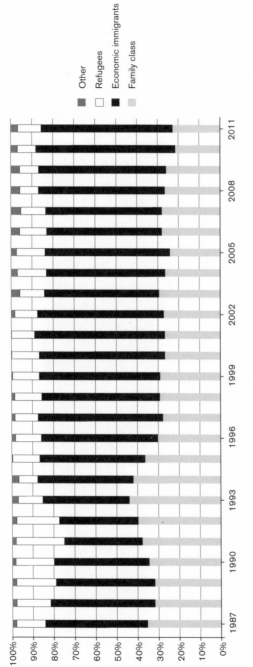

Legend:
■ Other
□ Refugees
■ Economic immigrants
▨ Family class

Source: Citizenship and Immigration Canada, http://www.cic.gc.ca/
english/resources/statistics/facts2011/permanent/01.asp.

Fig. 8.1 Canadian Immigration by Admissions Category

a sponsor to be considered for admission. Immigrants sponsor themselves, with success dependent on the accumulation of points under the criteria just noted. If they meet a certain point threshold, they are admitted to Canada as permanent residents. Like current policy in the United States, the Canadian system also allocates some slots for family members as well as for refugees. For the most part, however, immigrants to Canada enter as human-capital migrants, bringing with them the kinds of skills and talents that Canadians most value today. No immigrant is tied to any particular job, and no underclass of "temporary" or "seasonal" workers exists to placate a particular industry or interest group.[9]

The result is that among immigrants to Canada today, 55 percent have college degrees, 82 percent speak a Canadian language well, their household incomes exceed $50,000, and over 70 percent become citizens.[10] In comparison, among current legal U.S. immigrants, only 26 percent have completed college, 47 percent speak English well, household incomes average under $40,000, and only 40 percent seek citizenship.[11]

AMERICAN IMMIGRATION REFORM TODAY—MAYBE

Given the enormous importance of immigration—and deciding which immigrants to admit—it is most encouraging that we may finally be on the verge of adopting a coherent, human-capital-oriented national immigration policy. As noted earlier, a bipartisan bill to reform American immigration policy was proposed in 2007, only to die because of bitter disagreement in Congress over what to do about current illegal immigrants. As of this writing, the U.S. Senate has passed a bill along the same lines, addressing many of the issues raised in this chapter. Its provisions for new immigrants are far more geared to human-capital concerns than present law and, by putting to rest the polarizing issue of illegal immigration—past and future—it indirectly generates additional human-capital benefit. Reviewing the bill's fine print, one might quarrel with its mix of quotas and several other provisions, but overall it is probably as good an immigration policy as one could hope for, given the issue's complexity, Washington partisan gridlock, and competing constituency interests (immigrant advocates, business, labor, and "Tea Party" opponents of illegal immigrant "amnesty").

Although the bill is heavily weighted with text addressing illegal immigration, it provides four major reforms to *legal* immigration.

It increases the quotas for high-skilled workers with the following provisions:

The quota for high-skilled workers (H-1B) is raised from 65,000 currently to 110,000, with 25,000 more set aside for applicants with advanced degrees in science and engineering. Based on "need," the cap could be raised further to 180,000. Unfortunately, the legislation also includes an economically foolish proviso (included under pressure from labor unions) that immigrants brought in under this quota must be paid according to a scale set by the Secretary of Labor, presumably to ensure that they do not take jobs away from American workers in these fields.

There is an open-ended visa category for immigrants with "extraordinary abilities" (defined as Ph.D. holders, executives, and athletes) who, along with foreign-born graduates of American universities with science and technology job offers, are exempt from the high-skilled cap.

Most significantly, following Canadian precedent, a quota of 250,000 "merit visas" are made available under a point system that awards points on the basis of education, employment, and other considerations.

Foreign entrepreneurs seeking to establish a business in the United States can be admitted under a new visa category.

The Diversity Visa lottery is eliminated.

Low-skilled workers in construction, long-term care, hospitality, and other industries are admitted under a new visa category (W) of 200,000.

Family immigration preferences are altered, leaving the likely total relatively unchanged: Citizens can no longer sponsor siblings or married children over age thirty-one; Lawful Permanent Residents (i.e., Green Card holders) can sponsor spouses and children with no quota cap (currently this quota is capped).

On the illegal immigration front, which dominated the debate in the Senate and may prove the bill's undoing in the House of Representatives, these are the main provisions:

Employer verification: By 2017, all employers must use Homeland Security's electronic verification system, E-Verify, to determine the legal status of *all* job applicants.

Border security: A number of measures are mandated, including doubling the number of Border Patrol agents (to 38,405); adding 350 miles of new fencing along the Mexican border; and setting up an electronic database to track the timely exit of visitors with temporary visas.

Path to citizenship: All currently undocumented aliens (i.e., illegal immigrants) who arrived in the United States before December 31, 2011, and maintained continuous residence since then can obtain registered "provisional immigrant status" that will permit them to work, drive, send their children to school, and more or less engage in daily life without jeopardy, but will not allow them to receive federal welfare, health, or unemployment benefits.

The provisional status is for six years, but can be renewed for another six years. To register, they must pay a $500 fine; have no felony and fewer than three misdemeanor convictions; and to renew their provisional status they must pay another $500.

After ten years in provisional status and continuous residence in the United States, if they pay a fine of $1,000, they can apply for a Green Card (i.e., become a Lawful Permanent Resident).

Illegal immigrants brought to the United States as children will be able to get Green Cards in five years and apply for citizenship shortly after.

SUMMING UP

Immigration has been one of America's most important and, until recently, relatively unique human-capital boons. Immigrants have always brought fresh and diverse skills, a fierce work ethic, and a patriotic appreciation of their new country's freedom and opportunity. There can be no doubt that without its immigrants, in an ever-evolving ethnic mosaic, the United States would never have become the world's richest and most powerful nation. The precise level of national benefit from immigration does depend, however, on the contours of national immigration policy.

If the United States is to replicate its earlier success in attracting highly capable immigrants, it must now do so by design. While most debates of immigration policy today concern the question of what to do about the country's 10 to 12 million illegal immigrants, a more fruitful policy discussion would focus on the politically less sensitive issue of which immigrants we should admit going forward. Therefore, policies to attract the most capable immigrants must address issues of both legal and illegal immigration. The federal government's failure to stem illegal immigration over three decades has so poisoned the national dialogue on all aspects of immigration that a prerequisite to any reform is a policy of "zero tolerance" for future illegal immigrants. Settling the illegal immigration issue once and for all would then pave the way for a thorough reconsideration of the criteria for admitting legal immigrants. To the extent that it is politically achievable, the overall national quota of somewhat more than 1 million immigrants should be incrementally redirected away from family-sponsored relatives and toward increasing numbers of educated, skilled, and, ideally, English-speaking "self-sponsored" immigrants. One easy way to begin such a transition is to give Green Cards to (i.e., admit as Lawful Permanent Residents) all foreign students graduating from American colleges and universities who wish to stay.

Happily, the immigration reform legislation that passed the U.S. Senate in June 2013, while not perfect, largely accomplishes these objectives. It credibly secures the border while also immediately allowing most of the country's huge cohort of currently illegal residents to legalize their status and, if they want to, eventually gain citizenship. More important, it greatly increases the quotas for talented immigrants (including foreign students who wish to stay) and makes room for low-skilled immigrants in needed corners of the job market, while leaving the most popular provisions for family reunification largely intact. As I write, the bill has not yet passed the House of Representatives. It may yet die there, or emerge in unrecognizable form. In any case, whatever happens, the country has begun to take immigration seriously as a *human-capital* issue. That is indeed good news.

Getting It Done

This book was written to further the appreciation of the United States' strongest attribute, the capabilities of its people—what economists call *human capital*—and to show how it can be raised even further. This attribute has been, from the first settlers to the present day, the secret to Americans' economic and social success and their happiness. As chapter 1 documents, it is to America's great credit that it always devoted more resources to developing human capital, and distributing it more broadly, than any other contemporary country; this is how the United States became the world's "smartest" society. But we cannot rest on our laurels; thus the rest of the book lays out what we might do to maintain our centuries-long lead.

In these pages, I have used an expansive definition of human capital. Certainly, the development of human capital begins with education. Accordingly, chapters 2 through 5 take a detailed look at America's educational system from preschool through college and show where educational policies fall short. But there is more to human capital than education. So, consistent with the most recent work of economists specializing in the subject, three chapters have been devoted to two other vital determinants of human capital. Chapters 6 and 7 deal with how human capital is translated into productivity in the workplace. Chapter 6 considers the quality of workplace technology and its dependence on research; since productivity also depends on how much people work, chapter 7 considers the impact of public policies on overall American work effort. Because human capital needn't be entirely homegrown—it can be *imported* by taking in immigrants—chapter 8 reviews American immigration policy.

Finally, I have aimed at being specific; calls for raising America's human capital are commonplace today, but usually lacking in thought-out ways to achieve it. Viewing policies affecting American education, workplaces, and immigration as the country's "human-capital tripod," the preceding chapters have presented concrete recommendations for how we can sharply upgrade the educational attainment of Americans from preschool through college; how we can have more technologically advanced workplaces, and more people working in them; and how we can add to our stock of human capital by recruiting the world's most talented immigrants. In each case, achieving these goals does require actions by government, and it always has. But it is also true that this needn't mean *more* government, because in each area government policies are already determinative; it does mean that we need *changes* in these policies. I have outlined what these changes might be, and why we need them.

But how might these changes be accomplished? Taking each leg of the human-capital tripod in turn, in this final chapter I summarize this book's policy recommendations and discuss the prospects of their implementation, with a focus on how much has already been proposed or is being done; the obstacles—substantive or political—that stand in the way of implementation; and what the reform agenda might cost, in dollars or in disruption of the status quo.

CHAPTER 3: CLOSING THE MEGAGAP

The work of E.D. Hirsch and other specialists in educational development has shown that socioeconomically disadvantaged children do badly in school mainly because of cultural deprivation in early childhood—what Hirsch refers to as a deficit in "cultural literacy." The earlier this cultural deprivation is attended to the better, and the most empirically validated way to do this is by enrolling such children in preschool. That is the rationale for Head Start, the country's biggest federally funded preschool program, but Head Start has largely failed in its eponymous mission because it has been run as a social service program by social service agencies, rather than as an early education program for instilling cultural literacy. For preschool to work as intended, it must be an early childhood educational enrichment program, run by educational agencies. The most effective way to do this is by making it the responsibility of local school districts that can tie it into their K–12 curriculum.

Even when Megagap children benefit from preschool, there is a risk that the progress they make cannot be sustained in later grades. Numerous trials around the country have shown that extending instructional time for children who are falling behind academically is effective in keeping them academically on grade level. These experiments have also shown that how the time is extended (by a longer school day, school year, or through summer school) matters.

Recommendations

1. Introduce district-operated, universal-access, and free preschool, funded initially with federal grants—perhaps at first on a pilot basis to gain national support, then nationally

if it is shown to be effective. The reason to make preschool universal and free is threefold: all children benefit (even if the culturally deprived benefit the most); for the preschool curriculum to be continuous with that of later grades, it is best that all local children participate; and it is the only way to ensure its long-term local support.

2. Introduce Extended Learning Time in districts with Megagap children, also kick-started with federal grants on a pilot basis. After experimenting with alternative ELT formats, settle on the most effective format.

Discussion Recommendation 1, of preschool for socioeconomically disadvantaged (Megagap) schoolchildren, has the support of leading experts in educational development, notably including Hirsch, who is among the most well-respected scholars of education policy, and economics Nobel laureate James Heckman. Something along the lines of this recommendation was proposed by President Obama in his February 12, 2013, State of the Union address. Although the speech was short on details, the Department of Education has indicated that the preschool initiative would be implemented through grants to the states (rather than by expanding Head Start). Many states (with both Republican and Democratic administrations) have already experimented successfully with non–Head Start preschool programs; with federal funding most states would undoubtedly get on board. While Head Start as it currently operates has largely failed in its mission, it is a "foot in the door" in terms of the concept; it is not a huge policy leap to redirect the money spent on Head Start toward this proposal.

In the current, highly polarized partisan political environment, it may be difficult to persuade Congress that preschool can have the kind of game-changing impact on disadvantaged schoolchildren's later performance that the experts (and this author) claim. Another serious obstacle to implementation is the proposal's sizable potential cost. Chapter 3 outlines in detail how universal preschool might be paid for, but the proposal requires redirecting funds away from Head Start (which would be ended), federal Title I school aid, and roughly a third of federal aid for special education, all of which would be highly controversial. Also, given the proposal's Megagap-closing rationale, perhaps the hardest sell is making preschool universal, rather than means-tested. Nevertheless, as noted earlier, for it to be viable in the long term, preschool must become an integral part of America's education system rather than a segregated outlier.

Regarding recommendation 2, a growing number of states across the country have already lengthened instructional time in their schools, and many local school districts have gone beyond their state mandates. Most significantly, the most successful charter schools have made ELT a core feature of their instruction. Behind the scenes, several reputable national organizations like the National Center on Time and Learning and the Wallace Foundation have advocated for ELT and publicized its benefits.

Three issues stand in the way of ELT becoming universally adopted. The first, obviously, is cost. However the extra time is configured, teachers will have to be paid more, with the cost being proportional to the amount of instruction added. (Some educators supporting ELT, skeptical of the educational benefits of smaller classes, suggest the cost be absorbed by modestly increasing class sizes.) The second obstacle is uncertainty as to its efficacy. Even its proponents agree that the benefits of ELT depend on when the extra time is added and how it is used. Massachusetts, before implementing ELT, experimented with different formats before settling on the most proven. That is why I advocate it be tried on a pilot basis initially. Finally, not all students need ELT. An effective program would excuse high-achieving students, or allow them to use the time in accordance with their ability and interests.

CHAPTER 4: CLOSING THE MAINSTREAM LEARNING GAP

Despite the long-standing concern with America's academic Megagap, the country's most extensive educational achievement gap, in terms of numbers of children, is the one separating most non-disadvantaged American schoolchildren from their foreign and American upper-middle-class peers. The Mainstream learning gap is, however, a much easier educational problem for the country to tackle. All it takes is to raise academic expectations, and then follow through to make sure they are met. For school districts to close their Mainstream gap requires implementing four key reforms.

Recommendations

1. Institute a rigorous academic curriculum for each grade, consistent with the best national and international academic standards.
2. Ensure that students are mastering the curriculum by instituting a program of feedback and continuous improvement through grade-by-grade testing.
3. Hire teachers knowledgeable in the subjects they teach.
4. Offer academic high school diplomas only to those graduates shown to be capable of doing college-level work.

Discussion The biggest stride forward in the direction of recommendation 1 is the near-universal adoption by all but five U.S. states of the Common Core State Standards Initiative (CCSSI). The CCSSI is far from perfect, but for most states it is a great improvement over current curricular standards. Recommendation 2 is built into the requirements for No Child Left Behind, but districts need to use it—as Massachusetts does—to raise the performance of mainstream students, not just the "left behind." Recommendation 3 is not at all controversial; it just needs to be heeded. On the positive front, it is strenuously advocated by the Education Trust and most respected education reformers. The proposal's implementation does depend, however, on the reform of teacher training at its source, the teacher education schools. One heartening sign that this may be happening is the more rigorous standards being imposed by their accrediting organizations, the National Council for the Accreditation of Teacher Education and the Teacher Education Accreditation Council as they merge into the Council for the Accreditation of Educator Preparation (CAEP). Half of all American states *think* they are implementing recommendation 4; that is, they administer high school exit exams as a condition of receiving a diploma—the only problem is that these exams aren't rigorous. But the fact that they are being administered is hopeful; states just have to be persuaded to use tougher exams—preferably the ACT or SAT, as recommended in the chapter.

While none of these recommendations is necessarily controversial, the challenge in most states is to put teeth into their administration. If the states did so, these recommendations *would become* controversial because recommendations 1, 2, and 4 would inevitably raise student failure rates for *mainstream* students (the ones, remember, who are supposed to be doing okay), upsetting both parents and school officials; recommendations 1, 2, and 4 would also require a change in school culture and practices, much to the discomfiture of teachers and principals; and recommendation 3 would upend teacher education as we know it, causing an uproar there. That is why the chapter recommends that, to effectively reform mainstream schools, we turn to charter schools (where they would do much more good than in their typical venue, troubled inner-city neighborhoods). To reform teacher training, we should increasingly rely on selective liberal arts colleges—with subsequent on-the-job pedagogy training—rather than traditional teachers colleges. One other point: Massachusetts already has curricular standards exceeding those of the CCSSI; it should stick to them; the CCSSI should only be implemented where it is superior to local practice.

Regarding cost, virtually all the recommendations are costless; indeed, if they improved mainstream students' academic outcomes, they might actually save money for both school districts and colleges (in remediation) and parents (in supplemental tutoring and test-prep). The politics, happily, seems to be converging. The promotion of aggressive school reform by President Obama and countless liberal Democratic mayors—in defiance of teachers' unions and other traditional liberal constituencies—indicates a growing convergence with long-held conservative education policy views.

CHAPTER 5: MAKING COLLEGE PAY OFF

America may have the world's best higher-education system; nevertheless, in terms of its contribution to human capital, it has five serious deficiencies. Too many academically capable students can't afford to go to college; too many academically unprepared ones are going; too many colleges give short shrift to instruction in the arts and sciences, especially for freshmen and sophomores; too many college administrators (and students themselves) are unconcerned about whether students graduate; and when they leave (even when they don't graduate), too many college students are heavily burdened with debt.

Federal financial aid to students in the form of loans and grants is the primary source of funding for college attendance in the United States. Thus, without spending more than currently, changes in policy governing the terms of this aid can be a powerful lever to ameliorate all five problems. Recommendations on how this might be done are outlined below, with details provided in chapter 5.

Recommendations

1. To make college affordable for all academically prepared but financially constrained students, make low-interest loans available to cover the full expense (pegged to the cost of efficient state colleges) of college attendance.

2. To motivate high schools to adequately prepare their students for college, condition financial aid on college readiness.

3. To motivate both students and college administrators to take program completion seriously, and to reduce post-graduate indebtedness, waive a portion of the loan to be repaid for students who graduate on time.

4. To motivate colleges to take undergraduate instruction seriously, limit eligibility for student financial aid to those that do.

Discussion Changing well-entrenched federal college student aid policies is, admittedly, a challenge. On the positive side is the fact that something similar to these recommendations is being proposed by the conservative Cameron government of Britain, and also the increasing frustration, across party lines, with the status quo. Realistically, the kinds of reforms being advocated must be implemented piecemeal. The least controversial proposal, on its face, would be to end the complex, means-tested application process for student loans. Close behind is the idea of keeping student loan interest rates low. The issue is being resolved in Congress as this is being written; given current historically low interest rates in financial markets, a bipartisan compromise that has been agreed on ties student loan rates to prevailing market interest rates plus a minor surcharge to cover administration and defaults. Forgiving debt for college graduates might also be politically attractive—

except for its cost; and the proposed use of Pell funds to pay for this might raise hackles among liberals. The idea of conditioning student aid on college readiness will encounter strenuous resistance from liberals; conditioning a college's eligibility on its instructional practices will encounter strong opposition from conservatives.

Perhaps the most plausible reason that a reform agenda tied to federal student aid isn't being considered is that no one has, to my knowledge, ever proposed it. My hope is that the recommendations here will at least provoke a political dialogue on the subject.

CHAPTER 6: THE HIGH-TECHNOLOGY WORKPLACE

The return to individuals and society on the human-capital investment that people acquire through education and training, their *productivity*, depends heavily on what happens once they start working. A key determinant is the quality of the technology they have to work with. For well over a century and a half, America's workplace technology has been the world's most advanced: first in agriculture, then in infrastructure and industrial mass manufacture, and today in biomedicine and electronics. But the rest of the world (think of China) is catching up. Because all technology is grounded in research, for the United States to maintain its technological lead, it must also maintain its lead in research—both applied and basic. Although private firms conduct half of all U.S. research today, given the advanced state of science today, even applied research is too expensive for them to shoulder without subsidies, and basic research, given its nonproprietary nature, is wholly unprofitable. That is why the U.S. government currently underwrites, both directly and indirectly, a large share of the cost of American research. But in order to maintain the country's lead, it must do more.

A less costly form of governmental support of workplace technology, as old as the country itself, is maintaining a viable patent system. Currently, the U.S. Patent and Trademark Office (USPTO) is badly backlogged in processing patent applications and has not aggressively countered the practice of "patent trolling," by which unscrupulous firms, through the acquisition of dubious patents and costly litigation, blackmail undercapitalized inventors, seriously undermining the invention process and inhibiting cutting-edge start-up ventures. It is easy enough to clear the backlog: hire more patent examiners. Developing an effective strategy to end patent trolling is legally complex, but, given the depth of available legal expertise, should not be too challenging.

Recommendations

1. To promote private-sector research, make the corporate research tax credit (which currently needs to be periodically reauthorized) more generous and permanent.

2. To promote basic research—mainly at American universities—on which applied research and technology is dependent, set the level of federal appropriation for basic research (which currently fluctuates erratically from year to year) at a fixed percent of GDP.

3. To ensure that all inventions can quickly enter the U.S. technological bloodstream, give the U.S. Patent and Trademark Office the funds it needs to clear its backlog and keep abreast of new patent applications.

4. To protect the intellectual property of inventors and start-up technology firms, authorize the U.S. Attorney General, with technical guidance from the USPTO, to go after "patent trolls" aggressively.

Discussion Few politicians in Washington disagree with the premise behind these recommendations. Further helping them is the fact that they are not especially costly—a rounding error in the federal budget at most. That is the good news. The problem is, as with many worthwhile, uncontroversial government expenditures, the proposals lack politically powerful constituencies. The business community clearly favors recommendation 1, a permanent and more generous research tax credit, but not enough to fight for it as strenuously as for other, more lucrative, tax breaks. The biomedical community has been pretty effective in fighting for recommendation 2, in the form of support for the budget of the National Institutes of Health, but we need serious basic research funding in other fields as well. Shortsightedly, while no political constituency is against Patent Office reform, and its cost is negligible (not even a rounding error), it consistently falls off the Washington political radar. My hope is that, with arguments like those made in this book, and perhaps a more favorable budgetary and political climate as the U.S. economy improves, these recommendations will get enacted on their merits.

CHAPTER 7: ENDING IDLENESS AS WE KNOW IT

Besides technology, the other great determinant of returns on human-capital investments in education and training is how much people work. Americans have long been the hardest workers of any rich country, which accounts for a significant share of the United States' greater productivity. But for that to continue, Americans' work effort should not be undercut by income-support programs that get people to rely on government checks rather than paychecks. Three government programs stand out both in the number of people being withdrawn from the workforce and in their amenability to reform. The most egregious is disability insurance, whose rolls have grown wholly out of proportion to the incidence of disability, or even the condition of the economy. However, unemployment insurance, while less subject to abuse, also needlessly subsidizes idleness. In the case of the United States' largest income-support program by far, Social Security (meaning its old-age pension component), the challenge is to motivate seniors to delay their retirement. Finally, most U.S. states and localities, through collective bargaining agreements, allow their public employees to retire with generous "defined-benefit" pensions at absurdly young ages. This has drawn much attention lately because of its ruinous cost; the concern here is with its drain on human capital.

Recommendations

1. To minimize disability insurance fraud, rigorously monitor the validity of disability insurance claims (which would save billions of dollars).
2. To keep all workers who are not seriously disabled employed, place eligible workers in jobs suitable to their disability.
3. To keep laid-off workers employed, and to prevent degrading of skills, use unemployment insurance funds to underwrite their continued employment or reemployment.
4. To keep as many seniors as possible working, reconfigure Social Security rules to make delayed retirement more profitable than getting a Social Security check.
5. To keep state and local public employees working until normal retirement age (and to stabilize state/local finances), place all new employees in defined-contribution pension plans.

Discussion Politically, recommendations 1 and 2 concerning disability insurance should be the easiest of these to implement. There is already widespread alarm at the growth of the program, even among liberals; it is a candidate ripe for reform. Recommendations 2 and 3, representing forms of "welfare to work," have important precedents both in the United States and abroad, starting with the stunningly successful welfare reform legislation of 1996, and policies in some of the world's most generous welfare states, Denmark and Germany. Recommendation 4, regarding Social Security, has a precedent within existing policy: the current delayed-retirement benefit increments—they just have to be made more generous. The hardest nut to crack may be recommendation 5, putting all new public employees in defined-contribution pension plans. Several states, including New York, Pennsylvania, and Washington, are considering this, but are encountering strong opposition from organized labor. Ironically, as with some of the other recommendations in this chapter, the welfare states of Europe are ahead of us; defined-contribution pensions are already a fact of life in Britain and the Scandinavian countries. Although it is proposed here for human-capital considerations, what will ultimately tip the balance across the United States is the growing unaffordability of state and local defined-benefit pension plans.

As to cost, every one of these proposals would save money—many billions of dollars, in fact. As noted in the chapter, just reforming disability insurance alone would pay for every other recommendation in this book several times over. State/local pension reform will, in many cases, spell the difference between bankruptcy and fiscal solvency. But there are also significant savings to be had in the proposed reforms of unemployment insurance and Social Security. The biggest financial benefit, however, will accrue to the subject workers, whether they realize it or not. The disabled, the unemployed, and seniors look to get far more money from paychecks than they can ever hope for in government stipends—not to mention the dignity and satisfaction they will get from working. Even public employees in defined-contribution pension plans stand to gain, in the first instance in the increased earnings from working longer, but also because the potential return from funds invested in such plans are likely to outstrip the guaranteed payouts of defined-benefit plans.

CHAPTER 8: IMPORTING SMART AMERICANS

Immigrants have been one of the great human-capital secrets to American success. Not only has the United States, founded by immigrants, realized enormous economic gains from continuously welcoming subsequent foreign cohorts; just as important, it has profited from immigration much more than other countries because it has been uniquely able to turn its immigrants into full-fledged patriotic fellow citizens. While the tradition persists to this day, for the United States to enjoy the maximum human-capital benefit from its new immigrants, it must have a more human-capital–driven immigration policy—something it clearly lacks today.

Because the tangible human capital generated by immigration does depend on the abilities of the immigrants admitted and the circumstances of their admission, the following proposals, if adopted, would tip the scales more toward admitting immigrants with greater human-capital endowments; no longer allow unfettered illegal entry to make a mockery of America's formal immigration policy; wrest the maximum human capital out of the illegal population already here by ending their anomalous status; and restore America's singular tradition of immigrant assimilation by curtailing promotion of "multiculturalism" and bilingual education.

Recommendations

1. Greatly increase the quotas for educated and skilled immigrants.
2. Minimize the quotas for unskilled immigrants.
3. Allow qualified immigrants to sponsor themselves (as opposed to depending on sponsorship by families or employers).
4. Rigorously enforce border security with electronic verification and other measures.

5. Bring current illegal immigrants out of their legal purgatory through a carefully crafted path to legitimation and ultimate citizenship.

6. Foster assimilation of all immigrants by promoting English language proficiency and American values.

Discussion How to recast America's immigration policy has been one of the most contentious political issues of the last decade. Ever since a highly constructive bipartisan immigration reform initiative collapsed in 2007—one supported by the Republican president at the time, George W. Bush, and a bipartisan coalition of leading senators—the issue has appeared to be beyond resolution. Immigration policy was a seriously divisive issue among Republican presidential candidates in the run-up to the election of 2012, and it continued as a divisive partisan issue in the subsequent presidential campaign. However, the attribution of Republican political losses in 2012—both presidential and congressional—to the alienation of Hispanic voters appears to have cleared the way for a renewed bipartisan immigration reform effort. Its fruit, as of this writing, is an immigration reform package broadly similar to the aborted 2007 bill, but with tougher provisions on border security. The legislation is now under consideration in the Republican-controlled House of Representatives, where its fate is very much in doubt.

Although this legislation is not without flaws, it incorporates many of the recommendations of chapter 8. It increases quotas for educated and skilled immigrants (recommendation 1); it has a window for self-sponsorship in its 250,000 "merit" visas for immigrants admitted under a Canadian-style point system (recommendation 3); it incorporates electronic verification by mandating employer use of E-Verify (recommendation 4); and, most controversially—and perhaps its legislative downfall—it offers current illegal residents a path to legalize their status and, after a long transition, to become citizens (recommendation 5). If Congress passes this legislation or something close to it, this will represent a great step forward toward a human-capital–based immigration policy.

CONCLUSION

This book is grounded in my profound belief in the greatness of the United States. We are not only the freest people on the face of the earth, but also the most dynamic. By that I mean we are never content with the status quo; we are always looking to improve ourselves—both as individuals and collectively—and we generally succeed in doing so. Americans have certainly faced their share of crises, both economic and social, and their share of moral dilemmas, the most persistent being the condition of African Americans. But, in the end, to paraphrase Winston Churchill, we always do the right thing.

As I write this, we are near the end of another bout of intense national hand-wringing over worries that because of globalization or other "structural" factors our economy will never recover; that rampant income inequality will only get worse while socioeconomic mobility will never get better; that our physical infrastructure is beyond repair; that we are drowning in debt or that we don't have enough of it; that we are destined to continue our descent in all manner of international rankings: life expectancy, educational attainment, even happiness. I believe all this gloom and doom is unwarranted, and this book in many of its particulars explains why. On the positive side, however, when Americans become self-critical and soul-searching, it is almost always a prelude to a round of serious institutional reform. That, I hope, will be the case today. Among the things that are most in need of reform are the policies that have made America a smart society. This book's mission has been to offer some concrete proposals, all grounded in strong empirical evidence, on how we might proceed.

If even a fraction of the book's recommendations are implemented, the value of American human capital will take off from its already high level. The ripest target today is educational reform, a subject already high on the national agenda. Among the plethora of reform ideas being considered, this book offers suggestions as to the most fruitful to vigorously pursue. We tend to forget that a large share of our human capital is actually generated in the workplace: that technology is the main engine of productivity, and also that there is no productivity without work—meaning not just jobs, but the hours and years spent working. My hope is that this book increases policy makers' attention to this sphere. In the political realm, the least appreciated leg of America's human-capital tripod is immigration. Most liberals view immigration primarily as an imperative of compassion; too many conservatives fear its social and economic disruption. My hope is that this book will refocus attitudes toward immigration squarely on its human-capital impact.

One final thought. There are those who fear that we might be in danger of having too much human capital; that if we actually succeed in raising our stock of human capital, American workers will possess more qualifications—and aspirations—than the U.S. labor market can absorb. Given the declining level of young Americans' educational attainment currently and the large army of unskilled immigrants—legal and illegal—in the United States, this looks like a distant and far-fetched worry, but it needs to be addressed. If this book's recommendations are followed, will the new crop of high school, college, and professional school graduates, supplemented by well-educated immigrants, find well-paying jobs to match their skills? And who will be left to do the dirty work? Not to worry. A considerable body of labor market research clearly indicates that no national economy is permanently tied to a fixed proportion of skilled (or unskilled) jobs; that labor markets rapidly adapt to the rising skill sets of their workers, resulting in higher productivity and wages. The worst that might happen is that some of the work currently being done by America's lowest-skilled workers—domestic and foreign—might have to be performed by teenagers, homeowners, parents, customers, or—most advantageously—machines. In the meantime, we can draw reassurance from the unassailable reality that in the United States, more than two centuries' worth of increasing human capital has yielded spectacular corresponding increases in prosperity and well-being for all its people.

Appendix

BASICS OF THE UNITED STATES IMMIGRATION SYSTEM

U.S. immigration law is very complex, and there is much confusion as to how it works. The Immigration and Naturalization Act (INA), the body of law governing current immigration policy, provides for an annual worldwide limit of 675,000 permanent immigrants, with certain exceptions for close family members. Congress and the President determine a separate number for refugee admissions. Historically, immigration to the United States has been based upon three principles: the reunification of families, admitting immigrants with skills that are valuable to the U.S. economy, and protecting refugees. This fact sheet provides basic information about how the U.S. legal immigration system is designed.

I. FAMILY-BASED IMMIGRATION

Family unification is an important principle governing immigration policy. The family-based immigration category allows U.S. citizens and lawful permanent residents (LPRs) to bring certain family members to the United States. There are

Reprinted with permission from the Immigration Policy Center
at the American Immigration Council, November 2010.

480,000 family-based visas available every year. Family-based immigrants are admitted to the U.S. either as *immediate relatives* of U.S. citizens or through the *family preference system*.

There is no numerical limit on visas available for immediate relatives, but petitioners must meet certain age and financial requirements. Immediate relatives are:

- spouses of U.S. citizens

- unmarried minor children of U.S. citizens (under 21 years old)

- parents of U.S. citizens (Petitioner must be at least 21 years old to petition for a parent.)

There are a limited number of visas available every year under the family preference system, and petitioners must meet certain age and financial requirements. The preference system includes:

- adult children (married and unmarried) and brothers and sisters of U.S. citizens. (Petitioner must be at least 21 years old to petition for a sibling.)

- spouses and unmarried children (minor and adult) of LPRs

In order to balance the overall number of immigrants arriving based on family relationships, Congress established a complicated system for calculating the available number of family preference visas for any given year. The number of family preference visas is determined by subtracting from 480,000 the number of immediate relative visas issued in the last year and the number of aliens paroled into the U.S. for at least a year. Any unused employment preference immigrant numbers are then added to this sum to establish the number of visas that remain for allocation through the preference system. By law, however, the number of family-based visas allocated through the preference system may not be lower than 226,000. Consequently, the total number of family-based visas often exceeds 480,000.

Below is a table summarizing the family-based immigration system:

FAMILY-BASED IMMIGRATION SYSTEM

Preference	U.S. Sponsor	Relationship	Numerical Limit
"Immediate Relatives"	U.S. Citizen adults	Spouses, unmarried minor children, and parents	Unlimited
Total Family-Sponsored Visas Allocation (floor = 260,000)			**480,000**
1	U.S. Citizen	Unmarried adult children	23,400*
2A	LPR	Spouses and minor children	87,900
2B	LPR	Unmarried adult children	26,300
3	U.S. Citizen	Married adult children	23,400**
4	U.S. Citizen	Brothers and Sisters	65,000***

* Plus any unused visas from the 4th preference.
** Plus any unused visas from 1st and 2nd preferences
***Plus any unused visas from the all other family-based preferences

In order to be admitted through the family preference system, a U.S. Citizen or LPR sponsor must petition for an individual relative (and establish the legitimacy of the relationship), meet minimum income requirements and sign an affidavit of support stating that they will be financially responsible for their family member(s) upon arrival to the United States.

II. EMPLOYMENT-BASED IMMIGRATION

Temporary Visas

The United States provides various ways for immigrants with valuable skills to come to the United States on either a permanent or a temporary basis. There are more than 20 types of visas for temporary nonimmigrant workers. These include L visas for intracompany transfers, P visas for athletes, entertainers and skilled performers, R visas for religious workers, A visas for diplomatic employees, and a variety of H visas for special occupations such as nursing and agriculture. Most of the temporary worker categories are for highly skilled workers, and immigrants with a temporary work visa are normally sponsored by a specific employer for a specific job offer. Many of the temporary visa categories have numerical limitations as well. The United States Citizenship and Immigration Services (USCIS) website contains a more complete list of temporary worker categories.

Permanent Immigration

Permanent employment-based immigration is set at a rate of 140,000 visas per year, and these are divided into 5 preferences, each subject to numerical limitations. Below is a table summarizing the employment-based preference system:

PERMANENT EMPLOYMENT-BASED PREFERENCE SYSTEM

Preference Category	Eligibility	Yearly Numerical Limit
Total Employment-Based Immigrants		140,000 for principles and their dependents
1	"Persons of extraordinary ability" in the arts, science, education, business, or athletics; professors and researchers, some multinational executives.	40,000*
2	Members of the professions holding advanced degrees, or persons of exceptional abilities in the arts, science, or business.	40,000**
3	Skilled shortage workers with at least two years of training or experience, professionals with college degrees, or "other" workers for unskilled labor that is not temporary or seasonal.	40,000*** "Other" unskilled laborers restricted to 5,000
4	Certain "special immigrants" including religious workers, employees of U.S. foreign service posts, former U.S. government employees and other classes of aliens.	10,000
5	Persons will invest $500,000 to $1 million in a job-creating enterprise that employs at least 10 full time U.S. workers.	10,000

*Plus any unused visas from the 4th and 5th preferences
**Plus any unused visas from the 1st preference
***Plus any unused visas from the 1st and 2nd preferences

Per-Country Ceilings

In addition to the numerical limits placed upon the various immigration preferences, the INA also places a limit on how many immigrants can come to the United States from any one country. Currently, no group of permanent immigrants (family-based and employment-based) from a single country can exceed 7% of the total amount of people immigrating to the United States in a single year.[1] This is not a quota that is set aside to ensure that certain nationalities make up 7% of immigrants, but rather a limit that is set to prevent any immigrant group from dominating immigration patterns to the United States.

III. REFUGEES AND ASYLEES

Protection of Refugees, Asylees and other Vulnerable Populations

There are several categories of legal admission available to people who are fleeing persecution or are unable to return to their homeland due to life-threatening or extraordinary conditions.

Refugees are admitted to the United States based upon an inability to return to their home countries because of a "well-founded fear of persecution" due to their race, membership in a social group, political opinion, religion, or national origin. Refugees apply for admission from outside of the United States, generally from a "transition country" that is outside their home country. There are also preference or priority categories for refugees based upon the degree of risk

---

1. There are exceptions to this limit, mainly in the area of family-based immigration. For example, 75% of the second family preference immigrants are exempt from the per-country limit. See Wasem, Ruth Ellen, "U.S. Immigration Policy on Permanent Admissions." Washington, D.C.: Congressional Research Service, July 20, 2009.

they face, membership in a group that is of special concern to the United States (designated yearly by the President of the United States and Congress) and whether or not they have family members in the U.S.

Each year the President, in consultation with Congress, determines the numerical ceiling for refugee admissions. The total limit is broken down into limits for each region of the world as well. After September 11th 2001, the number of refugees admitted into the United States fell drastically, but the numerical limits have been increased in the past several years.

For Fiscal Year 2010 the President announced that up to 80,000 refugees could be admitted to the U.S. under the following regional allocations:

Africa	15,500
East Asia	17,000
Europe and Central Asia	2,500
Latin America/Caribbean	5,000
Near East/South Asia	35,000
Unallocated Reserve	5,000
TOTAL	**80,000**

Asylum. Persons already in the United States who were persecuted or fear persecution upon their return may apply for asylum within the United States or at a port of entry at the time they seek admission. They must petition within one year of arriving in the U.S. There is no limit on the number of individuals who may be granted asylum in a given year nor are there specific categories for determining who may seek asylum.

Refugees and asylees are eligible to become Lawful Permanent Residents (LPRs) one year after admission to the United States as a refugee or one year after receiving asylum.

IV. OTHER FORMS OF HUMANITARIAN RELIEF

Temporary Protected Status (TPS) is granted to people who are in the United States but cannot return to their home country because of "natural disaster," "extraordinary temporary conditions," or "ongoing armed conflict." TPS is granted to a country for six, 12, or 18 months and can be extended beyond that if unsafe conditions in the country persist.

Deferred Enforced Departure provides protection from deportation for individuals whose home countries are unstable, therefore making return dangerous.

Certain individuals may be allowed to enter the U.S. through **parole**, even though he or she may not meet the definition of a refugee and may not be eligible to immigrate through other channels. Parolees may be admitted temporarily for urgent humanitarian reasons or significant public benefit.

The Diversity Visa Lottery

The Diversity Visa Lottery is a program to allow the entry of immigrants from countries with low numbers of people admitted to the United States. Each year 50,000 visas are made available in the Diversity Visa Lottery. To be eligible for a diversity visa an immigrant must have a high school education (or its equivalent) or have, within the past five years, a minimum of two years experience working in a profession requiring at least two years of training or experience. A computer-generated random lottery drawing chooses selectees for diversity visas. The visas are distributed among six geographic regions with a greater number of visas going to regions with lower rates of immigration, and with no visas going to nationals of countries sending more than 50,000 immigrants to the U.S. over the last five years. No one country within a region may receive more than seven percent of the available visas in any one year.

V. U.S. CITIZENSHIP

In order to qualify for U.S. citizenship, an individual must have had LPR status (a green card) for at least 5 years (or 3 years if he obtained his green card through a U.S. citizen spouse or through the Violence Against Women Act, VAWA). There are other exceptions for members of the U.S. military who serve in a time of war or declared hostilities. Applicants for U.S. citizenship must be at least 18 years old, demonstrate continuous residency, demonstrate "good moral character," pass English and U.S. history and civics exams, and pay an application fee.

Notes

CHAPTER 1

1. *Global Views on Life Satisfaction, National Conditions, and the Global Economy*, The Pew Global Attitudes Project, Pew Research Center, 2007. John Helliwell, Richard Layard, and Jeffrey Sachs, eds., *World Happiness Report*, The Earth Institute, Columbia University, 2012.

2. The World Bank, *GDP Per Capita (Current US $)*, 2012.

3. Helliwell, Layard, and Sachs, eds., *World Happiness Report* (cited in n. 1).

4. Claudia Goldin and Lawrence F. Katz, *The Race between Education and Technology* (Cambridge, Mass., and London: The Belknap Press of Harvard University Press, 2008), 5.

5. Paul E. Peterson and Eric A. Hanushek, "The Vital Link of Education and Prosperity," *Wall Street Journal*, September 11, 2013.

6. Jared Diamond, *Guns, Germs, and Steel: The Fates of Human Societies* (New York: W.W. Norton, 1997).

7. Isaac Ehrlich, "The Mystery of Human Capital as Engine of Growth, or Why the US Became the Economic Superpower in the 20th Century," National Bureau of Economic Research, Working Paper 12868, 2007.

8. Tyler Cowen, *The Great Stagnation: How America Ate All the Low-Hanging Fruit of Modern History, Got Sick, and Will (Eventually) Feel Better* (Dutton, 2010).

CHAPTER 2

1. Robert L. Church, *Education in the United States* (The Free Press, 1976), Part I.
2. Ibid., pp. 16–20.
3. Ibid., Part II.
4. Lawrence A. Cremin, ed., *The Republic and the School: Horace Mann on the Education of Free Men* (Teachers College Press, 1968), p. 33.
5. Frederick M. Binder, *The Age of the Common School, 1830–1865* (New York: John Wiley and Sons, 1974), chap. 3.
6. Church, *Education in the United States* (cited in n. 1), pp. 261–69.
7. Ibid., chap. 9.
8. Ibid., chap. 12.
9. Sarah Carr, "Can School Reform Hurt Communities?," *New York Times*, June 16, 2013.
10. Anna A.E. Vinkhuyzen, "Reconsidering the Heritability of Intelligence in Adulthood: Taking Assortative Mating and Cultural Transmission into Account," *Behavior Genetics* (March 2012).
11. Kenneth Clark and Mamie Clark, testimony to U.S. Supreme Court in connection with *Brown v. Board of Education*; K.B. Clark, *Dark Ghetto: Dilemmas of Social Power* (Hanover, N.H.: Wesleyan University Press, 1965).
12. Jonathan Kozol, *Death at an Early Age* (Boston: Houghton Mifflin, 1967); Rudolf Franz Flesch, *Why Johnny Can't Read: And What You Can Do about It* (New York: Harper and Row, 1985).
13. The National Commission on Excellence in Education [David Pierpont Gardner, chairman], *A Nation at Risk: The Imperative for Educational Reform* (Washington, D.C.: U.S. Department of Education, 1983).
14. U.S. Department of Education, National Center for Education Statistics, Digest of Education Statistics, 2011.
15. Teach for America website, "Our History."
16. Common Core State Standards Initiative website.
17. Paul Peterson et al., *Globally Challenged: Are U.S. Students Ready to Compete?* (Harvard's Program on Education Policy and

Governance, Taubman Center for State and Local Government, Harvard University, August 2011).

18. Mark S. Barajas, "Academic Achievement of Children in Single Parent Homes: A Critical Review," *The Hilltop Review* 5, no. 1 (Fall 2011): 15.

19. James S. Coleman et al., *Equality of Educational Opportunity* (U.S. Department of Health, Education, and Welfare, Office of Education, 1966).

20. Peterson et al., *Globally Challenged* (cited in n. 17).

CHAPTER 3

1. Mark S. Barajas, "Academic Achievement of Children in Single Parent Homes: A Critical Review," *The Hilltop Review* 5, no. 1 (Fall 2011).

2. Jonathan Guryan, "Desegregation and Black Dropout Rates," *American Economic Review* 94, no. 4 (2004).

3. Sarah J. Reber, "Court-Ordered Desegregation: Successes and Failures Integrating American Schools since *Brown versus Board of Education*," *Journal of Human Resources* 40, no. 3 (2005).

4. Abigail Thernstrom and Stephan Thernstrom, *No Excuses: Closing the Racial Gap in Learning* (New York: Simon and Schuster, 2003), chap. 9.

5. Steven Malanga, "The Court That Broke Jersey," *City Journal* (Winter 2012).

6. Fatih Unlu, "California Class Size Reduction Reform: New Findings from the NAEP," Princeton University, unpublished, November 2005.

7. Eric A. Hanushek, "Improving School Achievement: Is Reducing Class Size the Answer?," Policy Brief, Progressive Policy Institute, June 1998.

8. Matthew G. Springer et al., *Teacher Pay for Performance: Experimental Evidence from the Project on Incentives in Teaching* (National Center on Performance Incentives, Vanderbilt University, 2010).

9. "The Debate over Teacher Merit Pay: A Freakonomics Quorum," Freakonomics.com, September 20, 2011.

10. Phillip Gleason et al., *The Evaluation of Charter School Impacts* (National Center for Education Evaluation and Regional Assistance, 2010); Caroline M. Hoxby, *Achievement in Charter Schools and Regular Public Schools in the United States: Understanding the Differences* (National Bureau of Economic Research, 2004).

11. Casey Cobb, *Review of Three Reports from the Comprehensive Longitudinal Evaluation of the Milwaukee Parental Choice Program* (National Education Policy Center, 2012).

12. Kara Finnigan et al., *Evaluation of the Public Charter Schools Program: Final Report* (U.S. Department of Education, 2004).

13. Caroline M. Hoxby et al., *How New York City's Charter Schools Affect Achievement* (Cambridge, Mass.: New York City Charter Schools Evaluation Project, September 2009), vii.

14. Ibid., viii.

15. E.D. Hirsch, Jr., *Cultural Literacy: What Every American Needs to Know* (New York: Houghton Mifflin, 1987).

16. Lynn A. Karoly and Gail L. Zellman, "Promoting Effective Preschool Programs," RAND Corporation Research Brief RB-9427, 2009.

17. James J. Heckman and Dimitriy V. Masterov, "The Productivity Argument for Investing in Young Children," *Review of Agricultural Economics* 29, no. 3: 446–93, 447.

18. Alfie Kohn, "Early Childhood Education: The Case against Direct Instruction of Academic Skills," *The Schools Our Children Deserve* (Boston: Houghton Mifflin, 1999).

19. Grover J. Whitehurst, "Is Head Start Working for American Students?," *Up Front* blog, Brookings Institution, January 21, 2010.

20. W. Steven Barnett et al., "Principles for New Federal Early Education Policy Initiatives," *Preschool Matters . . . Today!* blog, National Institute for Early Education Research (NIEER), February 8, 2013.

21. W. Steven Barnett, *Preschool Education and Its Lasting Effects:*

Research and Policy Implications (Boulder and Tempe: Education and the Public Interest Center and Education Policy Research Unit, 2008), p. 5.

22. Lawrence J. Schweinhart, "Benefits, Costs, and Explanation of the High/Scope Perry Preschool Program," Paper presented at the Meeting of the Society for Research in Child Development, Tampa, Florida, April 26, 2003.

23. Promising Practices Network, Programs That Work, "The Abecedarian Project," Promising Practices Network website, 2012.

24. Andrea McLaughlin et al., "Depressive Symptoms in Young Adults: The Influences of the Early Home Environment and Early Educational Child Care," *Child Development* 78, no. 3 (May/June 2007): 746–56.

25. Promising Practices Network, Programs That Work, "Child-Parent Centers," Promising Practices Network website, 2012.

26. Barnett, *Preschool Education and Its Lasting Effects* (cited in n. 21).

27. Wade F. Horn and Douglas Tynan, "Revamping Special Education," *National Affairs* 144 (Summer 2001).

28. E. D. Hirsch, Jr., "A Wealth of Words," *City Journal* (Winter 2013).

29. Barack Obama, State of the Union address, February 12, 2013.

30. Barnett, *Preschool Education and Its Lasting Effects* (cited in n. 21).

31. Gail Collins, "The State of the 4-Year-Olds," *New York Times*, February 13, 2013.

32. What Works Clearinghouse, Early Childhood Education Reviews, http://ies.ed.gov/ncee/wwc/reports/.

33. W. Steven Barnett, "Better Teachers, Better Preschools: Student Achievement Linked to Teacher Qualifications," *Preschool Policy Matters*, no. 2, National Institute for Early Education Research (December 2004).

34. Ibid.

35. W. Steven Barnett, "Low Wages = Low Quality: Solving the Real Preschool Teacher Crisis," *Preschool Policy Facts*, National Institute for Early Education Research (March 2003).

36. Barnett et al., "Principles for New Federal Early Education Policy Initiatives" (cited in n. 20).

37. Horn and Tynan, "Revamping Special Education" (cited in n. 27).

38. Malcolm Gladwell, *Outliers* (New York: Little Brown and Company, 2008).

39. David C. Berliner, "What's All the Fuss about Instructional Time?," *The Nature of Time in Schools: Theoretical Concepts, Practitioner Perceptions* (New York and London: Teachers College Press; Teachers College, Columbia University, 1990).

40. National Center on Time and Learning, *Time Well Spent: Eight Powerful Practices of Successful, Expanded-Time Schools* (National Center on Time and Learning, 2011).

41. Zakia Redd et al., *Expanded Time for Learning Both Inside and Outside the Classroom: A Review of the Evidence Base* (Wallace Foundation, August 2012).

CHAPTER 4

1. Nationwide, NAEP eighth-grade reading scores for public school whites are 272, for blacks 248, a difference of 24; the difference between suburban whites in New Jersey and Nevada or West Virginia is 22.

2. Massachusetts Department of Elementary and Secondary Education, Education Reform Progress Report, May 1997.

3. Ibid., Progress Reports 1998–2012.

4. Stephen Jirka and Ronald K. Hambleton, *Comparison of Trends in NAEP, Massachusetts-NAEP and MCAS Results*, Center for Educational Assessment, University of Massachusetts, Amherst, July 2004.

5. Paul E. Peterson et al., *Globally Challenged: Are U.S. Students Ready to Compete?*, PEPG Report no. 11-03 (Cambridge, Mass.: Harvard University Taubman Center for State and Local Government, August 2011). U.S. Department of Education, National Center on Education Statistics, Digest of Educational Statistics, 2011.

6. New York State Regents report on college readiness, as reported by Sharon Otterman, "Most New York Students Are Not College-Ready," *New York Times*, February 7, 2011.

7. Common Core State Standards Initiative website, http://www .corestandards.org.

8. Chester E. Finn, Jr., and Michael J. Petrilli, "Foreword," in *The State of State Standards—and the Common Core—in 2010*, by Sheila Byrd Carmichael et al., Thomas B. Fordham Institutute, July 2010.

9. Ibid.

10. Javier C. Hernandez and Robert Gebeloff, "Test Scores Sink as New York Adopts Tougher Benchmarks," *New York Times*, August 7, 2013.

11. Jirka and Hambleton, *Comparison of Trends* (cited in n. 4).

12. Arne Duncan, U.S. Secretary of Education, "Teacher Preparation: Reforming the Uncertain Profession," October 22, 2009, http:// www2.ed.gov/news/speeches/2009/10/10222009.html.

13. Randi Weingarten, President, American Federation of Teachers, speech at the National Press Club, November 17, 2007.

14. Arthur Levine, *Educating School Teachers*, The Education Schools Project, 2006.

15. National Council on the Accreditation of Teachers of Education, Newsletter, Report on CAEP, July 15, 2013.

16. Alternative Teacher Preparation Program, New York State Department of Education, Office of Teaching Initiatives, April 2013.

17. *The Condition of College and Career Readiness 2012—National*, ACT, 2012.

18. *State High School Tests: Changes in State Policies and the Impact of the College and Career Readiness Movement*, Center on Education Policy, December 2011.

19. *The Condition of College and Career Readiness 2012—National* (cited in n. 17).

20. Ibid.

CHAPTER 5

1. Charles Murray, *Real Education* (New York: Random House, 2008).

2. Anthony P. Carnevale et al., *What's It Worth? The Economic Value of*

College Majors, Georgetown Public Policy Institute, Georgetown University, 2011. See also The Education Trust, http://www.edtrust .org/; and Complete College America, http://www.completecollege .org.

3. Sandy Baum and Jennifer Ma, *Education Pays: The Benefits of Higher Education for Individuals and Society*, The College Board, 2007.

4. Miroslav Beblavý et al., "Education Policy and Welfare Regimes in OECD Countries: Social Stratification and Equal Opportunity in Education," Organisation for Economic Co-operation and Development, 2011.

5. Richard Arum and Josipa Roksa, *Academically Adrift: Limited Learning on College Campuses* (Chicago: University of Chicago Press, 2011).

6. These organizations are the American Association of State Colleges and Universities (AASCU), the American Council on Education (ACE), the American Council of Trustees and Alumni (ACTA), the American Association of University Professors (AAUP), the Association of American Colleges and Universities (AAC&U), the Association of American Universities (AAU), the Association of Governing Boards of Universities and Colleges (AGB), and the Association of Public and Land-Grant Universities (APLU).

7. Peter D. Salins, "The Test Passes, Colleges Fail," Opinion, *New York Times*, November 17, 2008.

8. Lord [John] Browne of Madingley, chairman, *Securing a Sustainable Future for Higher Education: An Independent Review of Higher Education Funding and Student Finance*, 2010.

CHAPTER 6

1. Steve Olsen and Stephen Merrill, *Measuring the Impacts of Federal Investments in Research* (Washington, D.C.: The National Academies Press, 2013).

2. Battelle, *2012 Global R&D Funding Forecast*, December 2011, http:// battelle.org/docs/default-document-library/2012_global_forecast .pdf?sfvrsn=2.

3. Adam Jaffe, "Economic Analysis of Research Spillovers: Implications for the Advanced Technology Program," December 1996, http://www.atp.nist.gov/eao/gcr708.htm.

4. Lexikon's History of Computing, http://www.computermuseum.li/Testpage/99HISTORYCD-ARPA-History.HTM.

5. National Science Foundation, "National Patterns of R&D Resources: 2009 Data Update," http://www.nsf.gov/statistics/nsf12321/.

6. Martin Meyer, "Does Science Push Technology? Patents Citing Scientific Literature," *Research Policy* 29 (2000).

7. *Ariad v. Eli Lilly*, 2010.

8. National Science Foundation, National Center for Science and Engineering Statistics, "Survey of Federal Funds for Research and Development: Fiscal Years 2009–11," July 2012.

9. World Intellectual Property Organization (WIPO), *World Intellectual Property Indicators 2012* (Geneva, Switzerland: World Intellectual Property Organization, 2012).

10. Electronic Frontier Foundation, "How Patents Hinder Innovation," https://www.eff.org/issues/how-patents-hinder-innovation.

11. Economics and Statistics Administration and U.S. Patent and Trademark Office, "Intellectual Property and the U.S. Economy: Industries in Focus," U.S. Department of Commerce, March 2012, http://www.uspto.gov/news/publications/IP_Report_March_2012.pdf.

12. A utility patent is "issued for the invention of a new and useful process, machine, manufacture, or composition of matter, or a new and useful improvement thereof." See http://www.uspto.gov/web/offices/ac/ido/oeip/taf/patdesc.htm.

13. Brian T. Yeh, "An Overview of the 'Patent Trolls' Debate" (Congressional Research Service, April 16, 2013), p. 1, http://www.fas.org/sgp/crs/misc/R42668.pdf.

14. Jessica Lee and Mark Muro, "Cut to Invest: Make the Research and Experimentation Tax Credit Permanent," Brookings Metropolitan Policy Program, November 2012, http://www

.brookings.edu/~/media/research/files/papers/2012/12/06%20
federalism/06%20research%20experimentation%20tax.pdf.
15. Ibid.
16. Ibid.
17. National Science Foundation, WebCASPAR Integrated Science
and Engineering Resources Data System, "Survey of Federal Funds
for Research and Development, 1951–2012."

CHAPTER 7

1. U.S. Department of Labor, Bureau of Labor Statistics, Labor Force
Statistics from the Current Population Survey, 1950–2013.
2. Bart van Ark, Mary O'Mahoney, and Marcel P. Timmer, "The Productivity Gap between Europe and the United States: Trends and
Causes," *Journal of Economic Perspectives* 22, no. 1 (Winter 2008): 25–44.
3. Casey B. Mulligan, "Work Ethic and Family Background,"
Employment Policies Institute, April 10, 1997, http://epionline.org/
studies/mulligan_05-1997.pdf.
4. International Social Survey Programme, Work Orientation III,
2005, accessed through http://zacat.gesis.org/webview/index
.jsp?object=http://zacat.gesis.org/obj/fStudy/ZA4350.
5. Ibid.
6. Peter Gray, "Play Makes Us Human V: Why Hunter-Gatherers'
Work Is Play," July 29, 2009, http://www.psychologytoday.com/
blog/freedom-learn/200907/play-makes-us-human-v-why-hunter
-gatherers-work-is-play.
7. The flip side, however, is that the prevalence of warfare in
Paleolithic times led to about 0.5 percent of the population dying
annually; for comparison, this would have come to about 2 billion
people dying from warfare during the twentieth century, according
to Lawrence H. Keeley's *War before Civilization: The Myth of the
Peaceful Savage* (Oxford University Press, 1996). There is good
reason to think that the nature of war in Paleolithic societies would
have also led hunter-gatherers to have higher discount rates (to be
more present-focused) and thus greatly discount the value of work
relative to leisure.

8. Roger B. Hill, "History of Work Ethic," http://workethic.coe.uga
.edu/hatmp.htm.

9. Max Weber, *The Protestant Ethic and the Spirit of Capitalism*, 1904,
translated by Talcott Parsons in 1930.

10. Deborah Schildkraut, "Americanism in the 21st Century: Public
Opinion in the Age of Immigration," http://www.russellsage.org/
research/immigration/public-opinion-about-being-an-American
-in-the-age-of-immigration.

11. OECD StatExtracts, http://stats.oecd.org/Index.aspx?DatasetCode
=LFS_SEXAGE_I_R.

12. A recent survey finds that even wealthy individuals in the United
States tend to keep working past retirement age; this indicates
that a need for supplemental retirement income is not the only
driving force. Michael Nairne, "Working to a Ripe Old Age,"
Financial Post, March 3, 2011, http://www.financialpost.com/
Working+ripe/4377530/story.html.

13. Alberto Alesina, Edward Glaeser, and Bruce Sacerdote, "Work
and Leisure in the U.S. and Europe: Why So Different?," Working
Paper 11278 (Cambridge, Mass.: National Bureau of Economic
Research, April 2005), http://www.nber.org/papers/w11278.pdf.

14. Ibid., p. 61, Table 16.

15. Alesina, Glaeser, and Sacerdote, "Work and Leisure" (cited in n. 13).

16. Thomas Friedman, "How to Get a Job," *New York Times*, May 28,
2013.

17. Paul Krugman, "Sympathy for the Luddites," *New York Times*, June
13, 2013.

18. U.S. Department of Health and Human Services, Office of Family
Assistance, AFDC/TANF caseload data, 1996 and 2012.

19. Robert F. Schoeni and Rebecca M. Blank, "What Has Welfare
Reform Accomplished? Impacts on Welfare Participation,
Employment, Income, Poverty, and Family Structure," National
Bureau of Economic Research, March 2000, http://www.nber.org/
papers/w7627.pdf.

20. David Autor and Mark Duggan, "The Growth in the Social
Security Disability Rolls: A Fiscal Crisis Unfolding," National

Bureau of Economic Research, August 2006, http://www.nber.org/papers/w12436.pdf.

21. Nicole Maestas et al., "Does Disability Insurance Receipt Discourage Work? Using Examiner Assignment to Estimate Causal Effects of SSDI Receipt," *American Economic Review* 105, no. 5 (2013): 1797–1829.

22. Autor and Duggan, "The Growth in the Social Security Disability Rolls" (cited in n. 20), pp. 28–29.

23. Julie Norstrand, "Denmark: Public Policy," Global Policy Brief no. 14, The Sloan Center on Aging and Work, Boston College, October 2010.

24. Center on Budget and Policy Priorities, "Policy Basics: How Many Weeks of Unemployment Compensation Are Available?," http://www.cbpp.org/files/PolicyBasics_UI_Weeks.pdf.

25. Casey Mulligan, *The Redistribution Recession* (New York: Oxford University Press, 2012).

26. Scott Baker and Andrey Fradkin, "The Impact of Unemployment Insurance on Job Search: Evidence from Google Search Data," May 27, 2013. Available at SSRN: http://ssrn.com/abstract=2251548 or http://dx.doi.org/10.2139/ssrn.2251548.

27. Jesse Rothstein, "Unemployment Insurance and Job Search in the Great Recession," National Bureau of Economic Research, October 2011, http://www.nber.org/papers/w17534.

28. The HIRE Act did this from February 2010 to January 2011; a more permanent solution would be preferable.

29. See Tom A. Coburn, "Help Wanted: How Federal Job Training Programs Are Failing Workers," February 2011, http://www.coburn.senate.gov/public/index.cfm?a=Files.Serve&File_id=9f1e1249-a5cd-42aa-9f84-269463c51a7d; and Diana Furchtgott-Roth, "Whither Workforce Training?," Manhattan Institute for Policy Research, August 2012, http://www.manhattan-institute.org/pdf/ir_21.pdf.

30. U.S. Social Security Administration, Research, Statistics, and Policy Analysis, Federal Benefit Rates, Total Annual Payments, and Total Recipients.

31. Andrew G. Biggs, "Why Expanding Social Security Is a Bad Idea," *The American*, April 16, 2013, http://www.american.com/archive/2013/april/why-expanding-social-security-is-a-bad-idea.

32. "Retirement Planner: Delayed Retirement Credits," http://www.socialsecurity.gov/retire2/delayret.htm.

33. Andrew G. Biggs et al., "Social Security and Marginal Returns to Work Near Retirement," April 2009, http://www.ssa.gov/policy/docs/issuepapers/ip2009-02.html.

34. Metlife Mature Market Institute, *Transitioning into Retirement: The MetLife Study of Baby Boomers at 65* (New York: Metropolitan Life Insurance Company, April 2012).

35. Ibid.

36. John A. Turner, "Promoting Work: Implications of Raising Social Security's Early Retirement Age," Center for Retirement Research at Boston College, August 2007, p. 3; Figure 3A: Percent of Persons Reporting Health Status as Fair or Poor, Age 50–64, 1982–2005.

CHAPTER 8

1. Peter Salins, "Assimilation, American Style," *Reason* (February 1997): 20–26.

2. Jacob L. Vigdor, "Measuring Immigrant Assimilation in Post-Recession America," Manhattan Institute for Policy Research, March 2013.

3. Ibid.

4. Joseph Plaud, "Historical Perspectives on Franklin D. Roosevelt, American Foreign Policy, and the Holocaust," Franklin D. Roosevelt American Heritage Center and Museum, 2007.

5. Immigration restriction deepened the Great Depression by way of its negative impact on U.S. population growth. Clarence L. Barber, "On the Origins of the Great Depression," *Southern Economic Journal* 44, no. 3 (January 1978): 432–56.

6. U.S. Department of State, "Visa Bulletin for May 2013," May 2013, http://www.travel.state.gov/visa/bulletin/bulletin_5927.html.

7. Peter D. Salins, "Use Social Security to Seal the Border," *New York Times*, July 3, 2007.

8. *Citizenship and Immigration Canada*, Government of Canada website, 2013, http://www.canadaimmigrationvisa.com/morevisa .html#ind.

9. Ibid.

10. Statistics Canada, 2011, Ethnic Diversity and Immigration, Immigrants and Non-permanent Residents, detailed tables from CANSIM.

11. Steven A. Camarota, *Immigrants in the United States, 2010: A Profile of America's Foreign-Born Population*, Center for Immigration Studies, August 2012.

Index

Page numbers in bold refer to tables and figures.

Biggs, Andrew, 211
blacks. *See* African Americans
Brin, Sergey, 22
Brookhaven National Laboratory,
18
Brookings Institution, 77, 179, 207
Browne Commission, 145–47
Brown vs. Board of Education, 13,
41, 64, 65, 99
Budde, Ray, 44
Bureau of Labor Statistics, U.S.,
126–27
Bush, George W., 13, 37, 228, 237,
260

California: anti-immigrant
sentiment in, 223–24; charter
schools in, 44; educational
achievement in, 55, 68;
educational reform in, 68
Canada: assimilation of
immigrants in, 222; education
in, 12, **13**, 29, **29**, 57, **126**;
immigration policy in, 238, **239**,
240, 260; labor productivity in,
155; material well-being in, 4;
minimum wage in, **191**; research
and development (R&D) in,
158; work ethic in, 184, 185;
working time in, 187, **188**
Carnegie, Andrew, 21
Carson, Rachel, 197
Carter administration, 42
Catholic immigrants, 186, 219
Celler, Emanuel, 226

charter schools, x, 13, 43, 44, 70–73,
118–19, 251
Chicago Longitudinal Study,
81–82
China: educational investment
wasted in, 154; immigration
to United States from, 21, 186,
223–24; patent volume in, **172**;
research and development
(R&D) in, 157, **158**, 176, 180, 254
Chinese Exclusion Act, 223–24
Churchill, Winston, 261
City University of New York
(CUNY), 141
civil rights movement, 31, 36
Civil War, U.S., 31
Clark, Kenneth, 41
class, socioeconomic: and
educational achievement, 40,
41–42, 49–50, 52, 53–55, 63–64,
73, 81, 129; and educational
opportunity, 8, 9–10, 29, 31, 35,
36, 41–42, 87, 131–32; elimination
of linguistic markers of, 30. *See
also* middle class; upper middle
class
Clinton administration, 198
Cold War, 35–36, 41, 42
Coleman Report, 53
Colgate University, 132, 137
collective bargaining, 9, 118, 189,
190, 191, 196, 257
college: and admission standards,
140–41; affordability of, 135–39,
145; and educational reform,